LUCIA DI LAMMERMOOR

By
GAETANO DONIZETTI

Translated and Introduced
by
ELLEN H. BLEILER

DOVER PUBLICATIONS, INC.

New York

This Dover edition, first published in 1972 contains
the following material:
The Italian text of *Lucia di Lammermoor* as it appears
in Donizetti's manuscript score of 1835.
A new English translation of the Italian text and of
the French text of *Lucie de Lammermoor* (see page 83 for
details), as well as varied supplementary material, all
by Ellen H. Bleiler.

International Standard Book Number: 0-486-22110-5
Library of Congress Catalog Card Number: 71-107668

Manufactured in the United States of America
Dover Publications, Inc.
180 Varick Street
New York, N.Y. 10014

CONTENTS

GAETANO DONIZETTI

On September 13, 1811, a sturdy, dark-haired boy about fourteen years old stepped out on a tiny stage in the conservatory of the Scuola Caritatevole di Musica, in Bergamo, Italy. He sat down at a small piano, and recited the following words:

Quale insolito fuoco	What a rare fire
Or mi serpeggia in seno!	Creeps through my breast now!
Qual mi destò folla di nuove idee	What a mass of new ideas
La bella passeggiata mattutina!	A fine morning walk has awakened in me!
Di musica mi scuote un fervid'estro.	A frenzy of music shakes me.
Non perdiamo il momento...	Let us not lose the moment...
Certo un pezzo farò da gran maestro	Certainly I shall write a masterpiece
E giorni di vacanza	And during the vacation,
Mi sturberà nessuno,	No one shall disturb me,
A mio bell'agio qui potrò studiare.	And at my leisure here I shall be able to study.
Son proprio in vena, or or farò portenti,	I really have it in me to perform prodigies,
Dall'armoniosa penna	From my harmonious pen
Mi pioveranno incantatori accenti....	There shall rain upon me charming notes....

Taking a manuscript from a satchel, the boy sets pages on the piano rack, reads them, and then starts to improvise, playing a short waltz. When he has finished playing, he writes music on the pages, and says:

Ah perbacco con quest'aria	Ah, by Bacchus, with this aria
Avrò un plauso universale,	I shall receive universal applause.
Mi diran: bravo maestro!	People will say to me, "Bravo, maestro!"
Io con aria assai modesta	I, in a very modest manner,
Inchinando andrò la testa,	Shall walk about with bowed head;

Avrò elogi nel giornale,	I'll have rave reviews in the newspaper,
Saprò rendermi immortale...	I can become immortal...
Vasta ho la mente,	My mind is vast,
Rapido l'ingegno,	My genius is swift,
Pronta la fantasia	My fantasy is ready,
E nel comporre un fulmine	And at composing, a thunderbolt
Son io.	Am I.

The event was an exhibition at end of the school term, and the boy performer, who had written the music he played, was Domenico Gaetano Maria Donizetti. The diversion itself foreshadowed much of Donizetti's life.

Gaetano Donizetti (1797–1848) was descended from an undistinguished line of weavers and laborers in the Italian foothills of the Alps.* His immediate family was desperately poor, and was often on the edge of starvation. His father, Andrea Donizetti, never attained a higher post than the janitorship of the municipal pawnshop in Bergamo, and much of the time the family lived in a windowless crypt in the poorest section of the town. In this dungeon, as he later called it, Gaetano Donizetti was born. Three sons reached maturity in this environment: an older brother, Giuseppe, who became bandmaster to the Sultan of Turkey; a second brother, who was mentally defective; and Gaetano, one of the most gifted musicians that Italy has produced.

Bergamo, where the Donizettis lived, lies in the lower ranges of the Alps, about twenty-five miles northeast of Milan. A mill town and municipal center for the Austrian government of the area, it had long been the center of a flourishing musical culture, and it was famous for its splendid medieval architecture. During Donizetti's formative years Bergamo's two ornaments were the cathedral, Santa Maria Maggiore, dating in part from the eleventh century, and its *maestro di cappella*, Johann Simon Mayr, who was probably the most famous musician of the day in Italy, as well as the founder and director of the Scuola Caritatevole di Musica.†

---

* The statement, sometimes met in the older literature, that Donizetti was descended from a Scot named Donald Izett is nonsense. During the nineteenth century very little was known about Donizetti's life, and this ludicrous story may have been invented to accompany Donizetti's "Scottish" music in *Lucia di Lammermoor*.

† Johann Simon Mayr (1763–1845) has been called one of the most neglected men in the history of music. Born in Bavaria, he first studied at the Jesuit seminary in Ingolstadt, and then on the expulsion of the Jesuits took up civil law. His interests lay in

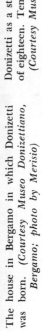

The house in Bergamo in which Donizetti was born. (*Courtesy Museo Donizettiano, Bergamo; photo by Merisio*)

Donizetti as a student in Bologna at the age of eighteen. Tempera painting by B. Martini. (*Courtesy Museo Donizettiano, Bergamo*)

Virginia Vasselli at about the time of her marriage to Donizetti. (*Courtesy Museo Donizettiano, Bergamo*)

Johann Simon Mayr, Donizetti's instructor and mentor. Painting by Gaetano Barabini, 1827. (*Courtesy Museo Donizettiano, Bergamo*)

At the age of nine Donizetti entered Mayr's school, where he was to receive training as a singer. He attended under some disadvantage at first, since he did not have an especially good voice, but his remarkable musical talents were obvious, and Mayr managed to retain him as an assistant teacher after his voice had broken and become impossible for the church choir. Cordial feelings arose between the scholarly teacher and the enthusiastic student, and throughout his life Donizetti remained in close contact with Mayr.

When Donizetti was seventeen, Mayr persuaded local philanthropists to pay Donizetti's tuition to the Liceo Filarmonico Comunale in Bologna. It was at this same school, headed by Padre Stanislao Mattei, the most highly regarded teacher in Italy, that Rossini had studied several years earlier. Here Donizetti studied counterpoint and classical harmony thoroughly, and received a technical background that served him well in later years.

An anecdote from this period shows the calibre of Donizetti's mind. Mayr had placed an opera with a local company, which staged it but refused to return the manuscript. Mayr was in despair, for it seemed as if his work was lost to him. Donizetti thereupon attended three performances of the opera, and wrote down the entire opera from memory, presenting the manuscript to Mayr. Mayr was so impressed with the feat—which parallels Mozart's famous adventure in the Sistine Chapel —that he drew his gold watch from his pocket and gave it to Donizetti. The watch is still preserved in the Museo Donizettiano in Bergamo.

During this early nineteenth century, musical advancement took a very limited form. There was little interest in instrumental music;

music, however, and with the financial support of a wealthy patron he left for Italy to continue his musical studies. He soon discovered that the Italian schools, which were then at a low point, had little to offer him, and he settled in Venice, where he made a small living as a composer of church music. At the urging of Piccini, the renowned operatic composer, Mayr attempted opera, and his first work, *Saffo* (1794), was so successful that his livelihood was assured. All in all, he wrote more than seventy-five operas, and was probably the most popular composer in Italy in the period immediately before Rossini. In 1802 Mayr became *maestro di cappella* of Santa Maria Maggiore, and in 1805 he founded the Scuola Caritatevole di Musica, which was one of the first free music schools in Northern Italy. Mayr died in 1845, universally mourned as a very generous and amiable man who had often exerted himself to help worthy pupils. Mayr was almost a foster father to Donizetti.

Musically, too, Mayr was very important. More than any other single person he was responsible for introducing the more advanced symphonic and orchestral techniques of Northern Europe into Italy. He was also an important innovator: according to P. H. Lang, many of the concepts and techniques usually attributed to Berlioz were really created by Mayr, who also originated many of the operatic devices that later made Rossini famous.

indeed, it is almost impossible to name an important non-operatic composer for all nineteenth-century Italy. All musical creativity was focused on opera, which was the absorbing passion of the entertainment world. The major cities had many opera houses, ranging from poor sheds with bad singers to palaces with the finest singers in the world. Even the smallest villages might see touring operatic troupes. For the most part, this musical activity was living opera, created freshly for each season, rather than the standard repertory of the past, as is the case with us now, and the various opera houses were in perpetual bitter competition to bring out new work. Most of these operas, produced under such circumstances, were shoddy and ephemeral, and died after a season or two—as did much of Donizetti's earlier work. Certain operas, on the other hand, attained sufficient quality to survive to our own time, as is the case with the better work of Rossini, Donizetti and Bellini.

The world of Italian opera was difficult to break into profitably, since competition was enormous and intrigues ever-present. But once a composer was accepted, he had opportunities to become extremely wealthy and influential. The music of Italy did not stop at the Alps, but continued over most of Western Europe, much of the New World, and even reached the European colonies and possessions in other parts of the world. Italian opera was supreme in many countries, and even where there were native developments, as in Paris and London, the Italians were powerful and influential, and Italian opera houses specialized in the latest music from the South.

Donizetti was ready to enter this world of music at the age of twenty-one, when he finished his course of study with Mattei at Bologna. He finished with many strengths and abilities. He was technically highly competent, and it would be a mistake to consider his training as primitive or second-rate, as was the case with certain of his contemporaries. He had a remarkable gift for melody, which he could pour out without effort. He was a rapid worker; he could write a whole cycle of songs "while the rice is cooking," and the results would be of high quality. He was a firmly self-disciplined worker, who could be depended on to finish his assignment on time. He was amiable personally, and did not suffer from the temperament that occasionally unbalanced Bellini or the lassitude that often paralyzed Rossini. He worked well with singers and management, orchestra and officials. He was an excellent administrator, in an area that has always been notoriously disorganized, and he eventually became the best producer in the world of Italian music.

In person he was tall, handsome and robust, with a large nose, dark eyes, and (eventually) a mustache and side-whiskers that did much to hide the kindliness that was easily seen in his face. In the general opinion of musical biographers, he was the most generous and likable of the composers of his day, free of occupational jealousy and eager to help his fellows. He was highly intelligent, and almost as gifted with words as with music.

These were the qualities and directional drives that Donizetti possessed when he emerged from his training.* Some were probably obvious at the beginning of his career; others were probably latent. But it would seem to have been only a matter of time before his gifts were recognized and appreciated. Unfortunately, he had no practical experience.

II

After spending some time in Bergamo writing non-operatic music, Donizetti took the first step toward his future livelihood and approached impresarios in Verona and Venice, offering to compose operas on commission. He received no encouragement, whereupon he then reversed the usual order of things, writing an opera first, then selling it. The result, his first opera,† *Enrico di Borgogna*, was accepted for the Teatro San Luca, one of the minor houses of Venice. Little is known about *Enrico di Borgogna*, since the music has been lost, but it had its première on November 14, 1818, and was advertised as being by a Signor Donzelletti. It was not markedly successful, apparently, since it did not run very long, but on the other hand it could not have been a failure, either, since Donizetti was commissioned to write a one-act farce, *Una Follia*, which followed within a month. This opera, too, has been lost.

It used to be believed that Donizetti had served in the Austrian army during this period. According to the traditional anecdote, he managed to obtain his release by composing an opera for his commanding officer. Unfortunately for anecdotes, the truth seems to be that a wealthy lady, who had accepted him as a protégé, purchased his exemption from military duty. During the years 1818–21, instead of serving in the army,

---

* There are several amusing nineteenth-century anecdotes about Donizetti's training period at the Conservatory at Naples. Donizetti did not attend the Conservatory as a student.

† Juvenile works, of earlier date, are *Il Pigmalione*, 1816; *L'Ira d'Achille*, 1817; *L'Olimpiade*, 1817.

Donizetti wrote now-forgotten operas for the minor houses of Venice*
and a certain amount of instrumental and sacred music. Probably these
very early operas were musically trivial, but they at least offered
Donizetti practical experience and permitted him to list works actually
performed on his applications for new commissions.

Donizetti's first stroke of good fortune came in the latter part of 1821,
when through Mayr's connections and his own previous experience, he
obtained a contract for an opera with the Teatro Argentina in Rome, a
leading house which specialized in *opera seria*. He was assigned a libretto
and was paid 500 Roman scudi. He wrote part of the opera in Bergamo,
and then set out for Rome, where he completed the opera and assisted in
staging it. *Zoraide di Granata* had its première on January 28, 1822,
although it had a close escape from being cancelled. The tenor on whom
Donizetti had counted burst a blood vessel while straining to create an
effect and died about two weeks before the opening. Donizetti had to
rewrite the tenor's part for a woman singer.

Zoraide di Granata pleased both critics and audiences. Indeed, the
audience, after one of the performances well into the season, gave
Donizetti and Donzelli, the *primo uomo*, a torchlight parade through
Rome—the contemporary equivalent of the old Roman triumphal
march. Although *Zoraide di Granata* did not stay in the repertory long,
and is now forgotten, it had the important result of establishing
Donizetti as a professional whose work had to be taken seriously.

Armed with further letters of introduction, Donizetti proceeded
south to Naples, then the capital of the Kingdom of the Two Sicilies, and
the second operatic center of Italy, Milan being first. Mayr had many
friends in the musical world of Naples, and Donizetti was made welcome.
In May and June 1822 he produced two successful operas† and sus-
tained his Roman reputation. In *La Lettera anonima*, a one-act farce,
Donizetti was fortunate enough to have as his tenor Giovanni Battista
Rubini, who was then on the way to becoming the greatest tenor of the
early nineteenth century.

Now that two strongholds of music had fallen to him, Donizetti
approached Milan, and in October of the same year, 1822, produced
Chiara e Serafina at La Scala, with a good cast, including the foremost
baritone of the day, Tamburini. This opera, however, was only

---

* *Piccioli Virtuosi ambulanti*, 1819; *Il Falegname di Livonia, o Pietro il grande, czar delle
Russie*, 1819; *Le Nozze in villa*, 1820-1.

† *La Zingara* and *La Lettera anonima*.

moderately successful, and it does not seem to have aroused enthusiasm among either the audience or the critics.

After his visit to Milan, Donizetti returned to Naples, which in some sense can be considered his home until 1839; from Naples he commuted to Rome, Milan, Venice, Palermo, Genoa and other cities at a break-neck pace that would have destroyed a less vital man. After 1835, indeed, his schedule included Paris. The amount of mileage that Donizetti covered in staging his operas throughout much of the world of Italian music is almost incredible, especially when one remembers that there were no railroads or steam vessels, and that coaches and sailing ships were the common carriers.

From the end of 1822 until the end of 1830 Donizetti's musical career continued relatively smoothly, without important events. He composed many operas, most of which are now forgotten.* During these eight years Donizetti gradually rose in the musical world, with increased critical recognition, higher fees and certain official positions. Yet it still cannot be said that he had reached the topmost pinnacle attainable by an operatic composer in early nineteenth-century Italy. He was recognized as an extremely competent craftsman, but up to this point, after some ten years of professional work, he had not achieved the enthusiastic following that Bellini, Verdi, and Rossini achieved in a much shorter time. This semi-failure was due, understandably, to the fact that he had not yet reached his musical maturity.

Donizetti's musical personality, however, became firmly established during this period. His working speed was almost unbelievably great; he could write a whole opera in a matter of days, and no matter how forced and rapid his composition was, he could be depended on to complete a very acceptable piece of work to fit the impresario's schedules. It was this great facility which brought him to the top musically, and as might be expected, it was this need for haste which sometimes let him produce work that did not meet his own highest standards.

Part of this remarkable productivity lay in his firmly disciplined method of working. The opposite of the temperamental musician who can work only when the mood strikes him (like Bizet or Bellini),

* *Alfredo il grande*, 1823; *Il Fortunato inganno*, 1823; *L'Ajo nell'imbarazzo*, 1824 (the first of Donizetti's operas to circulate extensively in Italy); *Emilia di Liverpool*, 1824; *Alahor di Granata*, 1826; *Il Castello degli invalidi*, 1826; *Elvida*, 1826; *Gabriella di Vergy*, 1826; *La Bella Prigioniera*, 1826; *Olivo e Pasquale*, 1827; *Otto Mesi in due ore, ossia Gli Esiliati in Siberia*, 1827; *Il Borgomastro di Saardam*, 1827; *Le Convenienze ed inconvenienze teatrali*, 1827; *L'Esule di Roma, ossia Il Proscritto*, 1828; *Alina, regina di Golconda*, 1828; *Gianni di Calais*, 1828; *Il Giovedì grasso*, 1828; *Il Paria*, 1829; *Elisabetta al castello di Kenilworth*, 1829; *I Pazzi per progetto*, 1830; *Imelda de' Lambertazzi*, 1830.

Donizetti kept a rigorous work schedule. He started to write at 7 A.M., and worked through until late afternoon. Sometimes he worked with a piano, sometimes completely on paper. He normally wrote the voice parts first, then filled in the bass, harmonies, and orchestration.

Despite the fact that he lived in the Romantic period of music and literature, Donizetti did not consider his music primarily a means of self-expression. For him the prime reason for composing was economic: to provide money for his own life, to support his parents, to keep his incompetent brother on a pension and to provide for the future. He had known great poverty in his youth, and while it would be absurd to claim that he was money-mad or miserly, Donizetti was interested in his finances in the hard-headed way that Alpine peasants often are; he shared this characteristic with Verdi. This business acumen stands in contrast to his notable generosity.

Nevertheless, Donizetti was a passionate musician, who could be a perfectionist in some matters, and in whom the force of creation could be overpowering. An incident is on record in which he begged one of his literary friends for lyrics, since the pressure of unreleased song in his mind was so great (after several days of inactivity) that he was ready to burst.

Donizetti came heavily under contract to the leading opera houses of Italy. He also received several official decorations, culminating in the post of Director of Music of the Royal Theatres of Naples, a somewhat shadowy post that apparently involved coordinating the various opera houses, which were under government supervision. He held this post from 1829 until 1839 or so; the exact date of termination is unclear.

During this same period, in June 1828, Donizetti married Virginia Vasselli, the sister of one of his closest friends. His marriage was idyllic in some ways, and he was passionately devoted to his wife. It was also tragic, since none of their three children lived more than a few days, and Virginia Donizetti herself died in her third childbed.

The music of this earlier period in Donizetti's life, up to the middle of 1830 or so, is generally considered immature. While occasional operas may undergo revivals as curiosities, most of this early work is now forgotten. This neglect may be unfortunate, since a couple of the early *buffa* operas, like *L'Ajo nell'imbarazzo*, are good minor works in the manner of Rossini. Most of this early work, indeed, may be characterized as Rossinian, what with elegant, witty turns of musical phrase, many of Rossini's technical characteristics (vocal parts written in thirds, unusual instrumentation, crescendos for dramatic effect, certain types of musical theme) and very elaborate coloratura.

Donizetti's first mature work, in the opinion of most scholars, is *Anna Bolena*, which appeared at the Teatro Carcano, Milan, on December 26, 1830. Felice Romani, generally considered the best librettist of the day, wrote the libretto, which was based on the life of Anne Boleyn, the wife of Henry VIII. The cast was splendid, including Giuditta Pasta (the leading soprano of the day, at whose villa Donizetti is said to have written much of the music), Rubini (the foremost tenor of the day, whose name still survives in the term "Rubini sob") and Luigi Lablache (perhaps the finest bass of all time). It has sometimes been claimed that Rubini was responsible for the great success of *Anna Bolena*, but this judgment ignores the fact that Rubini had sung in several previous Donizetti premières, and that the music itself had definite attractions. Despite its powerful cast *Anna Bolena* opened under some disadvantage, for the Milanese première of Bellini's *I Capuleti ed i Montecchi* was taking place at La Scala, with Grisi (the other great soprano of the day) as prima donna.

Anna Bolena marked a considerable step forward in Donizetti's work, and it received critical applause, old J. S. Mayr for the first time addressing Donizetti as "maestro." In *Anna Bolena* Donizetti broke with the Rossinian concepts of music and opera. Instead of employing irony and wit, Donizetti wrote with Romantic passion and dolor, with the result that *Anna Bolena* may be characterized as the first important thoroughly Romantic Italian opera. It had a prodigious melodic exuberance and showed great resources in harmony and orchestration. Important, also, was its concept of interrelating music and story; coloratura was held to a reasonable minimum, the music was dramatic, and there were successful attempts at musical characterization. This last point may now seem to be an obvious characteristic of music, but this concept of dramatic music was indeed somewhat strange to early nineteenth-century Italy.

The new opera spread rapidly over Italy, with traveling groups performing it in most of the major cities. Pirated performances, made possible by lack of copyright protection between the various independent Italian states, took place in Rome. In a very short time *Anna Bolena* spread beyond the bounds of Italy: London, July 1831; Paris, September 1831; Madrid, August 1832; Brünn, February 1833; Lisbon, February 1834; Dresden, March 1834; Havana, 1834; Berlin, 1841, etc. A French-language production appeared in Le Havre in 1835, Brussels in 1838, New Orleans in 1839 and New York and Philadelphia in 1843.

Translated into English, the opera played in New York and Philadelphia in 1844 and London in 1847, while translations into German, Swedish and Hungarian soon were performed. *Anna Bolena* became part of the standard operatic repertory for the middle nineteenth century, with periodic revivals during the later nineteenth century. Then, for unknown reasons, it fell from the repertory. When it was revived after World War II at Bergamo and at La Scala, Milan, it created a sensation At La Scala, in 1957, it was performed by Maria Callas, Giulietta Simionato, Nicolò Rossi-Lemeni, and later Cesare Siepi. The tapes from these performances, which were broadcast in the United States, created astonishment and enthusiasm among many listeners, who discovered that *Anna Bolena* is really a remarkable work with the lyricism of Donizetti's best later manner, a depth of orchestration and harmony that he did not always try to repeat, and a dramatic power that was certainly equal to Verdi's early and middle work. It is probably not an exaggeration to say that these broadcasts of *Anna Bolena* had much to do with reawakening present-day interest in Donizetti's music.

In 1831–2 Donizetti's fortunes continued to rise, although none of the operas in this period* between *Anna Bolena* and *L'Elisir d'amore* achieved any musical permanency.

III

The next important point in Donizetti's musical life was the well-known *Elisir d'amore*, which was first performed on May 12, 1832 at the Teatro della Canobbiana in Milan. As the story goes, the manager of the Canobbiana approached Donizetti in despair; an opera which had been promised to the theatre had been cancelled out, and there were only three weeks to obtain and stage a new opera. The manager proposed that Donizetti rework an old score, but Donizetti (who usually disliked to do this) indignantly rejected the proposal. According to his biographers he made the following offer:

"I have enough energy to prepare for you a new, a completely new opera in two weeks. I give you my word. Now send Felice Romani in here to me.... I am obliged," said the Maestro with a smile, to the poet, "to set a libretto to music in a fortnight. I can allow you one week to prepare it for me."

Romani, normally a procrastinating worker, responded and had his

* *Francesca di Foix*, 1831; *La Romanziera e l'uomo nero*, 1831; *Fausta*, 1831; *Ugo, conte di Parigi*, 1832.

book ready in time, adapting *Le Philtre*, a libretto by Scribe, the French dramatist and librettist. The story is simple and entertaining: A shy bumpkin, who is in love with the village heiress but afraid to speak of his love, begs a traveling mountebank to sell him a love-potion. The mountebank merely sells him a bottle of wine, but after many romantic mishaps the "potion" works and the bumpkin and the heiress marry.

L'Elisir d'amore was very successful both in Italy and the remainder of the operatic world. It has been translated into a score of languages, and has been performed hundreds of times, up to the present, in the United States alone. It was one of Caruso's major successes, in which he sang the role of Nemorino to perfection, ably supported by Marcella Sembrich (the heiress), Antonio Scotti (Belcore, an amorous soldier) and Marcel Journet (Dr. Dulcamara, the quack). Today, with *Lucia di Lammermoor*, it is one of the two Donizetti operas most frequently performed in the United States, even though it contains one of the most taxing tenor roles in the repertory.

Many critics have acclaimed *L'Elisir d'amore* as an important moment in both Donizetti's development and the evolution of opera. It is the first important comic opera to make good use of local color, to suggest the antics and peculiarities of the peasant background in Donizetti's own native land; it offers a new and firm technique of expressing individuality and characterization musically—the pompous and sly quack, the nimble-witted heroine and the amorous bumpkin. It also managed to express more varied emotional tones than had hitherto been possible. It could be comic and farcical, grotesque, joyous, and, when the situation demanded, its music could have tenderness and pathos. It was the first major breakthrough from the uniformly suave musical humor of Rossini, which had dominated the Italian operatic stage for a generation. Musically, too, it was vigorous and dynamic, tuneful and imaginative, and well orchestrated. It marked one of the first abandonments of the vocal arabesques that had hitherto overlain Donizetti's (and his contemporaries') melodic structures. While its approach was still *bel canto*, and the melody was still cantilena to be sung by virtuosi, it was a more restrained, more dramatic music.

Approximately one and a half years later, after four operas that are now almost unknown,* Donizetti's next major work, *Lucrezia Borgia*, appeared at La Scala, Milan, December 26, 1833.

---

* *Sancia di Castiglia*, 1832; *Il Furioso all'isola di San Domingo*, 1833; *Parisina d'Este*, 1833 —for a time Donizetti's own favorite among his works; *Torquato Tasso*, 1833. Donizetti's contemporaries considered these last three to be among his best work. *Parisina d'Este* and *Il Furioso* have recently been revived in Italy.

Lucrezia Borgia offered a new range of problems to the hard-working composer. Romani, procrastinating as usual, delayed the libretto until Donizetti began to be panicky about not having the music ready in time. The prima donna, Méric-Lalande, insisted stubbornly upon having a coloratura aria in a most inappropriate place, and refused to sing unless Donizetti provided such an aria. Donizetti was forced to yield. And the censors caused considerable trouble and threatened for a time to prohibit performances. Since Lucrezia Borgia was the daughter of a Pope, and a Borgia Pope was criticized by implication, the subject matter was sensitive from a religious point of view, and for a long time the opera could not be staged in parts of Italy.

The Italian reception of *Lucrezia Borgia* was very favorable, and it soon moved out of Italy, to France and other countries, eventually spreading over the operatic world. In France, however, it ran into difficulties. The play from which Romani had adapted the libretto had been written by Victor Hugo, and Hugo had the opera suppressed by legal action. The result was that Donizetti's music was performed to a new libretto (with a completely new plot): *Nizza di Granata* or *La Rinnegata*. In Italy still other plots and librettos were associated with the music.

Lucrezia Borgia has long been highly regarded, and is still alive, although it is not often performed, because of casting difficulties. The well-known Brindisi (drinking song) of Orsini has been a concert favorite with great contraltos, and is now most familiar to us from the recordings by Madame Schumann-Heinck. Caruso and Scotti starred in performances in New York just after the turn of this century.

By this time, the years 1833–5, success had finally begun to approach Donizetti.* He was receiving an adequate salary for his administrative work in Naples; had been appointed Maestro di Camera to the Prince of Salerno, and was chosen, on a pro tempore basis, Professor of Counterpoint and Harmony at the Royal College of Music in Naples. This last position, which Donizetti could fill well, because of his thorough grounding in classical techniques, was important and carried with it considerable prestige, since the Neapolitan College was one of the foremost musical institutions in Italy.

Donizetti also received the great honor of being invited by Rossini to provide an opera for the Théâtre-Italien in Paris. This invitation was a

---

* Minor, forgotten, or unsuccessful operas from this period also include *Rosmonda d'Inghilterra*, 1834, which later served as the source for an aria formerly substituted in *Lucia di Lammermoor*; *Maria Stuarda*, 1834, which was brilliantly revived a few years ago in Italy, and deserves to be better known; *Gemma di Vergy*, 1834; *Marin Faliero*, 1835.

true indication that he had really "arrived" and was now an important international figure in music. In January 1835 he arrived in Paris in time to see the première of Bellini's *I Puritani di Scozia*, and to witness the singing combination of Grisi, Rubini, Tamburini and Lablache—a remarkable group of well-coordinated singers which has probably never been surpassed on the opera stage.

This period also marked something of a rupture between the giants of Italian opera, Bellini and Donizetti. Vincenzo Bellini and Donizetti had met in Naples years before, and had been on reasonably friendly terms since that time, despite the fact that they really had little in common either in personality or in outlook on music. Bellini, who was practically the archetypal image of the Romantic composer, possessed the high passions and turbulence of his Sicilian origin; he was incredibly suspicious and distrustful, perpetually scenting non-existent conspiracies. Money and fame meant little to Bellini; the consciousness of being right was sufficient. Donizetti, on the other hand, was among the most affable of men, seemingly incapable of meanness or suspicion or envy. Donizetti considered himself a working craftsman, wrote very facilely and seldom revised his work. Bellini, on the other hand, identified himself passionately with his music, worked and reworked it over and over, until he was completely satisfied that he had achieved the best possible results for his intention.

The upshot of these differences was estrangement between the two composers, an estrangement marked by the exchange of letters with a mutual friend. Bellini called Donizetti a musical hack who deliberately sacrificed quality for the sake of money, while Donizetti accused Bellini of being a musical sponger upon elderly, wealthy ladies. As a result, the meeting and conflict of their musical works in Paris aroused ill feeling. Bellini sneered at *Marin Faliero*, when it was performed at the Théâtre-Italien in March 1835, while Donizetti was only perfunctorily enthusiastic about *I Puritani*, the sensation of the day. When Donizetti was appointed Chevalier of the Legion of Honor by Louis Philippe and was given a ring by the Queen, Bellini seems to have felt outraged. The two men continued to be estranged, a state which lasted until Bellini's untimely death a few months later.

IV

In April 1835 Donizetti was re-established in Naples, and had decided that Sir Walter Scott's *Bride of Lammermoor* was to serve as the subject for his next opera for the San Carlo. How or why this work was selected is not known, although Donizetti himself seems to have made the selection and submitted it to the management for approval. Donizetti may have read one of the French translations of Scott, or, as is more probable, he may have become acquainted with one of the French stage versions of the novel. It is almost certain that he knew Michele Carafa's opera *Le Nozze di Lammermoor*, which had been staged in Paris in 1829.

The story might have interested Donizetti from several points of view. It was by Sir Walter Scott, who still commanded an immense following all over Western Europe. It was a fine melodramatic story, with frustrated love, plenty of gore, persecuted heroines and many strong situations that would lend themselves well to staging. And probably not least, it provided a heroine who went mad. Madness was greatly in style in the opera of this period.* The subject of insanity offered a release from musical constrictions, permitting the singer to indulge in extravagant coloratura to the limit of her capabilities.

Salvatore Cammarano,† a Neapolitan who later wrote several librettos for Verdi, was selected to do the libretto, although administrative difficulties kept besetting the composer and librettist. The Neapolitan opera houses were in great financial difficulties, and feuds and quarrels among the administrators threatened to cause the entire musical edifice to collapse. By the end of May Cammarano still did not officially have the text in his hands. On May 29, 1835, Donizetti wrote an almost frantic letter to the Royal Neapolitan Theatres requesting approval and clearance.

Eventually, around the first of June 1835 Donizetti and Cammarano started to work, with Donizetti seizing the sheets of libretto individually, as fast as Cammarano could write them down, and setting them to music. Just what Cammarano used as his immediate source for com-

---

* Donizetti's own *Anna Bolena, Torquato Tasso, Il Furioso, Lucrezia Borgia, L'Esule di Roma* and *Maria Stuarda*; Meyerbeer's *Dinorah*; Bellini's *Il Pirata, La Sonnambula* (somnambulism) and *I Puritani*.

† Salvatore Cammarano (1801–52) was a member of a celebrated family of painters. He first studied art, but eventually turned to the theatre, where he was considered one of the best librettists of the day. He prepared libretti for many operas which are still performed or remembered: with Donizetti, *Lucia di Lammermoor, Belisario, Maria di Rohan, Maria di Rudenz, Poliuto*; with Persiani, *Ines de Castro*; with Mercadante, *La Vestale*; with Pacini, *Saffo, Stella di Napoli*; with Verdi, *La Battaglia di Legnano, Luisa Miller*, and *Il Trovatore*, which was not yet complete when he died. A proof of his skill as an artist can be seen in his excellent portrait of Donizetti, which is included in this volume.

Portrait drawing of Donizetti by Salvatore Cammarano, *c.* 1838.
(Courtesy Museo Teatrale alla Scala, Milan)

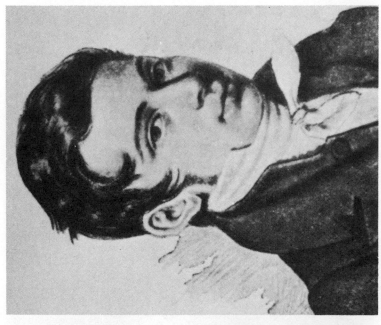

Salvatore Cammarano, librettist of *Lucia*, at the age of fourteen.

Felice Romani, librettist of nine Donizetti operas between 1822 and 1841. (*Courtesy Biblioteca Reale, Turin*)

position is not known, although the probabilities are that it was one of the French dramatic versions rather than the novel.

There are a few traditions associated with the creation of *Lucia di Lammermoor*, but it is now impossible to tell to what extent they are mere legend, and to what extent they reflect fact. One strong tradition is that Donizetti, dissatisfied with Cammarano's last act, worked and reworked the words until he finally cast it aside and rewrote it himself. This is not impossible, since Donizetti showed himself to be a very skilled librettist in *Betly* and *Il Campanello*.

Traditions are also associated with some of the arias in *Lucia di Lammermoor*. According to Tomaso Persico, one of Donizetti's closest friends, the composition of *Lucia* was attended with severe headaches. One evening when Donizetti's wife, Persico, the tenor Duprez and the soprano Fanny Persiani were playing cards in Donizetti's apartment, the door burst open and Donizetti half-staggered in, exhausted from his evening walk and quite ill. His wife put him to bed and the card game resumed. After a short time Donizetti's night bell was heard ringing frantically; the card players rushed to his room, where Donizetti, sitting up in bed, kept shouting, "Bring me a light and writing materials." His wife did not want to, but finally yielded, and Donizetti started writing feverishly. Only a short time later, Donizetti came to the card room and handed a sheaf of manuscript to Duprez, saying, "Here is your last aria." It was "Tu che a Dio spiegasti l'ali." Donizetti added that the pain was now out of his system. Duprez took the music reluctantly, prejudging it from the circumstances of its composition, but upon examining it, found it very much to his liking. It is true that Persico gives an incorrect date for this incident, but the situation is in character and is reasonably well attested.

Three other legends are recorded about the creation of *Lucia*. According to Persico the duet "Verranno a te sull'aure" came from the melodies of a street bagpiper, to whom Donizetti was listening avidly. Since Donizetti loathed street musicians and there is a similar melody in Bellini's *Il Pirata*, which Donizetti probably remembered subconsciously, the legend seems suspicious. A second story claims that when Donizetti first went to the theatre to hear Duprez rehearse, Duprez's ringing voice suffocated him emotionally and he had to be carried out of the theatre. This seems unlikely, despite Donizetti's illness at the time. The third legend, the prettiest and the most widely spread, is probably the falsest. Donizetti is said to have stated, when complimented upon *Lucia*, that he had written it as a sort of monument to his beloved dead friend Bellini. Bellini did not die until after *Lucia di Lammermoor* was written.

By the sixth of July Donizetti had finished his entire score, both melodies and orchestration. The manuscript still survives, and on the last page is written boldly in Donizetti's sprawling hand, " 1835 Iulio 6." But the management, even at this late date, had not settled the production, and Donizetti, in letters that mirror desperation, comments: "The crisis is close at hand; the public is getting disgusted; the *Società teatrale* is about to be dissolved; Vesuvius is smoking and the eruption is near." On August 20th the management finally officially accepted the score, and the copyists were put to work making individual parts for the singers and musicians. But even here there came further impasses: on the fifth of September, less than two weeks before the première, Donizetti wrote to his friend Giovanni Ricordi: "The *società* here is about to go broke. Persiani [Fanny Tacchinardi-Persiani], who has not been paid, refuses to rehearse, and I am protesting...." Somehow, Persiani's salary was settled, rehearsals began, and the opera was made ready.

Donizetti, as was his custom, directed the production, despite increasing physical discomfort from his headaches, and undertook the myriad tasks that went into staging a new work: the costumes, the settings, the actions of the singers, the rehearsals and coaching of individual members, conducting the orchestra, etc. He did have excellent material to work with, however, and this presumably made his task easier.

His prima donna in *Lucia di Lammermoor* was Fanny Tacchinardi-Persiani, the daughter of the composer Persiani. One of the half-dozen foremost sopranos of the day, she was young, attractive, and possessed a voice of remarkable flute-like agility, clear tones, large volume and great dramatic power. She was capable of handling with ease the difficult intervals and complex arabesques, as well as the smooth legato, that have troubled most singers of the part of Lucia since her time. Her Edgardo, Gilbert-Louis Duprez, a French tenor in voluntary exile in Naples at the time, was also first-rate; in the opinion of many enthusiasts he ranked with Rubini and Nourrit as one of the three great tenors of this period. While his voice was more martial and less flexible than Rubini's, he had a remarkable dramatic sense and an almost unequaled command of emotion. It was commented that Duprez's rendering of the final scene of *Lucia di Lammermoor* could be depended upon to overwhelm an audience.

Fanny Tacchinardi-Persiani, who created the role of Lucia, in costume for the part. Lithograph by E. Morton after a picture by A. E. Chalon *(Courtesy Bibliothèque et Musée de l'Opéra, Paris)*

Domenico Cosselli, the original Enrico. Lithograph after a picture by Antonio Dall'Ongaro. (Cabinet des Estampes, Bibliothèque Nationale, Paris; photo courtesy Bibliothèque Nationale)

Gilbert-Louis Duprez, the original Edgardo. Lithograph after a picture by Devéria. (Cabinet des Estampes, Bibliothèque Nationale, Paris; photo courtesy Bibliothèque Nationale)

With such a cast, it was not surprising that *Lucia di Lammermoor*, which opened at the San Carlo in Naples on September 26, 1835, was a fabulous success.

The appearance of *Lucia di Lammermoor* and its worldwide success established Donizetti as the foremost active composer of Italian opera— which still ruled most of the musical world in Europe and America. Of Donizetti's contemporary competition, Bellini had unfortunately died a few days before the première of *Lucia*, and Rossini was in retirement. It would be several years before Verdi would emerge as a musical threat to Donizetti.

In the next years, up to 1840, Donizetti's output was less. He wrote several minor operas* which are now but names to musicologists and two charming, short one-act farces: *Il Campanello* and *Betly*, both of which were produced in 1836. Donizetti himself wrote excellent libretti for both of these operas. *Il Campanello*, which contains one of the finest patter songs in *opera buffa*, tells of the tricks a young man performs to keep a druggist from consummating his marriage. According to French law, every druggist had to answer his night bell, which was available to the public. Donizetti based the work on a French play by a trio of vaude-villists. It was extremely popular and for decades was one of the leading one-act *opere buffe* in the repertory. It is still available on records, and is frequently performed in Italy, where its broad humor is appreciated.

Betly, which is based upon *Le Chalet* by the French dramatist Scribe, is set in the Alps. It is the story of a village beauty who refuses to marry her lover until her brother hoaxes her into marriage. It also is available on records.

The years after 1835, however, were years of deep personal tragedy for Donizetti. Cholera epidemics raged throughout Italy and interfered with his musical work greatly since many opera houses remained closed. Both his parents, to whom he was devoted, died of old age. And as a crowning tragedy, in July 1837 his wife, Virginia, died, together with their third child. It was years before Donizetti recovered from her loss; indeed, in some degree, he never fully recovered. Her death came not long after he had finally bought a permanent residence in Naples. He closed the door to her room and never opened it again.

Donizetti sought refuge from his sorrow in hard work, but found that this did not help him. For the first time in his life his powers of

---

* *Belisario*, 1836; *L'Assedio di Calais*, 1836; *Pia de' Tolomei*, 1837; *Roberto Devereux, ossia Il Conte di Essex*, 1837. The last opera has recently been revived in New York for Beverly Sills.

concentration failed him. Eventually, after several months of despair and fumbling work, he finished an opera, *Maria di Rudenz*, which the public considered too morbid and was a failure. This did not help his frame of mind.

Naples, too, began to be distasteful to him. For some time now, he had wanted to curtail his hectic productivity, and he had been eager to obtain an appointment something like Mayr's, which would offer both a settled income and an opportunity for creative work. The director of the Naples Conservatory of Music, one of the leading musical schools in Europe, died, and for a time Donizetti was appointed acting head. This seemed to be the position he had been looking for, and he tried desperately to have the appointment made permanent. His qualifications were outstanding: he was the leading Italian composer, he had a thorough knowledge of academic musical theory, he was a first-rate administrator, and a very cultured, intelligent man who could well uphold the general standards of the position. He failed, however; the job was given to Mercadante, a lesser man. Donizetti had felt sure that he would receive the appointment because of the close terms on which he stood with the Bourbon rulers of Naples. When he ventured to ask the King why he had been rejected, the King is said to have replied, "My dear Donizetti, if there had been two such positions, without question I would have given you the first and Mercadante the second. But since there is only one position and Mercadante is a Neapolitan, I must give it to him."*

Donizetti also tried to obtain the post of *censore* at the Milan Conservatory, but nothing came of this.

The crowning dissatisfaction with Italy, especially Naples, came with his opera *Poliuto*, which was based upon Corneille's play *Polyeucte*. The drama dealt with Early Christian martyrs, and while it would seem inoffensive to a modern reader, it was interpreted by the Neapolitan censorship as insulting to religious sensibilities, and was prohibited. No amount of pressure on Donizetti's part could get it released. Nourrit, the tenor who had been scheduled for the title role, fell into a depression at the ban, and eventually committed suicide.

In 1839 Donizetti took the important step of establishing himself in Paris, which remained the center of his activity for the remainder of his short life, although he still traveled frequently around Italy for special

---

* It is of course possible, although unlikely, that the Court was aware that Donizetti was suffering from syphilis, and hesitated to give an important position to a man whose lifespan could not be long. Against this theory, however, is the apparent fact that Donizetti himself did not suspect what his disease was.

assignments. In Paris he staged French versions of some of his earlier operas, including *Lucie de Lammermoor* (1839), and also presented new work. Among his major operas from this period are *La Fille du régiment*, *Les Martyrs* and *La Favorite*.

La Fille du régiment, which had its première at the Opéra-Comique in February 1840, was the first work Donizetti wrote to a French libretto. The public was cold to it at first, but warmed during later performances, until it became one of the most popular of Donizetti's operas. The French critics, however, reviewed the opera harshly, Berlioz accusing Donizetti of rewarming old music taken from his earlier operas. Donizetti denied this accusation angrily in a public letter, saying that he had no need to plagiarize from himself. (To a modern listener many parts of *La Fille du régiment* suggest earlier work by Donizetti, although other parts are fresh.) *La Fille du régiment* has remained popular in Europe, in French or Italian versions. During World War II it was revived in New York for Lily Pons, and recently for Beverly Sills.

In April 1840 Donizetti staged his opera *Poliuto* in Paris, but with a new title and libretto. Now called *Les Martyrs*, it was successful both popularly and critically. Berlioz, usually a severe if not hostile critic, praised the orchestration. In Naples, however, censorship prohibited even news of the performance.

In December 1840 Donizetti produced *La Favorite*, which after *Lucia di Lammermoor* is the most popular of his tragic operas. His cast was glittering, with Rosine Stolz and Gilbert-Louis Duprez, and the opera was very successful. Almost overnight Italian, German, and English translations appeared, and the opera progressed around the world with great rapidity. Around the beginning of the present century it was still popular in the United States, and since World War II it has been standard repertory in Italy. It is available on record sets.

After completing several less important works* Donizetti received a commission from the Kärnthnerthor Theatre in Vienna, which resulted in *Linda di Chamounix*. Nearly equal in importance to the Vienna commission was Donizetti's staging of Rossini's *Stabat Mater* in Bologna. This performance was so successful that it demonstrated Donizetti's right to be considered the leading operatic director in Italy. Rossini was so delighted with Donizetti's achievement that he gave him four diamond studs and letters of introduction to Vienna, including a letter to the most important political figure in Austria, Prince Metternich.

* *Gianni di Parigi*, 1839, before *La Fille du régiment*; *Adelia, o la Figlia dell'arciere*, 1841; *Rita, ou Le Mari battu*, 1841; *Maria Padilla*, 1841.

Donizetti travelled to Vienna, and on May 19, 1842, produced *Linda di Chamounix*, which was very well received. As an aftermath of this opera, Donizetti was appointed Maestro di Cappella e di Camera e Compositore di Corte (to the Imperial Court), with an annual salary of 12,000 lire and six months leave each year to attend to his outside interests. Donizetti accepted eagerly, since he had been looking for some such post for several years. He was understandably thrilled at holding the same office that Mozart had held nearly 75 years earlier. He was severely criticized in Italy for having accepted a post from the Austrian government (since Austria and the Italian states were on bad terms because of the question of *Italia Irredenta*), but he replied very frankly that he had to take what was offered to him, and he had been rejected from Italian posts because of political intrigues.

Donizetti rejoiced that his "Gypsy days" were now over, but he still had many commitments to meet. He returned to Paris late in 1842, to begin his last great opera, *Don Pasquale*, despite serious warnings of impending collapse. The progress of his disease was now more and more rapid, and to nervous irritability, occasional incoherent expression, and exhaustion was now added premature aging.

For many years the circumstances under which *Don Pasquale* was written were very obscure, and the libretto was long attributed to an Italian political exile named Michele Accursi. More recently, however, the true history has been revealed. Donizetti had been commissioned by the Théâtre-Italien to produce an *opera buffa* on the story of *Ser Marc'-antonio* by Angelo Anelli, which had previously been set to music by Stefano Pavesi in 1810. It was a simple story, reminiscent of Ben Jonson's *Epicoene*. An elderly retired gentleman takes it into his head to marry, a most unwise procedure for his age. His friends and/or relatives arrange a false marriage which is disastrous; he is so eager to escape that he promises never again to consider marriage if he is released.

The prominent librettist Ruffini was engaged to work on the opera with Donizetti, but Donizetti criticized Ruffini's work so harshly and altered so much that Ruffini refused to allow his name to be associated with it. According to tradition Donizetti wrote most of the last part of the book.

Donizetti spent considerable time on the music of *Don Pasquale*, from October to December 1842. It now apparently took him months to accomplish what he had previously been accustomed to do in weeks. He also worked with a hostile orchestra and stage group. Many of the musicians scoffed at his music as unvocal, while some of the singers

Self-caricature by Donizetti done in Paris in 1841. Inscribed: "My portrait done by myself." *(Courtesy Museo Donizettiano, Bergamo)*

Unsigned caricature of Donizetti that appeared in *Le Charivari*,
Paris, 1840. Donizetti is shown simultaneously composing an
opera seria with his left hand and an *opera buffa* with his right
hand. The inscription reads: "Donizetti, whose brilliant genius
has given us a hundred different masterpieces, will soon have
only one homeland—the entire universe."

termed his melodies more fit for jumping jacks than for singers. The singers resented Donizetti's now somewhat irritable coaching, and drew obscene cartoons upon their music, one surviving cartoon showing Donizetti being given a clyster.

The première of *Don Pasquale* took place at the Théâtre-Italien on January 3, 1843, with the remarkable cast of Grisi, Mario (Rubini's successor as greatest tenor), Tamburini and Lablache. Their performance proved that Donizetti was right and everyone else wrong about the quality of the music. In only one respect has posterity differed with Donizetti: he felt that the setting should be contemporary; the singers felt it should be performed in eighteenth-century costume. *Don Pasquale* is now universally given in costume of this period.

Don Pasquale is still very much alive in both Italy and America, as elsewhere, and it is generally considered one of the half-dozen or so greatest humorous operas, ranking with *Le Nozze di Figaro* by Mozart and *Il Barbiere di Siviglia* by Rossini.

V

By now Donizetti's health had become very bad, and severe headaches, fever and neural pain perpetually bothered him. He looked grey and worn, shrunken and aged, tottering and feeble, a mere shadow of the vivacious, effervescent Donizetti of a few years earlier. Gone was his buoyant good humor; in its place appeared long periods of irritable depression and mental disturbance.

After *Don Pasquale* Donizetti wrote only three more operas, *Maria di Rohan*, in Vienna, June 1843; *Dom Sébastien, roi de Portugal*, in Paris, November 1843; and *Caterina Cornaro*, which was produced without his supervision in Naples, January 1844. *Maria di Rohan* is still remembered for a few arias, as is *Dom Sébastien*. *Caterina Cornaro* was probably Donizetti's worst failure.

From the end of 1843 Donizetti's physical condition grew progressively worse. During 1844 he wrote no operas, and in the spring of 1845 he found it necessary to reject a commission from London, for the high price of 21,000 francs (perhaps $10,000 in present value), because he had only four months to write the music. This from the man who used to write good work in four days!

He now stayed in Paris, sick most of the time. By the middle of 1845 it became obvious to his friends that his condition was desperate, and physicians ruled against his traveling to Italy. Major symptoms of paresis were now obvious: his memory was collapsing rapidly, he had lost most of his physical coordination, and could no longer walk; he was in perpetual pain, and he suffered from delusions. In response to urgent calls from his friends, his nephew Andrea came from Istanbul to examine the situation. Donizetti was then taken to a clinic and rest home at Ivry, not far from Paris, in February 1846.

The remainder of his life is a pathetic history of further deterioration. By March 1846 he could no longer write coherently; by April he could not maintain a conversation or walk; and by May all concerned recognized that his situation was hopeless, and that nineteenth-century medicine could do nothing for him. The only problem remaining was where he should die. His nephew and other relatives felt that he should be moved to Italy, where perhaps he might be cheered enough by his surroundings to permit a medical miracle. The doctors were no longer unwilling to permit him to leave France, since they now recognized that there was no possibility of either arresting or reversing his disease, but for some mysterious reason, which is still not understood, the police of Paris refused to permit him to leave the country. A tug of war took place over the body of the helpless composer, with the police on one side and Donizetti's relatives on the other. Various reasons have been suggested for the behavior of the police: that Donizetti's banker had embezzled his money and could not stand an accounting, and had bribed the police; that the Opera was desperate to get the manuscript of the opera Donizetti had been working on for years (Le Duc d'Albe), and had bribed the police, etc. None of these reasons, however, seems particularly cogent today.

Eventually, it took diplomatic representations from the Austrian government, whose subject Donizetti was, both by birth and by his post at Vienna, to procure his release. Donizetti left Paris by train on September 19, 1847, a completely helpless invalid, incapable of recognizing anyone, incapable of performing most of his bodily functions, hunched into a strained position he could not leave.

His expected death came on April 8, 1848, in Bergamo, at the villa of friends, the Basonis, who had undertaken to care for him. He was buried at the Pazzoli chapel in Bergamo, with the largest funeral Bergamo had ever seen. But even death did not end his misfortunes. When his body was exhumed in 1875 to be placed beside that of his old friend Mayr in the church of Santa Maria Maggiore, it was discovered that the top of his skull was missing. After some investigation the authorities found his skull vault among the possessions of the doctor who had performed the autopsy. The fragment was placed in an urn in the Museo Donizettiano in Bergamo; there it remained until 1951, when it was placed with his other remains.

VI

After Donizetti's death there still remained unfinished musical business. He left two complete but unstaged operas, *Rita* and *Gabriella di Vergy*. *Rita*, a French-text one-act comic opera, written in 1841, was first performed at the Opéra-Comique in Paris in 1860. *Gabriella di Vergy*, an *opera seria* written in 1826, was first performed at the San Carlo in Naples in 1869. *Rita* is still alive and has been recorded, but *Gabriella di Vergy* is forgotten.

One problem of Donizetti's last days was the unfinished *Duc d'Albe*, which Donizetti had been writing to a libretto by Scribe and Duveyrier. When Andrea Donizetti took the composer back to Italy in 1847, he also took along manuscript material, including *Le Duc d'Albe*. This soon became an object of bitter international litigation. After Donizetti's death, his heirs (his two brothers) seem to have quarreled about the division of properties. Then the feeble-minded brother died, confusing the inheritance by the equivocal status of his illegitimate children. The Opéra in Paris also entered the quarrel by demanding Donizetti's manuscript as its right.

The question appeared to be settled in 1849, when the Tribunal of Bergamo took the easy solution of deciding that so little of the opera had been written that the manuscript had no commercial value. For a generation *Le Duc d'Albe* was forgotten, until in 1875 the publishing house of Lucca bought the manuscript from its current owners and assigned Donizetti's protégé and student Matteo Salvi to finish it.

As might have been expected, there was a tremendous outcry and Lucca and Salvi were accused of musical sacrilege. Eventually a committee that included the composer Ponchielli examined the papers and declared that since sufficient material survived to indicate Donizetti's intentions, the opera might be finished by Salvi. Salvi's version (with an Italian libretto, now called *Il Duca d'Alba*) was staged in Rome in 1882, followed by performances in Naples, Bergamo, and elsewhere. It then disappeared from the stage.

During the renewal of interest in Donizetti's music after World War II, Gian-Carlo Menotti revived *Il Duca d'Alba* at the Spoleto festival in 1959. Thomas Schippers, the conductor, undertook to remove most of

Salvi's material, and a truncated version of the opera was performed, with the fortunate presence of much of the original scenery from the 1880's. It has been taped by RAI and although not commercially available, it has been broadcast several times in the United States.

SCOTT AND "THE BRIDE OF LAMMERMOOR"

Sir Walter Scott (1771–1832) was at the height of his fame as the Great Unknown when *The Bride of Lammermoor* first appeared under a transparent pseudonym. He had achieved great fame with a succession of poetic works, including *The Lay of the Last Minstrel* (1804), *Marmion* (1808), *The Lady of the Lake* (1810) and *The Bridal of Triermain* (1813). He had been even more successful with several popular novels that captured the spirit of the times better than anything else current in English literature. These were: *Waverley* (1814), *Guy Mannering* (1815), *The Antiquary* (1816), *Old Mortality* (1816), *Rob Roy* (1817) and *The Heart of Midlothian* (1818). It was as a successful author with an assured public that Scott started to work upon his *Third Series of Tales of My Landlord*, which was ultimately to be remembered mostly as the source for the opera *Lucia di Lammermoor*.

Strangely enough, Sir Walter Scott's share of *Lucia* was as much conditioned by ill health and pain as was Donizetti's, for during 1818 and 1819 Scott's chronic malady of gallstones was at its most severe. He was unable to walk most of the time, and suffered from fevers, jaundice, nervous exhaustion and a partial blindness that enabled him to distinguish only the outlines of forms. Beyond administering narcotics medical science could do little or nothing for him, and Scott suffered from periodic attacks for almost a year. He was bled several times, was almost perpetually filled with one drug or another (opium and henbane were the two most favored), while hot salt was piled upon his chest as a local irritant. Perhaps the strangest remedy for his illness was suggested by one of his sources of folk tradition, who proposed gathering twelve stones from south-flowing streams and letting him sleep on the stones. Scott, whose humor seldom failed him, managed to ward off this proposal by insisting that the stones had to be wrapped in the petticoat of a widow who had never wanted to be remarried.

During this period of pain, Scott still worked at his usual very rapid rate. He could not write, but dictated to two secretaries, one of them his friend and printer, Ballantyne, the other a young Scottish neighbor, William Laidlaw. Ballantyne, as a sophisticated reader, simply took dictation; Laidlaw, according to Lockhart's biography of Scott, perpetually interrupted with "Gude keep us a'—the like o' that!" as thrilling moments emerged. At times Scott's pain was so severe that his iron control was relinquished, and his screams could be heard outside in the garden. Laidlaw in such instances wanted to stop work, but Scott would merely reply with never-failing good humor, "Nay, Willie, only see that the doors are fast."

It is further recorded that Scott, drugged and exhausted mentally, would sometimes stagger to his feet during the more action-filled portions of the story and enact the parts in different voices, while the secretaries took down the words. On occasion Scott apparently questioned his own mental balance, and set himself tests to see if his mind had failed.

Despite these circumstances, *The Bride of Lammermoor* was finished, and on June 10, 1819, it was published simultaneously by John Murray in London and Blackwood in Edinburgh. Scott, by now in better physical condition, looked at his work with curiosity: he still remembered the family traditions that had suggested the story of the Bride of Dunbar, but he was forced to read his novel as if it had been written by a stranger, since he had absolutely no memory of it.

"For a long time," it is reported he said to Ballantyne, "I felt myself very uneasy in the course of my reading, lest I should be startled by meeting something altogether glaring and fantastic. However, I recollected that you had been the printer, and I felt sure that you would not have permitted anything of this sort to pass." "'Well,' I [Ballantyne] said, 'upon the whole, how did you like it?' 'Why,' he said, 'as a whole I felt it monstrous gross and grotesque, but still the worst of it made me laugh.'"

In a foreword which he prepared for *The Bride of Lammermoor*, Scott discussed the family traditions that had served as sources for his story. According to these sources, a strange incident had happened in the family of William Dalrymple, the first Viscount of Stair. Stair, who has been characterized as the Coke of Scotland and the ablest lawyer that Scotland ever produced, lived in Scotland during the period of the Commonwealth and the Restoration. He was an extremely able justice, a clever politician, a first-rate diplomat, and one of the most important figures in the adjustment of Scotland to the various political powers that

Sir Walter Scott. Engraving by W. Walker after a painting by
Sir Henry Raeburn.

The marriage contract of David Dunbar and Janet Dalrymple.
The events connected with this wedding were the basis of
The Bride of Lammermoor.

ruled Great Britain during those changing times. He was seconded by his wife, Lady Stair, who was also able, but more ruthless and more passionately involved in seeking power for its own sake. Stair, who was in and out of trouble because of conscientious and legal scruples he had about the changing governments, seems to have been respected, but his wife was hated as a shrew and a termagant. In the eyes of the masses she was a witch.

The important event in the history of the Stair family, apart from the publication of Viscount Stair's *Institutes of Scottish Law*, was the marriage of Janet Dalrymple, Stair's daughter, to David Dunbar, Lord of Baldoon, on August 12, 1668. Janet had previously pledged herself to a Lord Rutherford, but pressure from her family caused her to break her oath and marry Dunbar. This incident, and the events that tradition claimed took place after it, served as the basis for *The Bride of Lammermoor*. Scott changed names, shifted the setting from the eastern Scottish borderlands to the western, and developed his sources into a full Romantic novel.

At the time that Scott gathered his information—for he broadened his family traditions by consulting such documents as he could find and by questioning descendants of the families concerned—popular memory knew the story of the Bride of Dunbar in a very fluid form. According to the strongest school of thought, Janet was forced into marriage by her parents. During the bridal night her screams aroused the household, and when they broke into the barred chamber, they found Janet cowering insane in a corner, while Dunbar lay stretched out, bloody, upon the bed. All that Janet could say was, "Tak' your bonny bridegroom." The assumption was that either Janet had stabbed Dunbar, or that Rutherford, her discarded fiancé, had somehow entered the room and stabbed Dunbar. Janet was said to have died shortly after this, never regaining her sanity. When Dunbar recovered from his wounds, he summoned his friends and relatives to a meeting, and told them that if any woman ever spoke to him about the events of his wedding night, he would never speak to her again; if any man spoke, a duel would follow.

Another tradition, familiar to Scott, held, however, that it was Janet who had been stabbed and that either Dunbar was a homicidal maniac or her former lover, Rutherford, had attacked her.

In both of these stories, in addition, the supernatural was not ruled out, just as it is not entirely ruled out in Scott's novel.

What really happened in the bridal chamber of Baldoon on that night in mid-August 1668?

We have no documents to guide us, for the institution of civil records was of more recent date in Scotland, and in any case the great Scottish families were often able to control news of their doings. This much, however, is certain: Janet Dalrymple had engaged herself to Lord Rutherford—though which Lord Rutherford is unclear, since there were two brothers who held the title in rapid succession at this time. Her parents objected to the match since Rutherford was poor, and her mother, quoting a verse from Leviticus to the effect that a maiden's vows are worthless if her father disapproves, pressed Janet into breaking her engagement. On August 12, 1668, her wedding to Baldoon took place, with Janet white and trembling.* The bridal party roistered at her parents' house for several days, after which they all trooped to Baldoon, near Wigton, and watched a masque.

There are two contemporary accounts of what happened next. The most colorful of these is a scurrilously violent pasquin on the Stair family. It was written by one William Hamilton, a bitter enemy of the Dalrymples, and as a reading of the scandalous, obscene and sometimes blasphemous poem will show, he considered nothing too vile for the Dalrymples to do. Lady Dalrymple, according to the pasquin, was an out-and-out witch, who cast murrains upon animals and people and attended his Satanic majesty. Her children were equally as bad: Janet's sister flew through the air "upon her rumple" and was a worse nymphomaniac than Messalina. About the incident of Janet Dalrymple's marriage with Dunbar (who happened to be Rutherford's nephew) Hamilton says:

> What train of curses that base brood pursues
> Where the young nephew weds the old uncle's spouse!
> . . . .
> In all Stair's offspring we no difference know,
> They do the females, as the males, bestow—
> So he of ane of his daughter's mariage gave the ward,
> Lyke a true vassal, to Glenlusse's laird;
> He knew what she did to her master plight,
> If she her faith to Rutherford should blight;
> Which, like his own, for greid he brek outright.
> Nick did Baldoon's posteriors right deride,
> And as first substitute did sease the bride,
> What e're he to his mistress did or said,

---

* The marriage contract with the signatures of Janet and Dunbar was still in existence at the beginning of the twentieth century (and probably still exists).

He threw the bridegroom from the nuptial bed,
Into the chimney did so his rivall maull,
His bruised bones ne're cured but by the fall.

According to this version of the story, Janet presumably swore an oath to Satan to marry Rutherford, and when she broke the oath, the Devil came and claimed her for his prey. The last line refers to Dunbar's death, some years later, by being thrown from his horse.

The only other contemporary account was written by the Rev. Andrew Sympson, who devoted a long, prolix poem to the marriage. According to this account, the aftermath to the wedding was a pedestrian tragedy:

She waned in her prime,
For Atropos with her impartial knife,
Soon cut her thread and therewithall her life.

The minister's elegy records nothing unusual about either the bridal night or the fate of the couple. Janet simply wasted away and died, while nothing at all happened to Dunbar.

Is it possible that a novel, several plays, and several operas have all been based upon a "historical incident" that never happened?

We will never know the full story of Janet Dalrymple and David Dunbar, perhaps because there is nothing to know. The entire complex of events reads almost like a case study in folklore. Violent local prejudice, which in Scotland in the late seventeenth century was interpreted in terms of witchcraft, seized on the death of Stair's daughter (for the family was saddled with tragedy), and a scurrilous rhymester swore that the Devil had raped her. (Not too many years later than this Daniel Defoe wrote a pamphlet detailing very minutely how the Devil had appeared and bodily snatched away one of Defoe's literary enemies.)

This tradition of witchcraft gradually degenerated, with the supernatural aspects becoming weaker and weaker, as the Stair family was forgotten, until by Scott's time only a few ambivalent descriptions remained. These descriptions could be interpreted, as they were by Scott, as attempted or successful murder. In the literary treatments since Scott's time, the supernatural aspects have completely disappeared, and Janet Dalrymple, as Lucia di Lammermoor, has become almost the type figure in literature and music of a pitiful girl whose life is destroyed by her greedy family, who force her into an unwanted marriage.

When Scott worked the traditions he had collected into a novel, he used as a basic framework the contemporary literary form best suited to carry such material; this was the Gothic novel. Like *The Bride of Lammermoor*, the Gothic novel was basically a story of persecutions, disinheritance, brooding ancestral curses, and often eventual tragedy. In motivating force *The Bride of Lammermoor* shares a peculiar characteristic with the Gothic work of Horace Walpole, Mrs. Radcliffe, M. G. Lewis and Maturin: the hero, Ravenswood, never initiates action; he is simply a pawn in the hands of larger forces, and he never can do more than rage. In characterization, too, Ravenswood is very similar to the later heroes of Gothic fiction (who had by this time assumed some of the characteristics of the earlier villains): he is morose, vengeful, proud, irascible, melancholic and egocentric. To a modern reader Ravenswood is not a particularly sympathetic personality.

Yet Scott did not stop with this Gothic layer; a more personal element came from his own preoccupation with history; it is for these elements that the development of the English novel is indebted to Scott. Although emotions within *The Bride of Lammermoor* may be high, and the speech of the major characters may be resoundingly rhetorical, in many other ways Scott never abandoned external verisimilitude. Everyday life is low, actions are reasonable, and the minor personalities are conceived realistically rather than symbolically.

As a result of this dual origin (the Gothic framework and historical realism) *The Bride of Lammermoor* sometimes seems strangely compounded. Along with scowling brows, ruined castles and vows of vengeance it contains a swarm of details of daily life in seventeenth-century Scotland; accurate descriptions of the countryside and of local history; evidences of social stratification, with the expedients that loyal retainers must use to obtain food for their penniless lairds who are both too proud and too incompetent to earn their own living, and the schemes of the peasants to avoid such levies; the high-flung code of honor and the duello; corrupt politics at the court at Edinburgh; the niceties of Scots legal contracts, and similar material by means of which Scott almost single-handedly lifted the novel out of the static Gothic pattern into the progressive Victorian channel.

The supernatural aspects of the story seem to have nonplused Scott somewhat, and it is a flaw in *The Bride of Lammermoor* that its author cannot bear to part with any of the multiple purposes that animate the book: a realistic picture of life in Scotland in the late seventeenth century; a melodramatic story with thrilling and pathetic situations; the humorous aspects of haughty pride helpless before financial reality; and the spooks and bogles that tradition associated with the Bride of

Dunbar. The result is a very strange mixture: an ancient curse by Thomas the Rhymer that is fulfilled; a woman with the second-sight; a ghost, and a few portents. Some of the men who reworked Scott's novel for the stage seem to have recognized that this mixture was too diverse, at least for their purposes, and rid their versions of certain elements. The earliest operatic version concentrated on the Scottish humor; the English-language stage versions, for the most part, concentrated on the melodrama; Cammarano dropped all pretense at historical accuracy and environmental realism, and concerned himself primarily with the melodramatic aspects of the story, with only a tinge of supernaturalism in Lucia's story of the haunted fountain—and even this was dropped in many performances of *Lucia di Lammermoor.*

Despite the strange mixture of sentimentalism and hardheaded intellectualism, Gothic rant and Scottish peasant dialect—or perhaps because of this weird intermingling of different levels—*The Bride of Lammermoor* was a success as a novel. Critics rated it with *Romeo and Juliet* as a story of pathetic love, and readers bought edition after edition. It would be safe to say that it was one of the best-known works of fiction in all Western Europe by the time that Donizetti and Cammarano began to work with it.

Scott's work was usually pirated almost immediately upon the Continent, and English-language pirated editions from Paris and French translations usually appeared almost simultaneously with their authorized British counterparts. According to the memoirs of one of the printers at a Paris establishment, marked galleys of Scott's novels made their way surreptitiously from London to Paris in a matter of days, and teams of typesetters and pressmen worked night and day to parallel or beat the British editions to the market. These unauthorized editions were then circulated all over Europe.

Scott's works were perpetually dramatized, too. Covent Garden, the Royal Theatre of Edinburgh, the Park Theatre in New York, Drury Lane in London, the Comédie-Française of Paris, the Vaudeville of Paris, the Gaîté of Paris, the Opéra-Comique of Paris and practically every other major theatre or opera house knew either dramatizations or operatic versions of Scott's novels, sometimes authorized, sometimes unauthorized.

The first dramatization of *The Bride of Lammermoor* took place at the Surrey Theatre in London in 1819, less than two weeks after the appearance of the novel. The author of *The Bride of Lammermoor, or, The Spectre at the Fountain* was Tom Dibdin, an extremely prolific dramatic hack who is said to have written over 200 plays, many of which were quite successful. His dramatization of Scott's novel, however, was not a success, either as box office or as literature. Its text has been lost, but Dibdin apparently altered the plot in several instances; Edgar, for example, is killed by a domestic rather than either committing suicide as in the opera or wandering into the quicksand as in the novel.

The second, and most important, English stage adaptation of Scott's novel was prepared by John W. Cole, an Edinburgh actor and official poet to the Theatre Royal, better known to his friends as Old King Cole and to the public as J. W. Calcraft. Cole paralleled Scott closely in many respects, although he did make some alterations: Lucy dies in Ravenswood's arms, and Ravenswood commits suicide by falling upon his sword. This is the first time in the history of the story that Ravenswood has committed suicide.

Despite a brilliant cast which included Calcraft, Mrs. Siddons and Mackay, the first performances of Calcraft's *Bride of Lammermoor* were not successful, but the play gradually gathered momentum, until by the end of the 1820's it had spread widely and successfully over the English-speaking world.

The first continental dramatization of *The Bride of Lammermoor* took place in Paris, 1827,* with a one-act opera entitled *Caleb de Walter Scott*, with book by Achille d'Artois and Eugène de Planard, and music by Adolphe Adam. The French authors stressed the humorous aspects of Caleb Balderstone, and provided a happy ending.

More important was *La Fiancée de Lammermoor* by Victor Ducange, which was first performed in Paris in 1828. A heroic drama, it is admittedly a somewhat free adaptation of Scott's story. While it introduces some new material and makes certain changes, it is still closer to Scott's novel than is Cammarano's libretto.

Ducange's play is located rather precisely in time, in 1689–90, during the attempted restoration of James II; the changing fortunes of the war between William and James affect the events and motivations of the play. On the whole, the sequence of events is much as in Carafa's opera (see below), but *La Fiancée de Lammermoor* does present some peculiar features. The Chancellor very consciously sets out to win Ravenswood's friendship when it seems likely that James will win the war. Edgard

---

* Henry A. White in his *Sir Walter Scott's Novels on the Stage* mentions *La Fiancée de Lammermoor* with music by Auber and libretto by Scribe. No other reference to this opera has been found and it seems to be mythical. Perhaps it arose from misinterpretation of the title of *La Fiancée*, by Auber and Scribe.

Lucy and Edgar in *The Bride of Lammermoor*. After a painting
by Sir John Everett Millais.

A lithograph by Eugène Delacroix from an 1830 French translation of Scott's novel, illustrating the passage in Chapter XXIX:
"The bird dropped at the feet of Lucy, whose dress was stained
with some spots of its blood." *(Courtesy Bibliothèque et Musée
de l'Opéra, Paris)*

saves the Chancellor and Lucie from assassins when the Ashtons have taken refuge from the storm in Wolfcrag. Lady Ashton and her brother, Lord Douglas, try to cause Edgard's arrest for treason, since warrants are out against members of Athol's party, but the Chancellor permits him to go free. The crux of the play consists of Lucie's agreement to marry Lord Seymours (Mrs. Ashton's candidate for Lucie's hand) to save Edgard from the scaffold. Lady Ashton is Lucie's stepmother rather than natural mother. When Edgard bursts in during the wedding, Lucie loses her mind and her memory, and does not recognize him; she regains her reason only as he is leaving. She follows Edgard to the sea, where Edgard intends to commit suicide. Both are trapped by the waves and are drowned, despite efforts to save them. Lucie's body is carried in by fishermen.

Michele Carafa's opera *Le Nozze di Lammermoor*, which was performed in Paris in 1829, is obviously adapted from Ducange's play, and many of the motivations and incidents in Carafa's work, which are not clear from the surviving vocal score itself, receive illumination from Ducange's play. Carafa's opera, as the first important opera based upon the heart-situation of Scott's novel, is discussed in some detail in Appendix A, page 157.

That Donizetti and Cammarano knew Carafa's work, and probably also Ducange's, would seem almost certain. Donizetti moved in the same circles in Paris as did Carafa, and Carafa's music was available in a piano transcription. Even if Donizetti had never attended a performance of *Le Nozze di Lammermoor*, he could still have been well aware of both the music and the libretto.

Donizetti did not borrow from Carafa's music, but the librettos of *Lucia di Lammermoor* and *Le Nozze di Lammermoor* share certain features. Both operas begin with a chorus of huntsmen (which is not too well motivated in *Lucia di Lammermoor*). Both develop the engagement scene between Lucia and Edgardo beyond Scott's brief mention of its occurrence. Carafa and the earlier versions of Donizetti's *Lucia di Lammermoor* call the castle where Lucia lives "Lammermoor"—which is really a district in Scotland—and both spell Lucia's last name as "Asthon." Both operas change the old blind seeress Alice into a servant for Lucia— Elisa and Alisa. Both treat the signing of the marriage contract as a form of wedding, and both portray the events at the contract-signing in vocal groups, an octet in Carafa, a sextet in Donizetti. Both have scenes set amid the tombs of the Ravenswoods. In both Edgardo commits suicide before the audience. There are many other points of resemblance.

Some of these likenesses can be explained as arising from dramatic necessity and operatic patterns, but the two operas have so much in common that it seems probable that Donizetti and Cammarano used Carafa and his librettist Balochi as a source. This borrowing should not be considered plagiarism, however, but simply fair use, well within the bounds of propriety.

II. Summary of Scott's Novel

Cammarano and Donizetti, when they prepared *Lucia di Lammermoor*, used only the central situation from Scott's *Bride of Lammermoor*, omitting all the Scottish local color, the political background, detailed personality studies and broad humor which Scott put into his novel. It is curious to note that Scott's novel is just as detailed and concrete in its background and setting as Cammarano's libretto is vague and abstract.

The Bride of Lammermoor is set in Southeastern Scotland, where the hills slope down to meet the seaside plains; it takes place not too many years after the Jacobite rebellion of 1689. As the novel begins, Sir William Ashton, a Whig lawyer and political opportunist, has acquired the hereditary holdings of the old and aristocratic Ravenswood family, who had been unfortunate enough to espouse the losing Jacobite cause. The loss of his property through legal chicanery has broken the heart of Allan, Lord Ravenswood, and he has just died, leaving his twenty-year-old son, Edgar, the last of the Ravenswoods. Edgar, penniless and a laird only by courtesy, takes up his abode in the crumbling tower of Wolf's Crag in the wilderness, all that remains to him of the vast former holdings of his family. A dark, brooding, Byronic young man, he has sworn vengeance upon the upstart usurpers.

Meanwhile, the Ashtons have established themselves in Ravenswood Castle. Besides Sir William, who has now advanced to the position of Lord Keeper, there are his wife Lady Ashton, a fiercely proud, violently ambitious termagant, who is the driving force behind her husband; her oldest son, Colonel Sholto Douglas, who is absent for most of the novel—he resembles his mother greatly in disposition; Lucy, approximately seventeen years of age, sweet-tempered and docile to a fault; and Henry, her younger brother, who is a rather spoiled self-centered youngster. Along with the estate the Ashtons have taken over many of the former retainers of the Ravenswoods.

One day when Edgar, still called locally the "Master" of Ravenswood, is prowling around the grounds of the Castle, looking for an opportunity to shoot Sir William Ashton, he sees Lucy and Sir William about to be attacked by a wild bull. He kills the bull with a well-placed shot, and although he repulses Sir William's thanks with scorn, he is instantly attracted to Lucy. He had intended, after killing Ashton, to seek his fortune at the French court of the Pretender, but he now decides to remain at Wolf's Crag, despite his poverty. He even offers sanctuary there to another Jacobite sympathizer, Frank Hayston, later Laird of Bucklaw, a young scapegrace with the certain expectation of inheriting a fortune and a title.

Sir William resolves to win the friendship of the sullen, unfriendly Master. He acts from mixed motives: he is really grateful that Ravenswood saved his and Lucy's lives; he fears the Master's revenge, for the Ravenswoods were notorious for bloody vendettas; he wishes to justify to his own conscience the somewhat shady tactics he had used to win the domain of the Ravenswoods; and, most of all, probably, he is afraid of the political future. There are signs of political reversals; the Parliament is about to sit in consideration of claims; and the Ravenswoods had very strong connections, particularly the Marquis of A[thol], whom Ashton fears desperately. In any case, the wily Keeper is successful in winning the confidence of the suspicious but naïve Master, and Ravenswood accepts an invitation to stay at the Castle.

Lady Ashton has been away during these manoeuvres, but she soon learns of her daughter's friendship with Ravenswood, and determines to break the relationship. Meanwhile, Lucy and Edgar have pledged their faith in secret; as a symbol of their betrothal, they have broken a piece of gold, each keeping half.

Returning hastily to the Castle, Lady Ashton forthwith orders Edgar Ravenswood to leave, since she wishes Lucy to marry Bucklaw, who has now acquired both his title and wealth. The malignant, strong-willed old woman overrides all objections to her action, and when Ravenswood's powerful relative sends him overseas on a mission, Lady Ashton sees to it that Lucy is totally unable to communicate with him, or even to hear any news about him. Subtly and gradually, she makes her daughter a virtual prisoner on the estate, perpetually undermining her spirit to make her agree to marry Bucklaw. The others in the family are incapable of resisting Lady Ashton, and Lucy remains alone and miserable in her opposition.

A year passes without word from Ravenswood. Lucy pines, with long periods of depression alternating with violent and unaccustomed outbursts of temperament. At last, growing alarmed over her daughter's health, Lady Ashton brings into the household the Reverend Mr. Bide-the-Bent, a kindly, well-intentioned (though naïve) clergyman who offers to communicate with the long-silent Edgar; if within a given period of time Edgar answers and affirms his prior claim to Lucy's affections, the girl will continue to refuse Bucklaw; if, however, Ravenswood does not answer, Lucy must yield. The Ashtons are now becoming more and more anxious that Lucy marry Bucklaw, for the Whigs are losing ground, and Ashton's possession of the Ravenswood estate is about to be questioned in Parliament.

When nothing is heard from Ravenswood within the prescribed time, Lucy agrees to marry Bucklaw. A marriage contract is drawn up, to be signed four or five days before the wedding. Only a small family group is present to celebrate the signing of the contract, and Lucy, the last to sign, is just finishing her signature when a commotion is heard outside the room. To the dismay of everyone, the long-absent Ravenswood strides in.

Furious words follow and bloodshed is avoided only by the intervention of Mr. Bide-the-Bent. Edgar demands an interview with Lucy, which is granted to him only on the condition that Lady Ashton is also present. Lucy stands dumbly by while Lady Ashton speaks for her. Ravenswood, disgusted at what he thinks is broken faith and fickleness, demands his love-token back, and leaves, cursing Lucy and her family. Lucy stands dejectedly, her hand feeling for her missing token. Colonel Sholto Ashton, who had returned for the wedding, accosts Ravenswood as he is leaving and challenges him to a duel. It is agreed that the duel will take place after Lucy's wedding, and Ravenswood, his blind rage turning rapidly to deep despondency, returns to Wolf's Crag.

The wedding takes place, with Lucy listless and impassive. According to the custom of the times, the bridal pair retire while the family and friends continue to celebrate the wedding. The festivities, however, are suddenly interrupted by a series of shrieks and cries from the bridal chamber. The guests break down the door and find Bucklaw, seriously but not mortally wounded by dagger thrusts; Lucy is presently discovered, her torn nightclothes stained with blood, huddled in a corner, grinning and gibbering. The unhappy bride lives only a few days longer, and never regains her sanity. Bucklaw recovers from his wounds, but firmly refuses to tell what had happened.

Shortly after Lucy's funeral, Ravenswood rides from Wolf's Crag to fight his duel with Colonel Ashton. He is now a broken man, and wants only to find death on Ashton's sword. According to an ancient prophecy the race of Ravenswood will perish in the nearby quicksands, and it is significant that Ravenswood, whose route passes the sands, never reaches the duelling ground and is never seen again.

This is the broad outline of the plot, which Scott embellished and interwove with a succession of other novelistic fancies. There is much detail about the political and social life of the period, about the technique of the hunt, about the customs of the fiercely independent tenants on the former Ravenswood holdings. The supernatural enters with the figure of Alice, an ancient blind retainer of the Ravenswoods, who is gifted with the second-sight. She sees the fatal outcome of the love between Edgar and Lucy long before the two young people are even aware that they are in love. Her ghost appears to Ravenswood as he passes the haunted Mermaiden's Fountain. There is also a fair amount of comedy, carried mostly by two persons, Craigengelt and Caleb Balderstone. Craigengelt, one of the most despicable toadies and cowardly braggarts in literature, is Bucklaw's parasite and evil genius. Balderstone, the last loyal retainer of the Ravenswoods, feels the family pride even more strongly than does the Master himself, and is perpetually in frantic endeavor to maintain the ancient standards of wealth and hospitality on an empty purse.

Almost all of this peripheral material was stripped away by Cammarano and Donizetti, who focused their attention upon a single basic situation, the frustrated love between Lucy and Edgar.

PERFORMANCE HISTORY

September 26, 1835 marked one of the high points of Donizetti's life. As he wrote to his friend Giovanni Ricordi on September 29th:

> *Lucia di Lammermoor* was performed, and permit me simply to say, in a friendly way, that I'm embarrassed, and that's the truth. It was liked, and it was liked very much, if I am to believe the applause and the compliments that I received. I was called out many times [for applause] and so were the singers, too. His Majesty's brother, Leopold, who was present and who applauded, paid me the most flattering compliments. The second evening I observed something very rare in Naples. That is to say, in the finale, after great *vivas* in the adagio section, Duprez was wildly applauded in the malediction, before the *stretta*. Every piece was listened to with religious silence and celebrated with spontaneous *vivas*.... Tacchinardi, Duprez, Cosselli and Porto carried themselves very well, especially the first two, who were miraculous.

Rossini, whose dictum was unquestioned in the world of opera, said of it, "This is the most beautiful opera by our young colleague."

From Naples *Lucia* spread out over the operatic world like sparks from a guttering torch. It was acclaimed as a masterpiece everywhere, and immediately became a favorite. This 1835 Italian version was in Vienna by April 1837; Madrid, August 1837; Paris, December 1837; Lisbon, January 1838; London, April 1838; Algiers, spring 1839; Odessa, summer 1839; Athens, January 1840; Havana, October 1840; Lima, 1841; Mexico City, July 1841; New York, September 1843; Warsaw, 1844; Constantinople, 1845, and so on, over the world.

Translated into other languages, it circulated equally widely. German versions, not always the same translation, appeared in Vienna, April 1837; Berlin, October 1838; Prague, October 1838; Ljubljana, February 1839; Budapest, January 1840. It was also translated, at various times, into Spanish (where it was turned into a *zarzuela*), Czech, Hungarian, Swedish, Russian, Polish and probably other languages.

The most important of these translations was the French, which appeared in Paris on August 6, 1839, with Donizetti's own staging. The

Italian *Lucia di Lammermoor*, it is true, had appeared several times earlier in Paris, but this new French translation, prepared by Alphonse Royer and Gustave Vaëz, became a force in itself. It differed in some ways, as will be shown, from the Italian version, and as it diffused throughout the world, it merged in various combinations with the earlier Italian version.

The première of the French *Lucie de Lammermoor* took place at the Théâtre de la Renaissance, which had been having financial difficulties at this time. Donizetti subscribed 5,000 francs as a loan to the theatre, and also agreed to revise *Lucia* for a French audience. Two veteran French librettists, Alphonse Royer and Gustave Vaëz, worked with him, and made considerable changes in the opera. In addition to alterations in individual lines, motivations and plot structure, the collaborators dropped the character of Alisa, enlarged the part of Normanno (whom they now called Gilbert) and changed many details of setting to conform to French customs in staging. These changes may be seen in the translation of the French libretto which is included in this book (Appendix B, page 165).

Donizetti also changed the music considerably to suit the needs of the new work. Some scenes were dropped from the Italian version, and new music was written for the new sections of libretto. Most of this new music, however, is recitative, either accompanied or unaccompanied, although there are a few melodic sections. There are also many minor changes within the material that was retained from the Italian version: additional notes are inserted to fit French prosody, other notes are dropped, certain sections are transposed to a different key (the soprano may have had difficulty with her lower register), and melodies are sometimes changed. It has not been possible to determine if there were any changes in the orchestration, since only a piano transcription and vocal score have been published.

In this French production of *Lucie de Lammermoor* Donizetti officially substituted the aria "Perchè non ho del vento" for the beautiful "Regnava nel silenzio" in No. 4 in the first act. For several decades "Perchè non ho del vento," which had been borrowed from Donizetti's earlier opera *Rosmonda d'Inghilterra*, was the music customarily sung at this point in the opera, in both the Italian and French versions.*

* It has been claimed that this substitution took place earlier in Italy with Fanny Tacchinardi-Persiani, but there does not seem to be any certain evidence for this claim. The close association of "Perchè non ho del vento" with the French *Lucie de Lammermoor* and its influences make it seem more likely that Donizetti himself made the exchange in Paris.

Donizetti was unhappy with the casting at the Renaissance, which could not afford top-flight singers, but was nevertheless pleased at the reaction of his audiences; as he wrote from Paris, August 9, 1839, to Tomaso Persico:

Which newspapers shall I send you? I'm embarrassed. Why? I've put on a French *Lucia* at the Renaissance with a company of *juvenes et cani* [children and old men], but it's as if I have a star protecting me.... All you need know is that while I was in bed with a headache after the opera, I had to get up because the singers, choruses and orchestra came with torches to repeat the choruses from *Lucia* under my window, and from on high, like royalty, I expressed my gratitude in between the screaming. Yesterday evening, the second performance, the theatre was packed. For this theatre, which had been going badly, I had subscribed 5,000 francs, and now the impresario has returned my money to me, saying that he doesn't need it any more.

The French *Lucie de Lammermoor* moved into the provinces of France, and started its own travels around the world. It appeared in Brussels in September 1839; Amsterdam, December 1839; New Orleans, 1841; Batavia, October 1842, and at Drury Lane, in London, in July 1845, although an earlier English translation, January 1843, had obviously been influenced by the French *Lucie*.

II

Although the French-language *Lucie de Lammermoor* had appeared in New Orleans in December 1841, with Nourrit's brother as Edgard, this seems to have been an isolated début, with no significance to American operatic history. Instead, the New York première, in September 1843, of the original Italian version is the true beginning of *Lucia di Lammermoor* in America.

Niblo's Garden, September 15, 1843, was the place and time, with Donizetti's opera performed by a cast that had been scraped together to make up an operatic season. Lucia was played by Signora Amelia Majocchi, Ashton by Attilio Valterllina, Edgardo by Cirillo Antognini and Raimondo by Temistocle Maggiori. The singers were not first-rate, and the performance was only mediocre; still, since it was the only *Lucia* available, it was well received.

Palmo's Opera House in New York, 1844, held the next sequence of performances. Eufrasia Borghese, a more capable singer than Majocchi, played Lucia and was appreciated. "Although evidently laboring under

Alphonse Royer (*left*) and Gustave Vaëz (*right*), co-librettists of *Lucie de Lammermoor*, Donizetti's French version of *Lucia*. The portrait of Royer is a lithograph after a picture by Benjamin; the photograph of Vaëz is by Franck. (*Both pictures courtesy Bibliothèque et Musée de l'Opéra, Paris*)

Two settings from an old Metropolitan Opera production of
Lucia: (*above*) for Act 1, Scene 2, and (*below*) for Act 2, Scene 2.

a severe cold, she gave her role last night in even more than her usual impassioned and thrilling manner... in the mad scenes she was indeed great," said one of the contemporary reviewers. Palmo's troupe performed again in the 1844-5 season; in 1845, when an English translation was used; and in 1847.

The first really good performance of *Lucia* took place at Niblo's Garden in 1850, with Marty's Havana Opera Company, directed by the excellent conductor Arditi, who is still remembered for some of his songs. Balbina Steffanone was Lucia, Federico Badiali was Ashton, and Lorenzo Salvi was Edgardo. Admission was one dollar top price. The "audiences ran wild."

Much the greatest *Lucia* heard in America was soon to follow, when Adelina Patti made her début at sixteen at the Academy of Music in New York, on November 24, 1859. Her Lucia was a triumph, both in the United States and later in Europe, and the role long continued to be one of her favorites. That she took the role seriously may be seen from the adventures that befell her at various points in her life as she performed it. During her début, one of the local gentry accidentally fired his pistol in the middle of the performance. The music stopped for a moment, but when it was recognized that no harm was meant, the performance went on. Years later, in Bucharest, *Lucia* was halted briefly during the mad scene, when a member of the audience fell into the pit atop a woman, and a shout of fire arose. Patti cried, "It is no fire," and continued to sing, quieting the house. But in Vienna, she had just started to sing the mad scene, when her dress really caught fire in the gas flare that lighted the stage. She simply ripped off the offending portion and continued her song. In San Francisco a lunatic threw a bomb onto the stage. The bomb exploded and the audience started to panic, but again Patti held them in their seats. Perhaps these incidents demonstrate that Patti had greater moral strength than Janet Dalrymple?

III

During the middle of the nineteenth century, as *Lucia di Lammermoor* was translated into most of the civilized languages of the world, alterations were often made to bring the opera into conformity with local cultural standards. In England, for example, while Italian and French versions were performed, native versions, unquestionably influenced by the "blood and thunder" stage, also emerged; in some cases these achieved considerable popularity.

The *English Version of Lucia di Lammermoor, a Grand Opera in Three Acts* follows the French text with reasonable closeness, departing principally in spoken portions, which are expanded, and in a few smaller details of plot. In this version, which is set in the last years of Charles II, the character Gilbert has been transformed into Lockheart, which name had been applied in Scott's novel to a servant of Ashton's; Lockheart does not have the comic aspects of Gilbert, nor is he bribed by Lucia, as was Gilbert, but otherwise he serves the same function in the story. Bucklaw dies in Bide-the-Bent's arms. Ashton does not appear in the last scene. And most important of all, Lucia wanders about the stage during the mad scene with a bloody dagger in her hand. This version of *Lucia di Lammermoor* was long popular in England and America, and was readily available in *Lacy's Acting Theatre*. It seems to have been performed in New York in the middle nineteenth century.

George Soane, the British dramatist, translator, and theatricalist, also created a new version of *Lucia di Lammermoor* for the British market. In Soane's version the arias and music were retained, but the spoken sections were changed. Lucy, for example, is not persuaded to marry Bucklaw by means of forged letters or counterfeit rings; she is overcome simply by the will of her brother. She does not go mad, but languishes offstage, while Ravenswood commits suicide before the wedding guests. Soane's version was imported to America and performed at Niblo's during the 1850's, as a variant to the Italian piece.

Donizetti's opera also undoubtedly served to keep Scott's novel alive, and several stage versions of the novel appeared during the later part of the nineteenth century. Leon Grus, in the last decades of the century, adapted and restaged Adolphe Adam's French opera *Caleb de Walter Scott*, while other now-lost versions of the play are known only from reviews. J. Palgrave's *Master of Ravenswood* was extremely popular in England and America; Dickens had a hand in its staging. Sir Henry Irving and Ellen Terry acted in still another version, *Ravenswood*, which was successfully performed in 1890–1. Irving's performance was considered remarkable.

The parodists did not hesitate to seize upon the story for their sport. *Lucy Did Sham Amour* with libretto by Dr. Northall and music by George Loder, appeared at the Chatham Theatre in New York in 1848. The point of the humor seems to have been librettoland.

The most important burlesque or parody of *Lucia di Lammermoor*, however, is Henry J. Byron's, which is one of a series of operatic parodies including *Little Don Giovanni, Norma*, etc. It was first performed at the

Prince of Wales's Theatre in London in 1865. Written in rhymed doggerel couplets, it is modern in setting and occasionally topical. The action and words burlesque Donizetti's work in a manner anticipatory of Gilbert and Sullivan.

Sometimes the burlesque is aimed at the personalities of librettoland:

> HENRY: The chief peculiarity in *me*,
> Is that I hate like poison all I see.
> My hatred doth embrace the worst and best,
> And all those I don't *hate* I detest.

Sometimes the individual lines of Cammarano's Italian libretto are scored:

> Atrocious creditors bombard my door!

Puns abound:

> LUCY: Oh! Kind fate doth pull it,
> And by a timely *bullet* is the *bull hit*.

Edgar's curse must have sounded frightful to Lucy:

> EDGAR: May you find that matrimony does not pay!
> May you soon find your fond adoring hub,
> Pass his whole time at his convivial club!
> Until you hate him, then when you can't bear him,
> May nothing from your presence ever tear him!
> May every play you go to turn out dull!
> May every evening party prove a mull!
> May he deny every debt by you incurred!
> May your dressmaker never keep her word!

The ending, however, is happy.

In some scenes (the duets between Lucy and Edgar, and Lucy and Henry) this parody used Donizetti's melodies, although they seem to have been reworked by J. C. Van Maanen. In other places traditional or popular tunes are indicated.

IV

Since Donizetti's lifetime Lucia has been one of the favorite roles of the prima donna, and it has been attempted by almost every important coloratura soprano of the last hundred years. In the period soon after Donizetti's death Giuletta Grisi was the most renowned Lucia; she was followed, for Northern Europe, by Jenny Lind. Adelina Patti, however, soon assumed the role and retained supremacy until her old age.

During the Golden Age and the modern period certain singers have specialized in the part of Lucia. Marcella Sembrich, who was the mainstay of the Metropolitan Opera in the last decade of the nineteenth century, made her début there as Lucia; other great sopranos who have excelled as Lucia include Nellie Melba, the brilliant Australian, whose recordings reveal much the maddest Lucia of all; Luisa Tetrazzini, whose dramatic sense and ability at pyrotechnics make her "Regnava nel silenzio" a remarkable experience on records; and Amelita Galli-Curci, perhaps the most pathetic and most tragic Lucia. Within more recent years the French soprano Lily Pons was the leading interpreter for the United States; since her vocal range was high, she transposed the music up, rather than down, as many other singers have been forced to do. In Italy the leading interpreters of Lucia were Toti Dal Monte and Lina Pagliughi. During the modern period Maria Callas, whose Lucia is in some ways the most intelligent, Joan Sutherland and Beverly Sills have led to further renewal of interest in the opera.

Many great tenors have excelled in the role of the unfortunate Edgardo. After Duprez, Mario and Nicolini, both associated with Patti, were outstanding performers. Within the recording period Caruso is preeminent; after his death John McCormack, Martinelli, Schipa and Gigli excelled in the role.

Ashton has been sung by many outstanding baritones, foremost of whom was Mattia Battistini; in more recent years Giuseppe de Luca, Pasquale Amato, and the moderns Merrill, Bastianini and Colzani have starred in the role. As basses Ezio Pinza and Cesare Siepi have been most effective.

At present *Lucia di Lammermoor* still has enormous vitality. It was selected to open the 1964 season of the New York Metropolitan Opera and it is one of the operas most frequently heard in the various reproduction media.

PLOT SUMMARY

BACKGROUND

Lucia di Lammermoor is set in Southwestern Scotland, in the somewhat nebulous time when "William is dead and Mary is ascending the throne,"* perhaps around 1700. This is a time of crisis in Scottish politics, and heads and fortunes have been falling with equal frequency. In the Lammermoor area the Ravenswoods were long the dominant family, but they have had the misfortune to back the wrong political party, and have lost their power, lands, and wealth. A new family, the Ashtons,† has risen to preeminence, and by various legal and political machinations has managed to acquire most of the property of the Ravenswoods, including Ravenswood Castle;‡ the Ravenswoods now have left to them only the half-ruined tower of Wolf's Crag.

At the time the opera takes place, the Laird of Ravenswood has died of a broken heart, and his son, Edgardo, the last of the family, blames the Ashtons and has sworn revenge. Enrico Ashton is the head of the hostile Ashton family, and is master of Ravenswood Castle and guardian of his younger sister, Lucia. Enrico is a choleric and vengeful man, who both fears and hates the Ravenswoods. New political upheavals are expected, and Enrico is justifiably afraid that the Ravenswoods may be returned to power and the Ashtons humbled. To assure his own safety Enrico wishes to form an alliance with Lord Arturo Bucklaw, a very powerful laird with strong political connections. Bucklaw would like to marry Lucia, and Ashton has repeatedly pressed her to consent. Lucia, however, has so far been successful in rejecting the marriage by claiming that she is still mourning her recently deceased mother and could not consider marriage at such a time. Enrico's affairs are growing desperate, and he feels that matters are approaching a crisis.

---

* Libretto, p. 113.
† Usually spelled "Asthon" in the earlier libretti and scores.
‡ Lammermoor Castle in the older librettos.

ACT ONE

SCENE ONE

In the grounds of Ravenswood Castle, Normanno, chief of Lord Enrico Ashton's guards and huntsmen, is exhorting his men to search for a stranger who has been sighted. The huntsmen hasten away to carry out their orders, while Enrico Ashton enters, accompanied by Raimondo Bide-the-Bent, a Presbyterian minister who is tutor and chaplain to the Ashtons.

Enrico reveals that he is greatly worried about the changing political situation: his only hope for besting his enemies lies in marrying his sister Lucia to a powerful neighbor, Bucklaw, but Lucia steadfastly refuses her consent. Raimondo comments that the girl cannot be blamed, since she is still mourning her mother and cannot be expected to think of love and marriage. Normanno, who is aware of events unknown to the others, laughs derisively; upon being questioned, he reveals that Lucia has fallen in love with a young man who had saved her from a wild bull some time before. Since that time Lucia has had a daily assignation with this man within the castle grounds.

Enrico is angry enough at hearing this, but his rage is boundless when he hears Normanno's suspicion that Lucia's lover is Edgardo di Ravenswood. The huntsmen return and confirm Normanno's words: while they were resting within the ruins of Wolf's Crag, they saw the object of their search, and a falconer recognized him as Edgardo. Enrico bursts into a rage; deaf both to Raimondo's entreaties for leniency toward Lucia and to the huntsmen's assurances that they will soon trap the trespasser, Enrico Ashton vows to put a bloody ending to the clandestine romance between his sister and his arch enemy.

SCENE TWO

Lucia Ashton and her maid and confidante, Alisa, are at the Mer-maiden's Fountain within the Castle grounds, waiting for Edgardo. As the women wait, Lucia tells Alisa of the supernatural experience she has had there: she has seen the ghost which haunts the fountain, and the ghost has beckoned to her. Alisa realizes that this means death, and urges her mistress to give up a love which can only end in ruin and disaster. But Lucia refuses to heed the warning.

Edgardo enters, and Alisa goes to stand guard for the lovers. To

Lucia's dismay, Edgardo tells her that he must go to France immediately, to serve the Jacobite cause. Before leaving, however, he wishes to make peace with the Ashtons, and seal the peace by marrying Lucia. Lucia, who knows her brother's hatred of Ravenswood, is opposed to telling Enrico, and Edgardo guesses her reasons. He reminds her that his oath of vengeance on the Ashtons is still binding. Lucia begs him to forget his hatred. Edgardo then suddenly urges her to exchange pledges of eternal love and faith with him; they exchange rings and vow love until death. Edgardo declares her his wife. Lucia begs Edgardo to write to her from France, saying that her knowledge of his love will sustain her. They bid each other farewell and part, Lucia back to the Castle, Edgardo to his ruined tower at Wolf's Crag, and from there to France.

ACT TWO

SCENE ONE

A considerable time has passed since the first act, perhaps several months. In Enrico Ashton's study in Ravenswood Castle Enrico and Normanno are busy plotting against the two lovers. Enrico has managed to intercept the correspondence between Edgardo and Lucia, but Lucia still refuses to marry Bucklaw, even though Enrico has made all arrangements for the wedding. As a last resort Enrico and Normanno plan to show Lucia a forged letter in which Edgardo seemingly admits loving another woman.

Lucia enters listlessly and Normanno leaves. She is worn and depressed by Enrico's perpetual badgering, but she still refuses to believe that Edgardo has deceived her. Enrico reminds her that the wedding date is drawing near, but Lucia only laments Enrico's harshness to her. Enrico rages at her, telling her that his care for the family reputation as well as the love he bears for her force him to be harsh, for her own good. She declares that she considers herself already married, whereupon Enrico shows her the forged letter.

Lucia reads the letter with horror, almost fainting at Edgardo's seeming faithlessness. Her misery increases as distant sounds of festivity are heard, indicating that Bucklaw is approaching. Enrico now delivers his final blow: he, her brother, will die beneath the headsman's axe unless she will save him by marrying Arturo. Can she live with this on her conscience? Enrico strides out as Lucia sinks weakly into a chair, begging death to release her from her misery.

Lucia is still in despair when Raimondo enters. She greets him with renewed hope, but collapses again when Raimondo tells her that Edgardo has not answered his letters. Raimondo has suspected that Enrico was intercepting correspondence and had secretly sent a personal letter to Edgardo. Since Edgardo has not answered, Raimondo declares, it must be accepted that he has not kept faith. Raimondo urges her to marry Arturo Bucklaw.

Lucia protests weakly that she is already bound to another man, but Raimondo scornfully replies that such a bond, unblessed by clergy, is worthless in the eyes of both man and Heaven. In the name of his office, by the memory of her mother, for the sake of her brother's life, he urges her to yield and marry Bucklaw. Such a sacrifice must be rewarded by Heaven. Wearily, Lucia surrenders.

Scene Two

A large hall in Ravenswood Castle has been made festive for the reception of Lord Arturo Bucklaw and the signing of the marriage contract. Retainers of the family and the guests sing in praise of Bucklaw: at the summons of love he has come as a powerful friend and ally, and he will reverse the tide of woes that threatens to submerge the Ashtons and their followers. Arturo and Enrico discuss the bride, Arturo asking whether there is any truth to the rumour that Edgardo was interested in Lucia. Enrico, in embarrassment, answers only vaguely; he is saved from further reply by the entry of a wan and despondent Lucia, supported by her maid Alisa and Raimondo. Again excusing his sister's appearance of grief, Enrico formally presents the bridal pair to each other. Lucia cannot hide her revulsion, and Enrico whispers a fierce admonition that she be more prudent. Enrico hastily shepherds the party to the table to sign the contract. Lucia, who is weak and trembling, is the last to put her name to the paper. She has just finished, when the door at the back of the hall is flung open so unceremoniously that everyone turns in surprise.

Edgardo is standing in the doorway, regarding the scene before him with horror and fury. Lucia faints. To a murmur of voices Edgardo states that he still loves her; Enrico is outraged by Edgardo's entry and yet he is beginning to feel the first pangs of remorse for his treatment of his sister; Lucia, Raimondo, Alisa, Arturo also comment, as do the onlookers.

Enrico and Arturo draw their swords and rush toward the unexpected guest, while Edgardo prepares to defend himself. Actual blows are prevented, however, by the intercession of Raimondo, who demands that his presence and the presence of Heaven be respected. Swords are sheathed, though insults continue to pass between Edgardo and Enrico as they glare with hatred at each other. Raimondo, trying to convince Edgardo that he should leave, bids him read the signed contract. Edgardo complies; seeing Lucia's signature on the document, he coldly demands whether it is indeed her handwriting. Overcome by emotion, Lucia replies with a barely audible "Yes." Enraged, Edgardo tears off the ring Lucia had given him at their last meeting, and demands that she return his ring. Lucia hardly seems to understand what she is doing. In a daze she takes the ring off her finger and hands it to Edgardo, who flings it to the floor, and with curses grinds it under his heel. His action arouses universal anger, and the principals and guests move threateningly toward him.

Proudly, Edgardo throws down his sword and bids his enemies kill him; his death will be a fine accompaniment to Lucia's wedding. Raimondo and others urge him to respect Lucia's future and his own life, and to leave before he is killed. Edgardo stands at bay for a time, then leaves, menaced by the angry and excited crowd.

ACT THREE

Scene One*

Edgardo has withdrawn to his ruined patrimony, the crumbling tower of Wolf's Crag. Here in a poorly furnished room he compares his own destiny to the fierce storm that rages outside. His thoughts are interrupted by the sound of horse's hooves nearing the tower; to his surprise Lord Enrico Ashton enters the room.

Edgardo asks how Enrico could be so insolent as to enter; and Enrico replies that Edgardo himself had recently been equally bold. Enrico now proceeds to taunt Edgardo with the *fait accompli* of Lucia's wedding and the joys of the nuptial bed to which she was just then presumably abandoning herself.

Edgardo, trying to hide the jealous anger that is overpowering him, accepts Enrico's challenge to a duel at daybreak, at the ancestral tombs of the Ravenswoods. They swear to kill each other, urging the sun to rise the sooner, so that the deadly enmity between them may be settled once and for all.

---

* This scene is often dropped completely from performances.

Scene Two

In the hall of Ravenswood Castle, the guests are celebrating the marriage, which signifies for them a renewal of their political well-being. The wedding ceremony has taken place and the bridal couple has retired. Suddenly, Raimondo, frantic with dismay, bursts into the room and orders the assembly to cease its merrymaking.

The astonished guests surround Raimondo, demanding to know what has happened. He relates a terrible event; just a little while before, he had heard such frightful shouts and screams from the bridal chambers that he rushed to discover the cause. To his horror, he found Bucklaw's bloody corpse, while not far from it stood Lucia, still clutching her husband's own sword, with which she had killed him. Seeing Raimondo, she gave a ghastly smile and said, "Where is my husband?" Raimondo declares that she must have gone completely mad.

The horrified guests agree with Raimondo, and fervently express the hope that Lucia's awful deed will not bring divine retribution upon all of them. At this point, the unhappy Lucia herself enters, wild-eyed and dishevelled. Unconscious of her surroundings, she slowly makes her way through the crowded hall as the guests stand back to let her pass. As she moves, she raves madly, imagining herself wed to Edgardo.

Enrico rushes in, frantic at the reports of what has happened during his absence. He is about to hurl himself at Lucia when the guests beg him to restrain himself, pointing out that Lucia has gone mad. As Lucia's ravings grow more pitiful, Enrico finally realizes his crime and is overcome by remorse. He brokenly admits that he will be tormented by his conscience for the remainder of his life.

Lucia collapses and is borne away by her attendants. Raimondo accompanies the women, but before leaving upbraids Normanno as the mischief-making informer who was the true cause of all this bloodshed and tragedy.

Scene Three

It is now daybreak the following morning, and Edgardo walks among the tombs of his ancestors, lamenting his fate. Without Lucia, he says, life is meaningless; his rage is now exhausted, and he intends to die by his enemy's sword. He ends his soliloquy by bitterly requesting the absent Lucia to show sufficient respect to his memory not to pass near his grave with her husband.

He is interrupted by a sombre procession from the castle. When he is informed that Lucia is dying, he becomes almost speechless with grief and horror. He tries to break away from the sad group, to rush to Lucia's side, but the passing-bell tolls mournfully in the distance: Lucia is dead.

Edgardo now realizes that Lucia has really been faithful to him, despite deceptive appearances. Praying that he may meet Lucia in the afterlife, he stabs himself and falls dead, while the chorus and Raimondo exclaim in horror.

ITALIAN OPERA

The century or so before Donizetti flourished had witnessed great changes in the world of Italian opera. The center of musical gravity had shifted from Northern Italy to Southern Italy; the polyphonic contrapuntal style associated with Venice had been replaced by the harmonic, melodic style of the Neapolitan school; and with the rise of the Neapolitan school the human voice had assumed absolute dominance over the orchestral portion of the music. No longer did voice and instrument act as equal partners; the voice had now become master and the instruments had become mere accompaniment.

Forms and subject matter, too, were in rapid evolution. Within the expanding Neapolitan school the static, highly conventionalized *opera seria* had first been most important.* As the *opera seria* waned, first the *opera buffa*† and then other operatic forms emerged. By the beginning of the nineteenth century the operatic range included melodrama (a play performed to background music), semitragedy (an opera in which certain characters were killed while others survived), tragicomedy (a mixture of romantic elements and tragic or seemingly tragic elements), farces (short pieces, often low comedy), modified *opera seria*, *opera tragica* (tragedies) and many other forms, most of which were not precisely delineated. During Donizetti's mature years these forms presented a

* The *opera seria* was characterized by a heroic attitude, classical or historical subject matter, and peculiar musical conventions. Every opera was really a collection of unrelated (or tenuously associated) arias, each of which expressed an emotional crisis reached by a character. These arias in turn were strung together with passages of recitative, but the arias were really independent and could be shifted from opera to opera—indeed, from one composer's work to that of another—like beads on strings. Violent action was seldom portrayed on the stage. Surprisingly enough, contrary to our modern expectations, this *opera seria* almost always had a "happy ending"—even to the point of violating the sources of the story.

† The *opera buffa*, which developed out of the comic interludes provided between the acts of the *opera seria*, was a new form, with stock figures and situations. It was much less constricted musically and dramatically than *opera seria*, and permitted new roles, new vocal groupings, and a wider range of situations. The dramatic plot could be linked to the arias, thus making it possible to carry out a story on the stage.

spectrum from which a composer might select according to his story line, his audience and his impresario. The terms were not too rigorously applied, for practice was more important than theory in early nineteenth-century Italy.

Within this explosive diversity of operatic forms and techniques, there was, however, one central situation which remained constant and conditioned all the circumstances that musical and dramatic evolution otherwise created. This was the supremacy assigned to the human voice. All musicians had to come to terms with the fact that the vocal part was supreme, that orchestral texture was less important than what the singer was doing, and that the way the singer performed was more significant than the words he sang.

Closely related to this absolute supremacy of the human voice in Italian opera (in a relationship which blends cause and effect) was the development of a very effective system of voice development, which flourished from the early eighteenth up through the early nineteenth century. While very few specific details are known about this training system, it seems clear that by present standards it demanded a very long period of training and remarkable self-discipline on the part of the student. The teachers, too, were unusual, for many were composers of distinction or first-rate musicians. Handel's rival Niccolò Porpora may be mentioned in this context as the teacher of both Caffarelli and Farinelli, the two outstanding castrati of the eighteenth century. Porpora's exact system was not recorded, but an anecdote will indicate its spirit. Porpora demanded five years from his students, and for five years he is said to have kept Caffarelli singing the same page of scales and exercises over and over; actual singing parts were ignored. At the end of the five years master dismissed student with the words, "You may leave now; you are the best singer in Europe"; and it was true.

This *bel canto* system produced singers with technical abilities that seem almost incredible today. It seems safe to say that there is not a singer in the world who could sing the ornaments that Farinelli is known to have inserted in his music, let alone sing them as well as Farinelli. The existence of these vocal athletes colored to a considerable extent the music that composers wrote. The audience demanded virtuosity and very often individual composers wrote music that emphasized the particular gifts of a singer. In the biographical section on Donizetti it has been mentioned that Donizetti created the part of Lucia with the abilities of Fanny Tacchinardi-Persiani in mind; in this tradition Bellini placed an *F* in alt in *I Puritani* for Rubini (with disastrous results for later singers), and Mozart wrote high chromatic intervals in the Queen of the Night's second aria for Josepha Weber that very few later sopranos have been able to master.

It was considered the singer's privilege, too, to adorn the composer's music with such ornament as he considered fitting. For men like Manuel del Pópulo García, who created the part of Almaviva in Rossini's *Barber of Seville*, Rossini's music (which few moderns can sing well) was far too simple, and he insisted upon intertwining it with an abundance of improvisations of his own. Many of these great singers, like García and his daughters Malibran and Pauline Viardot, were also good musicians, and their embellishments were justifiable to the extent that they were musically sound and pleasing. Not all other singers, however, were gifted with taste, and it is an unfortunate aspect of much late eighteenth and early nineteenth-century music that empty exhibition often took the place of good music.

The composers' reaction to this aspect of the opera "star system" was mixed. Some composers either did not care or were not strong enough to enforce discipline upon the singers. Others, like Rossini, fought bitterly to restrain the singers by writing out embellishments note for note and forbidding (with some success) other ornamentation. Other composers seem to have adopted a compromise: the singers had to sing what was written for most of the aria, but pauses were the singers' property, to fill with whatever cadenzas or figures they desired.

The vocal technique which was considered finest—and in turn affected operatic composition—stressed evenness and fluency of production, so that the quality of tone remained constant, whether the voice was in the upper or lower register. Speed per se (except for buffo basses) was considered less important than accuracy and agility; loud volume and sensational tricks were held in less esteem than musicianship. The voice was brilliant in texture; vibrato was rejected, and dramatic effects were attained by variations in the texture and volume of the voice in a manner that other schools of singing have not been able to equal.*

As many scholars have pointed out, this vocal situation created an operatic development that is almost incomprehensible to our times. In our aesthetics of the opera we tend to stress dramatic and emotional quality, the unities that are postulated for spoken dramatic work, and

---

* It is impossible to express the essence of *bel canto* singing verbally, since it consists of so many intangibles, but the reader who is interested should listen to original 78 rpm recordings (not the 33⅓ re-recordings) of the great baritone Mattia Battistini, who was for all practical purposes the only great *bel canto* singer to make recordings in his prime.

novelty in musical language. The early nineteenth century stressed performance and often saw opera as the means by which virtuosity fulfilled itself; it was relatively indifferent toward factors that we moderns tend to emphasize.

II

During Donizetti's working period Italian opera became subject to many new influences. First among these was the complex influence from across the Alps. Mozart, whose work was no longer considered "*porcheria tedesca*," came to be recognized as the preeminent figure in Neapolitan opera, and his work was studied by the major Italian composers. Rossini probably was not speaking only for himself when, asked which of his own works he liked best, he replied "[Mozart's] *Don Giovanni*." Similarly the Germanic orchestral technique was arousing serious attention in Italy. Donizetti, for example, studied Haydn and Beethoven assiduously. At this point, it seems reasonable to say, the Italian orchestral development (which was barely emerging from the Renaissance ensemble) was considerably behind the Germanic, and the Italians had much to learn—a process that was to continue through the nineteenth century to Verdi, Puccini and later composers.

During the early part of the nineteenth century the great names in Italian opera were four: Mayr, Spontini, Cherubini and Rossini. Mayr, who has been mentioned many times in the course of this book as Donizetti's teacher and mentor, was one of the principal sources for the diffusion of Northern music into Italy; his operas were preeminent for a decade or so, and were supplanted only by Rossini's. Spontini and Cherubini, much of whose major work was not written in Italy, but in France and Germany, also deepened Italian musical techniques. Although today Cherubini is nearly forgotten except for a single opera (*Medea*) and a symphony, he was a name to conjure with one hundred and fifty years ago; Beethoven considered him the outstanding contemporary composer.

Gioacchino Rossini (1792–1868), however, soon overshadowed and outweighed these three men. After a few lean years, his music suddenly "clicked" and almost overnight he became the major figure in the Italian music of his time. His brisk, sophisticated music showed an imagination (though within a limited range) that his immediate predecessors had lacked, and his operas soon captured Europe. Rossini moved to Paris in 1824, where he served for a time as director of the Théâtre-Italien and later as inspector-general of singing. It is difficult for a modern to comprehend the peculiar power that Rossini held, almost until his death. Although he was an enigmatic personality whose motivations have never really been understood, his brilliant wit, his intelligence, his affability and bonhomie, and his ability to captivate all social circles soon made him the most important personality in European music. He was the dean and arbiter of musicians between Beethoven and Wagner, a light-hearted Dr. Johnson of the operatic stage, whose nod was worth more than the applause of the rest of the world.

From the Italian generation immediately following Rossini, and overlapping with him, two men emerged: Donizetti and Vincenzo Bellini. They did little to change forms, since they worked within the contemporary mode, but their personalities soon transformed the musical understanding of the period. Bellini (1801–1835), Sicilian in origin, Neapolitan in training, was the Keats of Italian music, and just as Rossini had been accepted as dictator of music, Bellini was accepted as the exemplar of the Romantic genius. He was considered the native genius who, despite inadequate training, was able to reach the heights almost immediately by sheer ability. His forte was the elegiac manner, a music of simple classical beauty, sometimes serene, sometimes passionate, sometimes languorous, but always beautiful. It was a great blow to nineteenth-century Italian music that Bellini died young, before he had even reached his full maturity. His reputation remained, however, assuming almost legendary proportions, and later Italian composers, from Donizetti and Verdi up to the end of the century, were forced to come to terms with Bellini's remarkable musical personality. In many respects Donizetti's own work came to be a "conversation" with Bellini, and it is fascinating to speculate what Donizetti's own musical evolution might have been had Bellini lived ten years longer.

DONIZETTI'S MUSIC

For many years the music of Donizetti has languished under a critical cloud, a cloud very often perpetuated by critics who could not have had the opportunity either to hear or study much of Donizetti's work. "Has not stood the test of time well," "insipid melodies, stale harmonies, lack of dramatism," "skimpily developed, organ-grinder tunes, glibness" are comments that one frequently encounters, in these or similar words.

While it is not the purpose of this book to praise Donizetti as a musician, or to offer apologetics, it must still be pointed out that most of the criticism directed at Donizetti is either unjust or irrelevant, and sometimes inaccurate. His music is all too often damned by arguments that really have little or nothing to do with music.

The historical reasons for this deprecation of Donizetti's work are many. First, and perhaps most important, is the historical accident that Donizetti caught the full brunt of the Germanic attack on Italian opera hurled by Richard Wagner and others. For them Donizetti, as the leading Italian composer, was the *bête noire*; indeed, Wagner went so far as to classify Verdi as simply an imitation of Donizetti, and thereby automatically to be damned. Wagner gave several reasons for condemning Donizetti: Donizetti often wrote to trivial and foolish libretti; Donizetti did not care about integrating his libretto and his music and creating a music drama; Donizetti remained within the classical structure of aria and recitative; Donizetti pandered to the acrobatic propensities of his singers.

Wagner's musical genius has tended to give his critical theories in this area an acceptance that is sometimes undeserved. To put his argument into other, less specific terms, it simply amounts to the accusation that the Italians have not taken music seriously, or not seriously in the same way as did the German Wagnerites. Donizetti and his fellow Italians never felt the need to build a theoretical system comparable to the formal systems of German philosophy, which would embrace all the arts as handmaidens to music. They were content to retain operatic music as an entertainment, without larger purpose. Unfortunately, they do not seem to have defended their position in terms of aesthetics, and the debate has passed by default to the Germans; Donizetti has been automatically damned by standards developed in another land for another music.

Closely related to this last-mentioned critical judgment is the feeling of annoyance that arises in many listeners on learning that Donizetti remained dispassionate, as musicians go, toward his own music. Donizetti did not fit the ideal of the Romantic artist—a semidivine being who put into his creation an ineffable something that only he could give—as was the popular image of Bellini, and to a lesser extent Rossini. Donizetti worked hard, but did not rant about the flash of genius; he did not suffer over his music, and he saw himself as a working craftsman rather than as a high priest.

The nineteenth century (in which we often still find ourselves critically) was prone to interpret creativity in terms of Napoleon or Beethoven or Goethe or Lord Byron, and unless a figure fitted the cloud-straining, dynamic, spectacular pattern of these men, he was suspect. Donizetti, who was very easy-going and unegotistical, obviously does not belong in the same category as Byron. This usually unconscious aesthetic standard forgets that some of the greatest work in human culture has been produced by un-Promethean figures, by men who worked for a day, and then put aside what they had done, by men who were not obsessed by questions of theory, but simply worked. Only Shakespeare and J. S. Bach need be mentioned. It is not claimed that Donizetti is their equal, simply that he belongs to the same creative type.

Sneers have also been cast at Donizetti's working speed. When mention is made of the fact that Donizetti wrote a certain piece of music in a matter of days or weeks (which might have taken a slower composer weeks or months) the statement is usually made with a knowing look or raised eyebrows. This is, of course, completely irrelevant as a criterion of quality; it is the music, not the speed at which it was written, that must be judged. And even in matters of speed it should be pointed out that musicians have varied enormously in their working rate: Brahms and Debussy wrote somewhat slowly; Mozart wrote the overture to *Don Giovanni* in a single night.

Even the criticism that Donizetti's music might have been better if he had worked over it more is not wholly sound psychologically. The music that is generally conceded to be his best is often his most rapidly composed. His was the kind of genius that turned out good music very rapidly when the muse was with him. Prodigal talents do not always profit from revision.

The most severe criticism of all, however, is based upon the observation that Donizetti was not an innovator—that he used the traditional forms of his day; that he seldom broke from traditional harmonic practices, seldom experimented, seldom produced anything radically new: in short, that he drew on the backlog of Mozart, Haydn, Mayr, and Rossini. The critics who damn Donizetti for lack of originality may well be the same critics who are embarrassed by J. S. Bach's infrequent performance as an innovator.

Yet even the charge of lack of originality is somewhat out of historical perspective, since Donizetti did make evolutionary contributions, most of which have been overlooked because he has been so neglected critically in the past few generations. Donizetti employed a richer and more imaginative orchestral technique than did most of his Italian contemporaries; he strove to make the coloratura style of singing subordinate to expressiveness; he helped to establish a new kind of melodramatic opera; and he did much to open new channels in humorous opera.

If the usual unfavorable criticisms do not prove that Donizetti was a bad composer, refuting them does not prove that he was a great composer. The final answer to the question of his artistic stature lies in his music itself, not in the accidentals that have been often used to interpret it.

II

One reason that Donizetti's stature as a world musician cannot be measured precisely at present is the difficulty in meeting most of his music. Of his operas only three can be said to be permanently accessible: *Lucia di Lammermoor*, *L'Elisir d'amore*, and *Don Pasquale*. Another half dozen or so are sporadically available on records, though sometimes only on imported labels: *La Favorita*, *La Figlia del reggimento*, *Rita*, *Betly*, *Il Campanello*, and *Lucrezia Borgia*. Tapes from the Bergamo and Spoleto festivals and RAI performances may contribute another ten or twelve operas, which are broadcast perhaps once every ten years in the United States and are occasionally available surreptitiously in very expensive pirated tapes and disks. As a result, a resourceful musicologist with a long purse can have access to something like one third of Donizetti's operatic productivity. Unfortunately, much of this material is mangled and much of it is not Donizetti's most significant work. It may be a curiosity to perform Donizetti's first opera, *Il Pigmalione*, but we would much rather have an opera from the middle or late period. Almost fifty operas are not available, and who knows what they are like? It has been mentioned elsewhere that *Anna Bolena* caused a sensation in revealing a Donizetti of greater dramatic power than had been known.

It is a critical temptation to judge Donizetti by a single opera or two, to forget that within a range of over 70 operas there may be great variation. Such variation really exists for Donizetti; he is a much more varied composer than, say, Wagner or Bellini or even Rossini. There is obviously a personal element in Donizetti's work—the idiosyncratic melodies. They are usually very beautiful, but somehow they are not generally melodies that stick in one's mental vocal cords as do Verdi's or Bellini's. But there are equally great differences in every aspect of his work, from opera to opera. Some of his music is highly charged with coloratura; some of it is very simple. Some of his music is very thinly harmonized and simply orchestrated, so that the voice and words are stressed; some of his music is thoroughly orchestrated and imaginatively harmonized; some of his music is obviously routine; some is quite fresh and vivid. There are languishing elegiac operas like *Lucia di Lammermoor* that awaken all the pallid death eroticism of the early Romantics; there are boisterously joyous *opere buffe*, brimming with local color and broad humor, like *L'Elisir d'amore* and *Il Campanello*; there are somewhat subtle character studies, where the music shows personalities rather than stock humorous situations, like *Don Pasquale*; there are intensely dramatic works like *Anna Bolena* and *Maria Stuarda*, which are Donizettian in their melodies but reminiscent of middle-period Verdi in their musical techniques.

Even when Donizetti's operas are performed, they still suffer under a great disadvantage. Donizetti wrote mostly for a small band of vocal athletes, whose equal has not been seen for many years.

It is an unfortunate characteristic of the music of Donizetti's period—particularly that of Bellini and Donizetti—that it is extremely delicate in its emotional impact. If it is not sung to perfection, it simply does not come through to the listener. In this respect, it is quite different from most of the music of Verdi, Puccini, Bizet, Wagner and many of the moderns. This difficulty is recognized in performing circles, with the result that casting is an enormously frustrating problem, and the operas of Bellini and the unusual operas of Donizetti are very seldom staged. The risk is too great.

Despite all these factors that operate against him, it seems clear that by any fair test Donizetti should be considered among the great composers. He is not in the very top rank, with Mozart or J. S. Bach, but he almost certainly belongs in the group immediately below them. Yet that his genius did not always find fulfillment, that he sometimes turned out sloppy work to meet deadlines, and that his impatience did not permit him to rework material sufficiently are all probably equally true.

At this moment we are in the unfortunate position of being unable to see Donizetti as a totality. His prodigal output in areas other than opera is still not entirely gathered together and codified. To summarize the admittedly incomplete list that Guido Zavadini has established, Donizetti wrote 3 oratorios, 28 cantatas, 5 hymns, 116 miscellaneous pieces of religious music, 16 symphonies, 19 quartets, 3 quintets, 4 concerti, 1 sextet, 4 sonatas for violin, 26 piano pieces, 18 pieces for two pianos, 193 songs for solo voice, 45 vocal duets, 10 songs for vocal groups, and 50 or 60 miscellaneous works and significant fragments. Almost all of this work, unfortunately, is now completely unknown. Not only is it unperformed, most of it is unpublished; and what has been published is usually not in print and is difficult of access.

Donizetti's chamber music, which for the most part dates from his youth, is occasionally performed; it has been characterized by Francis Toye as good work in the tradition of Mozart and Beethoven. Once in a while songs by Donizetti are given in concerts and recitals; they vary considerably in style, although Rossini's influence is easily perceptible. Among his contemporaries Donizetti was considered to be a skilled composer in the strict forms of church music, but this music now seems completely overlooked. The Bellini *Requiem* is occasionally performed, however, and although not commercially available it has been broadcast at least twice in the United States. Still, by and large, it is safe to say that Donizetti's non-operatic work is unknown.

Most of Donizetti's operas are equally unknown. Who knows what exists in his unperformed works—which comprise about nine-tenths of his operatic writing? Among operas that are usually available, *Lucia di Lammermoor* is currently in print on about a half-dozen sets, while *Anna Bolena* has been broadcast in the New York area only four times in the past nine years, and is not commercially available. Another four or five operas can be purchased, depending upon one's access to foreign catalogues: *Roberto Devereux, Rita, La Figlia del reggimento,* * *La Favorita, Lucrezia Borgia, Il Campanello, Betly, Don Pasquale, L'Elisir d'amore, L'Ajo*

---

* The Italian version of *La Fille du régiment*.

[*text continues on page 76*]

DONIZETTI'S

OPERA	TYPE OF OPERA	LIBRETTIST	DATE OF COMPOSITION
Il Pigmalione	—	Unknown	Sept.–Oct. 1816
L'Ira d'Achille	—	Unknown	1817
L'Olimpiade	—	Unknown [perhaps Metastasio?]	1817
Enrico di Borgogna	Opera semiseria	Bartolomeo Merelli	1818
Una Follia	Farsa	Bartolomeo Merelli or Andrea Tottola	1818
Piccioli Virtuosi ambulanti	Opera buffa	Bartolomeo Merelli or Gherardo Bevilacqua-Aldovrandini	1819
Il Falegname di Livonia, o Pietro il grande, czar delle Russie	Opera buffa	Gherardo Bevilacqua-Aldovrandini	1819
Le Nozze in villa	Opera buffa	Bartolomeo Merelli	1820
Zoraide di Granata	Opera seria	Bartolomeo Merelli [and Jacopo Ferretti?]	1822
La Zingara	Opera seria	Andrea Leone Tottola	1822
La Lettera anonima	Farsa	Giulio Genoino	1822
Chiara e Serafina, o I Pirati	Opera semiseria	Felice Romani	1822

OPERAS

DATE OF FIRST PERFORMANCE	PLACE OF FIRST PERFORMANCE	ALTERNATE TITLES	COMMENTS
Oct. 13, 1960	Teatro Donizetti, Bergamo	—	—
Never performed	Never performed	—	MS in Library of Paris Conservatory.
Never performed	Never performed	—	Lost except for fragments in Museo Donizettiano, Bergamo.
Nov. 14, 1818	Teatro San Luca, Venice	—	Lost.
Dec. 15, 1818	Teatro San Luca, Venice	*Una Follia di carnovale* [Perhaps *Il Ritratto parlante*]	Lost.
Summer 1819	Scuola Caritatevole di Musica, Bergamo	*Piccoli virtuosi di musica ambulanti*	Lost.
Dec. 26, 1819	Teatro San Samuele, Venice	—	—
Jan. 23, 1821	Teatro Vecchio, Mantua	—	—
Jan. 28, 1822	Teatro Argentina, Rome	—	—
May 12, 1822	Teatro Nuovo, Naples	—	—
June 29, 1822	Teatro del Fondo, Naples	—	—
Oct. 26, 1822	Teatro alla Scala, Milan	—	—

OPERA	TYPE OF OPERA	LIBRETTIST	DATE OF COMPOSITION
Alfredo il grande	Opera seria	Andrea Leone Tottola	1823
Il Fortunato inganno	Opera buffa	Andrea Leone Tottola	1823
L'Ajo nell'imbarazzo, o Don Gregorio	Opera buffa	Jacopo Ferretti	1823–4
Emilia di Liverpool	Opera semiseria	Giuseppe Checcherini	1824
Alahor di Granata	Opera semiseria	"M.A."	1825
Il Castello degli invalidi	Farsa	Unknown	1826?
Elvida	Opera seria	Giovanni Federico Schmidt	1826
Gabriella di Vergy	Opera seria	Andrea Leone Tottola	1826
La Bella prigioniera	Farsa	Unknown	1826
Olivo e Pasquale	Opera buffa	Jacopo Ferretti	1826
Otto mesi in due ore, ossia Gli Esiliati in Siberia	Opera romantica	Domenico Gilardoni	1827

DATE OF FIRST PERFORMANCE	PLACE OF FIRST PERFORMANCE	ALTERNATE TITLES	COMMENTS
July 2, 1823	Teatro San Carlo, Naples	—	—
Sept. 3, 1823	Teatro Nuovo, Naples	—	—
Feb. 4, 1824	Teatro Valle, Rome	*Il Governo della casa; Don Gregorio*	—
July 28, 1824	Teatro Nuovo, Naples	*Emilia; L'Eremitaggio di Liverpool*	—
Jan. 7, 1826	Teatro Carolino, Palermo	—	MS lost.
Spring 1826?	Teatro Carolino, Palermo	—	Lost. Some question whether this opera ever existed or whether its production ever took place.
July 6, 1826	Teatro San Carlo, Naples	—	—
Nov. 22, 1869	Teatro San Carlo, Naples	—	Posthumous performance.
—	—	—	Lost except for fragments in Museo Donizettiano, Bergamo.
Jan. 7, 1827	Teatro Valle, Rome	—	—
May 13, 1827	Teatro Nuovo, Naples	*Gli Esiliati in Siberia; Die Macht der kindlichen Liebe; Elisabeth, ou La Fille du proscrit* (music adapted by Uranio Fontana)	—

OPERA	TYPE OF OPERA	LIBRETTIST	DATE OF COMPOSITION
Il Borgomastro di Saardam	Opera buffa	Domenico Gilardoni	1827
Le Convenienze ed inconvenienze teatrali	Farsa	Gaetano Donizetti	1827
L'Esule di Roma, ossia Il Proscritto	Opera seria	Domenico Gilardoni	1827
Alina, regina di Golconda	Opera buffa	Felice Romani	1828
Gianni di Calais	Opera semiseria	Domenico Gilardoni	1828
Il Giovedì grasso, o Il Nuovo Pourceaugnac	Farsa	Domenico Gilardoni	1828
Il Paria	Opera seria	Domenico Gilardoni	1829
Elisabetta al castello di Kenilworth	Opera seria	Andrea Leone Tottola	1829
I Pazzi per progetto	Farsa	Domenico Gilardoni	1830
Imelda de' Lambertazzi	Opera seria	Andrea Leone Tottola	1830
Anna Bolena	Opera seria	Felice Romani	1830
Francesca di Foix	Opera semiseria	Domenico Gilardoni	1831
La Romanziera e l'uomo nero	Opera buffa	Domenico Gilardoni	1831
Fausta	Opera seria	Domenico Gilardoni	1831

DATE OF FIRST PERFORMANCE	PLACE OF FIRST PERFORMANCE	ALTERNATE TITLES	COMMENTS
Aug. 19, 1827	Teatro Nuovo or Teatro del Fondo, Naples	—	—
Nov. 21, 1827	Teatro Nuovo, Naples	—	—
Jan. 1, 1828	Teatro San Carlo, Naples	*Settimio il proscritto; Il Proscritto; Settimio, ossia L'Esule di Roma*	—
May 12, 1828	Teatro Carlo Felice, Genoa	*La Regina di Golconda*	—
Aug. 2, 1828	Teatro del Fondo, Naples	—	—
Dec. 1828	Teatro del Fondo, Naples	—	—
Jan. 12, 1829	Teatro San Carlo, Naples	—	—
July 6, 1829	Teatro San Carlo, Naples	*Il Castello di Kenilworth*	—
Feb. 7, 1830	Teatro del Fondo, Naples	—	—
Aug. 23, 1830	Teatro San Carlo, Naples	—	—
Dec. 26, 1830	Teatro Carcano, Milan	—	—
May 30, 1831	Teatro San Carlo, Naples	—	—
Summer 1831	Teatro del Fondo, Naples	—	—
Jan. 12, 1832	Teatro San Carlo, Naples	—	—

OPERA	TYPE OF OPERA	LIBRETTIST	DATE OF COMPOSITION
Ugo, conte di Parigi	Opera seria	Felice Romani	1832
L'Elisir d'amore	Opera comica	Felice Romani	1832
Sancia di Castiglia	Opera seria	Pietro Salatino	1832
Il Furioso all'isola di San Domingo	Opera semiseria	Jacopo Ferretti	1832
Parisina	Opera seria	Felice Romani	1833
Torquato Tasso	Opera seria	Jacopo Ferretti	1833
Lucrezia Borgia	Opera seria	Felice Romani	1833
Rosmonda d'Inghilterra	Opera seria	Felice Romani	1834
Maria Stuarda	Opera seria	Giuseppe Bardari	1834

DATE OF FIRST PERFORMANCE	PLACE OF FIRST PERFORMANCE	ALTERNATE TITLES	COMMENTS
March 13, 1832	Teatro alla Scala, Milan	—	—
May 12, 1832	Teatro della Canobbiana, Milan	—	—
Nov. 4, 1832	Teatro San Carlo, Naples	—	—
Jan. 2, 1833	Teatro Valle, Rome	—	—
March 17, 1833	Teatro della Pergola, Florence	*Parisina d'Este*	—
Sept. 8, 1833	Teatro Valle, Rome	*Sordello; Sordello il trovatore*	—
Dec. 26, 1833	Teatro alla Scala, Milan	*Alfonso, duca di Ferrara; Elisa da Fosco; Eustorgia da Romano; Giovanna I di Napoli; La Rinnegata; Nizza di Granata; Dalinda*	—
Feb. 27, 1834	Teatro della Pergola, Florence	*Eleonora di Gujenna*	*Eleonora di Gujenna* performed in Naples, with music of *Rosmonda*, but new libretto.
Oct. 18, 1834	Teatro San Carlo, Naples	*Buondelmonte*	First performed with libretto *Buondelmonte*, by P. Salatino and Donizetti, in San Carlo. First performed as *Maria Stuarda*, with Bardari's libretto, at La Scala, Milan, Dec. 30, 1835.

OPERA	TYPE OF OPERA	LIBRETTIST	DATE OF COMPOSITION
Gemma di Vergy	Opera seria	Emmanuele Bidera	1834
Adelaide	Opera comica	Unknown	1834?
Marin Faliero	Opera seria	Emmanuele Bidera and Agostino Ruffini	1835
Lucia di Lammermoor	Opera seria	Salvatore Cammarano	1835
Belisario	Opera seria	Salvatore Cammarano	1835–6
Il Campanello	Farsa	Gaetano Donizetti	1836
Betly	Opera giocosa	Gaetano Donizetti	1836
L'Assedio di Calais	Opera seria	Salvatore Cammarano	1836
Pia de' Tolomei	Opera seria	Salvatore Cammarano	1836–7
Roberto Devereux, ossia Il Conte di Essex	Opera seria	Salvatore Cammarano	1837
Maria di Rudenz	Opera seria	Salvatore Cammarano	1837

DATE OF FIRST PERFORMANCE	PLACE OF FIRST PERFORMANCE	ALTERNATE TITLES	COMMENTS
Dec. 26, 1834	Teatro alla Scala, Milan	—	—
Never performed	—	—	Presumably never completed, but used as a source for *La Favorite*.
March 12, 1835	Théâtre-Italien, Paris	*Marino Faliero*	—
Sept. 26, 1835	Teatro San Carlo, Naples	*Lucie de Lammermoor*	*Lucie de Lammermoor*, performed at the Théâtre de la Renaissance, Paris, 1839, French adaptation by A. Royer and G. Vaëz, with additional music by Donizetti.
Feb. 4, 1836	Teatro La Fenice, Venice	—	—
June 6, 1836	Teatro Nuovo, Naples	*Il Campanello di notte; Il Campanello dello speziale*	—
Aug. 24, 1836	Teatro Nuovo, Naples	*Bettly; La Capanna svizzera*	Revised and enlarged for Palermo, 1837.
Nov. 19, 1836	Teatro San Carlo, Naples	—	—
Feb. 18, 1837	Teatro Apollo, Venice	—	—
Oct. 29, 1837	Teatro San Carlo, Naples	*Il Conte di Essex*	—
Jan. 30, 1838	Teatro La Fenice, Venice	—	Unsuccessful, and used as a source for *Poliuto*.

OPERA	TYPE OF OPERA	LIBRETTIST	DATE OF COMPOSITION
Poliuto	Opera seria	Salvatore Cammarano	1839
Gianni di Parigi	Opera comica	Felice Romani	1839
Le Duc d'Albe	Opera seria	Augustin-Eugène Scribe and Charles Duveyrier	1839 on
La Fille du régiment	Opéra comique	Jules-Henri Vernoy de Saint-Georges and Jean-François-Alfred Bayard	1839–40
La Favorite	Grand opera	Alphonse Royer and Gustave Vaëz	1839
Adelia, o La Figlia dell'arciere	Opera seria	Felice Romani and Girolamo Maria Marini	1840–41

DATE OF FIRST PERFORMANCE	PLACE OF FIRST PERFORMANCE	ALTERNATE TITLES	COMMENTS
Nov. 30, 1848	Teatro San Carlo, Naples	*Les Martyrs; Paolina e Poliuto; Paolina e Severo*	Banned by censors in Naples, rewritten libretto by A.-E. Scribe, performed as *Les Martyrs* at the Académie Royale de Musique, Paris, April 10, 1840.
Sept. 10, 1839	Teatro alla Scala, Milan	—	—
March 22, 1882	Teatro Apollo, Rome	*Il Duca d'Alba*	Left unfinished at Donizetti's death. The performances at the Teatro Apollo were finished by Matteo Salvi, to an Italian translation of the French libretto, by Angelo Zanardini. The Menotti production, Teatro Nuovo, Spoleto, June 11, 1959 removed most of Salvi's music.
Feb. 11, 1840	Opéra-Comique, Paris	*La Figlia del reggimento*	—
Dec. 2, 1840	Opéra, Paris	*La Favorita; Richard und Matilde; Leonore* (German translation); *Leonora di Guzman; Daila; Elda*	—
Feb. 11, 1841	Teatro Apollo, Rome	—	

OPERA	TYPE OF OPERA	LIBRETTIST	DATE OF COMPOSITION
Rita, ou Le Mari battu	Opéra comique	Gustave Vaëz	1841
Maria Padilla	Opera seria	Gaetano Rossi	1841
Linda di Chamounix	Opera semiseria	Gaetano Rossi	1842
Don Pasquale	Opera buffa	Giovanni Ruffini and Gaetano Donizetti	1842
Maria di Rohan	Opera seria	Salvatore Cammarano	1843
Dom Sébastien, roi de Portugal	Grand opera	Augustin-Eugène Scribe	1843
Caterina Cornaro	Opera seria	Giacomo Sacchero	1842–3

DATE OF FIRST PERFORMANCE	PLACE OF FIRST PERFORMANCE	ALTERNATE TITLES	COMMENTS
May 7, 1860	Opéra-Comique, Paris	*Deux Hommes et une femme*	—
Dec. 26, 1841	Teatro alla Scala, Milan	—	—
May 19, 1842	Kärnthnerthortheater, Vienna	—	—
Jan. 3, 1843	Théâtre-Italien, Paris	—	—
June 5, 1843	Kärnthnerthor-theater, Vienna	*Il Conte di Chalais*	—
Nov. 13, 1843	Opéra, Paris	*Don Sebastiano*	—
Jan. 12, 1844	Teatro San Carlo, Naples	—	—

nell'imbarazzo and *Linda di Chamounix*. Tapes from the Bergamo festivals, the Spoleto festivals, and RAI performances may contribute another half-dozen operas, which may be heard on the radio perhaps once every four or five years.

Yet even with this small sampling of music that can be heard, Donizetti's work stands high. He wrote two excellent major comedies, *L'Elisir d'amore* and *Don Pasquale*; one excellent minor comedy, *Il Campanello*; several good serious operas, *Poliuto, Anna Bolena, La Favorita, Lucia di Lammermoor, Maria Stuarda,* and *Lucrezia Borgia*. This is a great achievement for any man.

III

The list of Donizetti's operas on pages 62–75 is based primarily on the works of Zavadini and Weinstock. Other bibliographic sources occasionally give slightly different information on the early operas, particularly on dates of first performance. These differences, however, are unimportant and do not affect the basic chronological sequence of Donizetti's work.

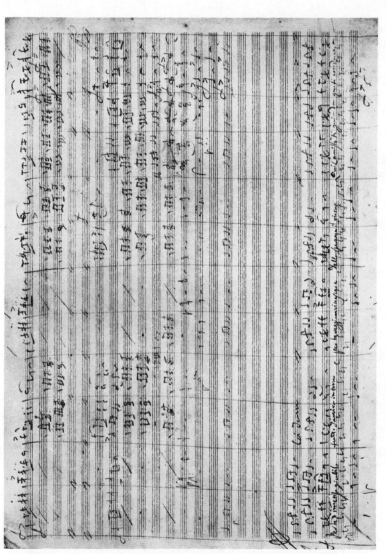

A page from Donizetti's autograph manuscript score of *Lucia*: The opening of the wedding chorus "Per te d'immenso giubilo" (Act 2, Scene 2).

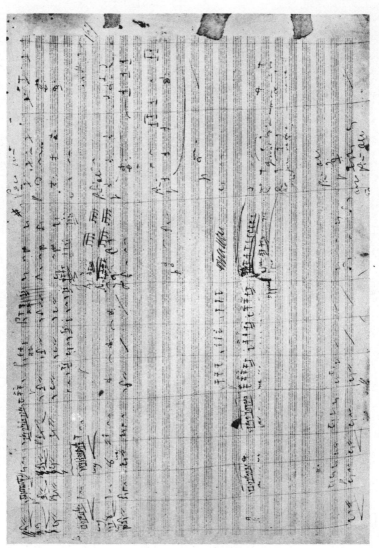

A page from the autograph manuscript of *Lucia:* The climax of Lucia's mad-scene aria "Spargi d'amaro pianto" (Act 3, Scene 2).

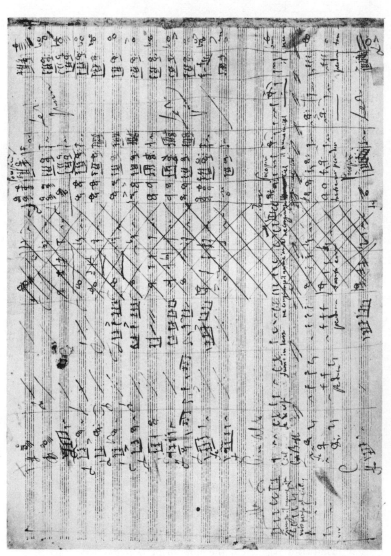

The next-to-last page of the autograph manuscript of *Lucia:* Raimondo and the male chorus accompany the end of Edgardo's aria "Tu che a Dio spiegasti l'ali" (Act 3, Scene 3).

A manuscript page from the libretto of *Don Pasquale* (Act 3, Scene 5) in Donizetti's hand. *(Courtesy Museo Donizettiano, Bergamo)*

MUSICAL ANALYSIS OF "LUCIA"

Lucia di Lammermoor starts with a brief orchestral prelude, in which the tympani enter, then strike octaves, whereupon horns enter with chords. Other wind instruments and finally the full orchestra join in. The piece ends softly and inconclusively with the sound of horns. This prelude is characteristic of the opera in its frequent use of horns and woodwinds, its minor mode and its close harmonies.

The first vocal number is the huntsmen's chorus, in which Normanno, the chief, sings a hornlike figure, with the chorus supplying the second portion of the phrase.

The first extended solo is Enrico's "Cruda, funesta smania," long a concert favorite with baritones:

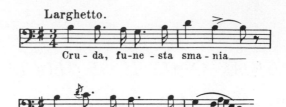

Lucia's first aria, "Regnava nel silenzio," which follows in the next scene, is most effective in its long melodic line, and the deft interweaving of broad melodic writing and coloratura passages.

During the long scene between Edgardo and Lucia a climax is reached with the duet "Verranno a te sull'aure i miei sospiri ardenti":

In Act Two high points occur in the duet sequence between Enrico Ashton and Lucia, as they sing related motives, with slight modifications and changes of pitch. Lucia's lament, "Soffriva nel pianto," when she sees the forged letter is related to the music of "Verranno a te sull'aure":

The second scene of Act Two begins with the brilliant chorus of the wedding guests:

In Act Two occurs the sextet, which is one of the most famous examples of concerted singing in Italian opera. Heed should be paid to the ingenious manner in which the voices combine, then separate and recombine with other voices, and to the way interjections are pieced into the melodic line. All voices end together in a sort of descending sigh.

The savage duet between Enrico and Edgardo, in Edgardo's tower, is an excellent example of passion expressed by broken rhythm:

The most famous moment in the opera is Lucia's mad scene. Divided into two parts by the interruption of the chorus and other characters, it recapitulates roughly the sequence of events in Lucia's tragedy. In the opening semirecitative "Il dolce suono":

Lucia imagines she is with Edgardo and the mood is pathos. At the outset of the second section, her happiness at earlier days is suggested by the orchestral presence of the opening phrase of "Verranno a te sull'aure," but suddenly she sees the spectre of the fountain step between her and Edgardo. Then she is in a frenzy of joy as she marries Edgardo by exchanging rings.

Raimondo, Enrico and the chorus interrupt her for a time, then Lucia resumes, indicating that she is hurt by Edgardo's rejection of her at the wedding. Finally, in despair she declares herself ready for death, and the music reaches its climax in the aria "Spargi d'amaro pianto":

The final portion of the aria is characterized by extremely difficult coloratura, what with prolonged trills preceded by eighth notes, heavy syncopation, unusual stresses, gliding chromatic runs, and wild large intervals which must be bridged very rapidly. The overall impression conveyed by this aria is that of insanity, pathos and the finality of death.

The last major aria in the opera, "Tu che a Dio spiegasti l'ali," is sung by Edgardo:

It resembles the first vocal music of the opera, the chorus of the huntsmen, in one of its themes. Donizetti often used this device of shared themes to link the first and last scenes of his operas, to create an impression of unity for the entire work.

II

The structure of *Lucia di Lammermoor* is typical of early nineteenth-century Italian opera. A brief overture, suggesting the mood of the work rather than using specific themes, is followed by a series of separate numbers (solos, duets, trios, and larger ensembles), each customarily prefaced by recitative. Parts are assigned according to the traditional vocal ranges, and each major character, according to tradition, should sing a solo aria and a duet with each other voice. In *Lucia di Lammermoor*, however, the contralto part (Alisa) has been somewhat slighted, for she does not have a solo. There may have been reasons for this in the original production situation: the contralto may not have been a good singer, or one of the other roles, probably Lucia, may have usurped the contralto aria.

Another convention of this phase of operatic writing is the stress given to the vocal element over the instrumental. The vocal line is considered to be the bearer of the emotional message. Other traditions of opera have relied on the capacity of harmony and evocative orchestration to indicate emotional tone, but Donizetti's *bel canto* opera preferred to relegate orchestra and harmony to the background and to create emotional tone by variations in the melodic line itself—its rhythms, its intervals, its speed, its phrasing, and particularly by the shadings and dynamics of the human voice. As a result, this is a very subtle form of writing, a highly stylized technique, since it renounces most of the aids that other operatic traditions have used. It should be emphasized that this treatment is not evidence of lack of musical inventiveness, but is rather a deliberate aesthetic device.

As a corollary of this same concept the musical texture of this type of opera is chordal rather than contrapuntal, since neither instrumental parts nor other vocal parts could be elevated to equality with the melody-bearing voice.

THE TEXT

The following Italian text has been established from the original manuscript which Donizetti wrote in 1835, as published in facsimile in 1941. It follows Donizetti's own hand, as he copied the text on his rough sheets, with the minor exception of personal names. Where Donizetti uniformly used "Asthon" and "Revensvood," possibly as a guide to Italian singers, we have used the standard forms "Enrico" [Ashton] and "Ravenswood." On matters of printing style, where Donizetti often did not bother to be precise, we have followed the Schirmer piano and vocal score, which is close otherwise to the manuscript.

As can be seen from Donizetti's manuscript, however, this version of the libretto was not exactly the text submitted to him by Cammarano, for Donizetti made quite a few minor changes as he composed the music. Cammarano's original libretto, without Donizetti's modifications, was printed and sold in Italy as the official book, and it seems to have been generally available in many places in the operatic world. When *Lucia di Lammermoor* was sung in Mexico City in 1841, for example, Cammarano's original text was reprinted with a few cuts.

In most cases the variant readings in Cammarano's original libretto have not been indicated here, since they are usually only changes of words or phrases and do not affect the sense of the libretto or the relations of music and text. In addition, since they were rejected by Donizetti they can have no critical value. There are, however, a few long passages in the original Cammarano libretto which do not occur in Donizetti's manuscript or more modern editions of *Lucia di Lammermoor*. These additional lines have been given in footnotes. What nineteenth-century singers did when they came to these passages we do not know, since no record is usually kept of individual performance traditions. It is quite possible that there was a gap between the printed libretto offered for sale in the theatre and the words that were sung, so that these passages were simply ignored. It is not an uncommon situation in opera for the official words and the performers' words to differ. Or the musicians and orchestra may have repeated or anticipated music to fill out the lines.

Besides Donizetti's version of the text (which is basically the modern version) and Cammarano's original text (which seems to be only a historical curiosity now) a third libretto type exists. This is the French libretto prepared by Royer and Vaëz for the Paris performance of 1839. It differs greatly from the Italian libretto in having different settings, different incidents, different characters, and different details of the story line. This French libretto, although it now seems to be dead, has been historically important in influencing translations of *Lucia di Lammermoor* into other languages. For example, the English translations which were produced in the middle and late nineteenth century were often based on the French revision rather than on the Italian original. A translation of Royer and Vaëz's work has been included as Appendix B to this book.

II

The complete vocal text of *Lucia di Lammermoor* has been printed here, including both the repeats and the passages that are ordinarily omitted in performance. As the user will discover, almost all performances of this opera are cut to some extent. In some cases only a few repeats and occasional lines are omitted; in other performances the text is mutilated to the point of inadequacy, both musically and dramatically.

LUCIA DI LAMMERMOOR

Opera in Three Acts
Music by Gaetano Donizetti
Libretto by Salvatore Cammarano

LUCIA DI LAMMERMOOR

Characters in the order of their appearance:

NORMANNO, captain of the guard at Ravenswood Castle, unscrupulous henchman of
Lord Enrico Ashton . . . . Tenor

LORD ENRICO ASHTON, present holder of
Ravenswood Castle, ruthless brother of
Lucia . . . . Bass (Baritone)

RAIMONDO BIDE-THE-BENT, clergyman, chaplain to the Ashtons . . . . Bass

LUCIA ASHTON, sister of Lord Enrico Ashton . . . Soprano

ALISA, servant and companion to Lucia . . Soprano
(Mezzo-Soprano)

EDGARDO RAVENSWOOD, dispossessed former
owner of Ravenswood Castle; enemy to
the Ashtons; lover to Lucia . . . . . Tenor

ARTURO BUCKLAW, suitor to Lucia; later en-
forced husband; murdered by Lucia . . . Tenor

Chorus of huntsmen, wedding guests, guards, servitors, etc.

Act One

Set design for Act 1, Scene 1, by Adriana Muojo. *(Courtesy Teatro di San Carlo, Naples)*

spiaggia – seashore, coast (handwritten)

ACT ONE

Scene One

The Lammermoor district of Scotland, about 1700. In the wooded grounds of Castle Ravenswood, Normanno, the captain of Lord Enrico Ashton's guards, instructs a group of huntsmen.

NORMANNO: Percorrete le spiagge vicine,—

TENORS, THEN BASSES: Percorriamo le spiagge vicine,—

NORMANNO: —della torre le vaste rovine:

TENORS, THEN BASSES: —della torre le vaste rovine:

NORMANNO: —cada il vel di sì turpe mistero,—

NORMANNO: —lo domanda, lo impone l'onor,—

HUNTSMEN: —cada il vel di sì turpe mistero,—

NORMANNO: —lo impone l'onor.

HUNTSMEN: —lo impone l'onor.

NORMANNO, HUNTSMEN: Splenderà l'esecrabile vero come lampo fra nubi d'orror,—

NORMANNO: Search through the neighboring shores—

TENORS, THEN BASSES: Let us search through the neighboring shores—

NORMANNO: —the vast ruins of the tower;

TENORS, THEN BASSES: —the vast ruins of the tower;

NORMANNO: —let the veil fall from this mystery so shameful—

NORMANNO: —honor asks it, honor demands it—

HUNTSMEN: —let the veil fall from this mystery so shameful—

NORMANNO: —honor demands it.

HUNTSMEN: —honor demands it.

NORMANNO, HUNTSMEN: The horrible truth will blaze like lightning through clouds of horror—

nasty, shameful (handwritten)

NORMANNO, TENORS: —splenderà, splenderà,—

BASSES: —splenderà, sì,—

NORMANNO, HUNTSMEN: —splenderà l'esecrabile vero come lampo fra nubi d'orror,—

NORMANNO, TENORS: —fra nubi d'orror.

HUNTSMEN: —fra nubi d'orror.

NORMANNO: Cada il vel di sì turpe mistero,—

NORMANNO: —sì,—

HUNTSMEN: —cada il vel—

NORMANNO, HUNTSMEN: —di sì turpe mistero,—

NORMANNO: —lo domanda, lo impone l'onore,—

NORMANNO: —sì,—

HUNTSMEN: —lo domanda,—

NORMANNO, HUNTSMEN: —lo impone l'onor,—

NORMANNO, TENORS: —cada il vel, cada il vel,—

BASSES: —che l'impone l'onor,—

NORMANNO: —sì, l'impone,—

NORMANNO, HUNTSMEN: —l'impone l'onor,—

NORMANNO, TENORS: —cada il vel, cada il vel,—

BASSES: —che l'impone l'onor,—

NORMANNO: —sì, l'impone,—

NORMANNO, TENORS: —it will blaze, it will blaze—

BASSES: —yes, it will blaze—

NORMANNO, HUNTSMEN: —the horrible truth will blaze like lightning through clouds of horror—

NORMANNO, TENORS: —through clouds of horror—

HUNTSMEN: —through clouds of horror.

NORMANNO: Let the veil fall from this mystery so shameful—

NORMANNO: —yes—

HUNTSMEN: —let the veil fall—

NORMANNO, HUNTSMEN: —from this mystery so shameful—

NORMANNO: —honor asks it, demands it—

NORMANNO: —yes—

HUNTSMEN: —asks it—

NORMANNO, HUNTSMEN: —honor demands it—

NORMANNO, TENORS: —let the veil fall, let the veil fall—

BASSES: —as honor demands it—

NORMANNO: —yes, honor demands it—

NORMANNO, HUNTSMEN: —honor demands it—

NORMANNO, TENORS: —let the veil fall, let the veil fall—

BASSES: —as honor demands it—

NORMANNO: —yes, honor demands it—

NORMANNO, HUNTSMEN: —l'impone l'onor,—

NORMANNO, HUNTSMEN: —honor demands it—

TENORS: —lo domanda, lo impone l'onor,—

TENORS: —honor asks it, demands it—

BASSES: —cada, cada,—

BASSES: —let it fall, let it fall—

NORMANNO: —cada,—

NORMANNO: —let it fall—

HUNTSMEN: —lo domanda, lo vuole l'onor,—

HUNTSMEN: —honor asks it, wills it—

NORMANNO: —lo vuol l'onor,—

NORMANNO: —honor wills it—

HUNTSMEN: —lo vuol l'onor,—

HUNTSMEN: —honor wills it—

NORMANNO, HUNTSMEN: —l'onor, lo vuol l'onor, lo vuol l'onor.

NORMANNO, HUNTSMEN: —honor, honor wills it, honor wills it.

The huntsmen hasten off in several directions. Lord Enrico Ashton enters, accompanied by Raimondo Bide-the-Bent. Ashton looks upset; Normanno approaches him and salutes respectfully.

NORMANNO: Tu sei turbato!

NORMANNO: You are disturbed!

ENRICO: E n'ho ben donde. Il sai: de' miei destini impallidì la stella; intanto Edgardo, quel mortale nemico di mia prosapia, dalle sue rovine erge la fronte baldanzosa, e ride! Sola una mano raffermarmi puote nel vacillante mio poter. Lucia osa respinger quella mano! Ah! suora non m'è colei!

ENRICO: I have good reason. As you know, the star of my destiny is waning; meanwhile Edgardo, that deadly enemy of my family, raises his bold brow from his ruined hold, and laughs! One hand alone can sustain me in my unsteady power. Lucia dares to refuse that hand! Ah! No sister of mine is she!

RAIMONDO: Dolente vergin, che geme sull'urna recente di cara madre, al talamo potria volger lo sguardo? Rispettiamo un core che trafitto dal duol, schivo è d'amore.

RAIMONDO: Should a sorrowing maiden, who is still moaning at the fresh grave of her beloved mother, turn her gaze to the nuptial couch? Let us respect a heart which, transfixed by sorrow, is averse to love.

NORMANNO: Schivo d'amor! Lucia d'amore avvampa.

NORMANNO: Averse to love! Lucia is ablaze with love.

ENRICO: Che favelli!

ENRICO: What are you saying!

RAIMONDO [*aside*]: (Oh detto!)

NORMANNO: M'udite: Ella sen già colà del parco nel solingo vial, dove la madre giace sepolta. Impetuoso toro ecco su lei s'avventa, quando per l'aria rimbombar si sente un colpo e al suol repente cade la belva.

ENRICO: E chi vibrò quel colpo?

NORMANNO: Tal che il suo nome ricoprì d'un velo.

ENRICO: Lucia forse?

NORMANNO: L'amò.

ENRICO: Dunque il rivide?

NORMANNO: Ogn'alba—

ENRICO: E dove?

NORMANNO: In quel viale.

ENRICO: Io fremo! Nè tu scovristi il seduttor?

NORMANNO: Sospetto io n'ho soltanto.

ENRICO: Ah, parla!

NORMANNO: È tuo nemico.

RAIMONDO [*aside*]: (Oh ciel!)

NORMANNO: Tu lo detesti.

ENRICO: Esser potrebbe Edgardo?

RAIMONDO [*aside*]: (Ah!)

NORMANNO: Lo dicesti.

ENRICO: Cruda, funesta smania tu m'hai svegliato in petto! È troppo, è troppo orribile, questo

RAIMONDO [*aside*]: (What has he said!)

NORMANNO: Listen to me. She was walking there, in the park, on the lonely path, where her mother lies buried. There, a wild bull came rushing at her, when a shot rang out through the air and in an instant the beast fell to the ground, dead.

ENRICO: And who fired that shot?

NORMANNO: One who shrouded his name in mystery.

ENRICO: And Lucia...?

NORMANNO: She fell in love with him.

ENRICO: Then she saw him again?

NORMANNO: Every dawn—

ENRICO: Where?

NORMANNO: On that path.

ENRICO: I am furious! And did you not recognize the seducer?

NORMANNO: I have only a suspicion.

ENRICO: Ah, speak!

NORMANNO: It is your enemy!

RAIMONDO [*aside*]: (Oh heavens!)

NORMANNO: The man you hate.

ENRICO: Could it be Edgardo?

RAIMONDO [*aside*]: (Ah!)

NORMANNO: You have said it.

ENRICO: You have aroused raw, baleful fury in my breast! It is too, it is too horrible, this fatal

fatal sospetto! Mi fa gelare e fremere, mi drizza in fronte il crin, ah, mi fa gelare e fremere, solleva in fronte, solleva in fronte il crin!

ENRICO: Colma di tanto obbrobio chi suora a me nascea! Ah!—

NORMANNO: Pietoso al tuo decoro, io fui con te crudel.

RAIMONDO [aside]: (La tua clemenza imploro; tu lo smentisci, o ciel!)

ENRICO [addressing the absent Lucia]: —pria che d'amor sì perfido a me svelarti rea,—

ENRICO: —se ti colpisse un fulmine,—

NORMANNO, RAIMONDO: Ciel!

ENRICO: —se ti colpisse un fulmine, fora men rio, fora men rio dolor,—

ENRICO: —ah! fora men rio, fora men rio, fora men rio dolor!

NORMANNO: Io fui con te, con te crudel, crudel!

RAIMONDO [aside]: (Tu lo smentisci, o ciel, ah! o ciel, o ciel!)

---

suspicion! It chills me, it makes me tremble, my hair stands on end, ah, it chills me, it makes me tremble, my hair stands on end, stands on end!

ENRICO: That one filled with such infamy could be born sister to me! Ah!—

NORMANNO: Out of respect for your honor, I spoke cruel truth to you.

RAIMONDO [aside]: (I beseech your mercy; refute it, O heavens!)

ENRICO [addressing the absent Lucia]: Before revealing yourself guilty of such treacherous love—

ENRICO: —if you had been struck by lightning—

NORMANNO, RAIMONDO: Heavens!

ENRICO: —if you had been struck by lightning, it would be less dreadful, it would be less dreadful sorrow—

ENRICO: —ah! it would be less dreadful, it would be less dreadful, it would be less dreadful sorrow!

NORMANNO: I spoke cruel, cruel truth to you!

RAIMONDO [aside]: (Refute it, O heavens, ah! O heavens, O heavens!)

The huntsmen return.

HUNTSMEN [to Normanno]: Il tuo dubbio è omai certezza.

HUNTSMEN [to Normanno]: Once and for all your suspicion is a certainty.

NORMANNO [*to Enrico*]: Odi tu?

ENRICO: Narrate.

HUNTSMEN: Oh, giorno!

Come vinti da stanchezza, dopo lungo errare intorno, noi posammo della torre nel vestibolo cadente: ecco tosto lo trascorre in silenzio un uom pallente. Come appresso ei n'è venuto ravvisiam lo sconosciuto: ei su rapido destriero s'involò dal nostro sguardo. Qual s'appella un falconiero ne apprendeva, qual s'appella.

ENRICO: E quale?

HUNTSMEN: Edgardo.

ENRICO: Egli! Oh, rabbia, oh! rabbia che m'accendi, contenerti un cor non può.

RAIMONDO: Ah, no, non credere, no, no—

ENRICO: No, contenerti un cor non può, no, non può, no, non può, no, no!

RAIMONDO: —deh sospendi—ella —ah!

RAIMONDO: M'odi!

ENRICO: Udir non vuo!

La pietade in suo favore miti sensi invan mi detta—se mi parli di vendetta solo intenderti potrò. Sciagurati! il mio furore già su voi tremendo rugge, l'empia fiamma che vi strugge io col sangue spegnerò, io col sangue, io col sangue l'empia

---

NORMANNO [*to Enrico*]: Do you hear?

ENRICO: Speak.

HUNTSMEN: Oh, day of woe!

When, overcome by fatigue after long searching, we stopped to rest in the crumbling entrance of the tower, suddenly a pallid man passed through it silently. As he passed close, we knew him for the unknown man [who saved Lucia]. He fled from our sight on his swift steed. A falconer informed us what his name is, what his name is.

ENRICO: And what is it?

HUNTSMEN: Edgardo.

ENRICO: He! Oh, fury, oh! A heart cannot contain you, oh fury that inflames me.

RAIMONDO: Ah, no, do not believe it, no, no—

ENRICO: No, a heart cannot contain you, no, cannot contain you, no cannot contain you, no, no!

RAIMONDO: —come, stop—she— ah!

RAIMONDO: Listen to me!

ENRICO: I will not listen!

Pity for her vainly enjoins tender feelings—I can understand you only if you speak to me of revenge. Wretches! My rage already roars about you terribly, I will quench with blood the impious flame that consumes you, with blood, with

fiamma che vi strugge spegnerò,
spegnerò, col sangue spegnerò!

HUNTSMEN: Ti raffrena, al nuovo albore ei da te fuggir non può,—

{ HUNTSMEN: —no, no, non può,—
RAIMONDO [*aside*]: (Ah! qual nube di terrore—)

HUNTSMEN: —ti raffrena, al nuovo albore ei da te fuggir non può,—

{ HUNTSMEN: —no, no, non può!
RAIMONDO [*aside*]: (—questa casa circondò!)

{ RAIMONDO [*aside*]: (Ah, qual nube di terror, ah, qual nube di terror, sì, questa casa circondò! ah, sì!)
HUNTSMEN: Ti raffrena, al nuovo, al nuovo albore ei da te fuggir non può, no, no.
ENRICO: Tacete! Tacete! Ah!

{ ENRICO: La pietade in suo favore—
RAIMONDO: Ah!

ENRICO: —miti sensi invan mi detta.

RAIMONDO: Ah! non credere!

ENRICO: Se mi parli di vendetta solo intenderti potrò.

RAIMONDO: Ah!

ENRICO: Sciagurati! il mio furore—

---

blood I will quench, quench the impious flame that consumes you, I will quench it with blood!

HUNTSMEN: Calm yourself, at the next dawn he cannot escape from you—

HUNTSMEN: —no, no, he cannot—
RAIMONDO [*aside*]: (Ah, what a cloud of terror—)

HUNTSMEN: —calm yourself, at the next dawn he cannot escape from you—

HUNTSMEN: —no, no, he cannot!
RAIMONDO [*aside*]: (—has encompassed this house!)

RAIMONDO [*aside*]: (Ah, what a cloud of terror, ah, what a cloud of terror, yes, has encompassed this house! Ah, yes!)

HUNTSMEN: Calm yourself, at the next, at the next dawn he cannot escape from you, no, no.

ENRICO: Be still! Be still! Ah!

ENRICO: Pity on her behalf—

RAIMONDO: Ah!

ENRICO: —vainly enjoins tender feelings.

RAIMONDO: Ah! do not believe it!

ENRICO: I can understand you only if you speak to me of revenge.

RAIMONDO: Ah!

ENRICO: Wretches! my rage—

ENRICO: —già su voi tremendo rugge, l'empia fiamma che vi strugge io col sangue spegnerò,—

RAIMONDO: Qual nube di terrore circondò! sì! sì!—

ENRICO: —io col sangue, io col sangue l'empia fiamma che vi strugge spegnerò, spegnerò, col sangue spegnerò,—

RAIMONDO: —questa casa circondò! questa casa circondò, questa casa circondò, circondò!

HUNTSMEN: Egli a te fuggir non può, no, non può, non può.

ENRICO: —l'empia fiamma che vi strugge io col sangue spegnerò,—

RAIMONDO: Qual nube di terrore questa casa circondò, sì, circondò!

ENRICO: —sì, col sangue spegnerò, l'empia fiamma che vi strugge,—

HUNTSMEN: Ei da te fuggir non può, fuggir non può.

ENRICO: —l'empia fiamma che vi strugge io col sangue spegnerò, sì,—

ENRICO: —spegnerò, sì, sì, col sangue spegnerò, sì, spegnerò, sì, spegnerò, spegnerò, spegnerò, col sangue spegnerò!

ENRICO: —already roars about you terribly, the impious flame that consumes you I will quench with blood—

RAIMONDO: What a cloud of terror has encompassed! Yes! yes!—

ENRICO: I will quench with blood, with blood the impious flame that consumes you, I will quench, I will quench with blood—

RAIMONDO: —has encompassed this house! has encompassed this house, has encompassed this house, has encompassed!

HUNTSMEN: He cannot escape from you, no, he cannot, he cannot.

ENRICO: —the impious flame that consumes you I will quench with blood—

RAIMONDO: What a cloud of terror has encompassed, yes, encompassed this house!

ENRICO: —yes, I will quench with blood the impious flame that consumes you—

HUNTSMEN: He cannot escape from you, he cannot escape.

ENRICO: —the impious flame that consumes you I will quench with blood, yes—

ENRICO: —I will quench, yes, yes, quench with blood, yes, quench, yes, quench, quench, quench, quench with blood!

RAIMONDO: Ah, questa casa circondò, sì, circondò, sì, circondò, circondò, circondò, sì, questa casa circondò!

HUNTSMEN: Fuggir non può, no, no, non può, no, no, non può, no, non può, no, non può, non può, no, no, no, non può!

RAIMONDO: Ah, has encompassed this house, yes, has encompassed, yes, encompassed, encompassed, encompassed, yes, encompassed this house!

HUNTSMEN: He cannot escape, no, no, he cannot, no, no, he cannot, no, he cannot, no, he cannot, he cannot, no, no, no, he cannot!

Exit all.

Scene Two

A park on the grounds of Ravenswood Castle, a short time later. In the foreground are a fountain and benches; in the background, a path leading to the castle. Lucia and Alisa approach the fountain from the direction of the castle. Both seem nervous and on their guard.

LUCIA: Ancor non giunse!

ALISA: Incauta! A che mi traggi! Avventurarti, or che il fratel qui venne, è folle ardir.

[run the risk]

LUCIA: Ben parli! Edgardo sappia qual ne circonda orribile periglio.

ALISA: Perchè d'intorno il ciglio volgi atterrita?

LUCIA: Quella fonte, ah! mai, senza tremar, non veggo. Ah, tu lo sai: Un Ravenswood, ardendo di geloso furor, l'amata donna colà trafisse, e l'infelice cadde nell'onda, ed ivi rimanea

LUCIA: He still has not come!

ALISA: Imprudent girl! Where are you leading me? It is madness for you to venture here now that your brother has returned.

LUCIA: You speak truth, but Edgardo must know what horrible danger surrounds us.

ALISA: Why do you gaze wildly about in such terror?

LUCIA: That fountain, ah! I never see it without trembling. Ah, you know the story. Over there, a Ravenswood, burning with jealous rage, stabbed the woman he loved and the poor

sepolta: M'apparve l'ombra sua—

ALISA: Che dici!

LUCIA: Ascolta.

Regnava nel silenzio alta la notte e bruna, colpìa la fonte un pallido raggio di tetra luna, quando un sommesso gemito fra l'aure udir si fe', ed ecco, ecco su quel margine, l'ombra mostrarsi, l'ombra mostrarsi a me, ah!

woman fell into the waters, and there remained entombed: Her ghost appeared to me—

ALISA: What are you saying!

LUCIA: Listen.

The deep, dark night brooded over the silence, and a pale ray from the dim moon struck the fountain, whereupon a low moan breathed through the air; and here, here on the brink of the pool the ghost appeared, the ghost appeared to me, ah!

She hides her face in her hands.

Qual che favella, muoversi il labbro suo vedea, e con la mano esanime, chiamarmi a sè parea; stette un momento immobile, poi ratta dileguò, e l'onda pria sì limpida di sangue rosseggiò, sì, pria sì limpida di sangue rosseggiò, sì, pria sì limpida, ah, sì, rosseggiò.

I saw her lips move as if she were speaking, and she seemed to beckon me to her with her lifeless hand; for a moment she stood motionless, then swiftly vanished, and the water, so clear until then, turned red with blood, yes, so clear until then, turned red with blood, yes, so clear until then, ah, yes, turned red.

ALISA: Chiari, oh Dio! ben chiari e tristi, nel tuo dir presagi intendo! Ah Lucia, desisti da un amor così tremendo.

ALISA: Oh, God, clear, most clear and painful forewarnings do I see in what you say. Ah, Lucia, abandon a love so filled with peril.

LUCIA: Egli* è luce a' giorni miei, è conforto, è conforto al mio, al mio penar.

LUCIA: He is the light to my days, he is solace, is solace to my, to my suffering.

---

* Before this passage the Cammarano 1836 libretto has the following lines for Lucia: " Io?—Che parli! Al cor che geme questo affetto è sola speme ... senza Edgardo non potrei un istante respirar'' (I?—What are you saying! To my sorrowing heart this love is the only hope ... without Edgardo I could not breathe an instant).

burning · Fsg — ecstacy

Quando rapito in estasi del più cocente ardore, col favellar del core, mi giura eterna fè, eterna fè, in estasi del più cocente ardore, col favellar del core, mi giura eterna fè, gli affanni miei dimentico, gioja diviene il pianto, parmi che a lui d'accanto si schiuda il ciel per me, si schiuda il ciel per me, si schiuda il ciel per me.

near · prepare

ALISA: Ah! giorni d'amaro pianto, ah! s'apprestano per te, sì, sì, giorni d'amaro pianto s'apprestano per te, per te, per te! Ah! Lucia! ah, desisti!

LUCIA: Ah! Quando rapito in estasi del più cocente ardore, col favellar del core, mi giura eterna fè, gli affanni miei dimentico, gioja diviene il pianto, parmi che a lui d'accanto si schiuda il ciel per me, si schiuda il ciel per me, si schiuda il ciel per me, a lui d'accanto si schiuda il ciel per me, ah! si schiuda il ciel, il ciel per me, a lui d'accanto si schiuda il ciel per me, ah! si schiuda il ciel, il ciel per me, sì, sì,—

LUCIA: —a lui d'accanto par si schiuda il ciel per me!

ALISA: Giorni d'amaro pianto, sì, s'apprestano per te!

When carried away in the rapture of the fieriest ardor, with heartfelt words he swears eternal faith, eternal faith to me, in the rapture of the fieriest ardor, with heartfelt words he swears eternal faith to me, I forget my afflictions, my tears turn to joy, it seems to me that by his side the heavens open for me, the heavens open for me, the heavens open for me.

ALISA: Ah! days of bitter weeping, ah! are approaching for you, yes, yes, days of bitter weeping are approaching for you, for you, for you! Ah! Lucia! ah, refrain!

LUCIA: Ah! When carried away in the rapture of the fieriest ardor, with heartfelt words he swears eternal faith to me, I forget my afflictions, weeping turns to joy, it seems to me that by his side the heavens open for me, the heavens open for me, the heavens open for me, by his side the heavens open for me, ah! the heavens, the heavens open for me, by his side, the heavens open for me, ah! the heavens, the heavens open for me, yes, yes—

LUCIA: —by his side the heavens seem to open for me!

ALISA: Yes, days of bitter weeping are approaching for you!

She listens.

EGLI s'avanza! La vicina soglia io cauta veglierò.

He is coming! I shall keep a careful watch at the nearby entrance.

Alisa withdraws toward the castle, and Edgardo enters.

EDGARDO: Lucia, perdona se ad ora inusitata io vederti chiedea: ragion possente a ciò mi trasse. Pria che in ciel biancheggi l'alba novella, dalle patrie sponde lungi sarò.*

EDGARDO: Lucia, forgive me for asking to see you at this unwonted hour; strong reasons have forced me. Before the next dawn whitens the sky, I shall be far from the shore of my homeland.

LUCIA: Che dici!

LUCIA: What are you saying!

EDGARDO: Pei franchi lidi amici sciolgo le vele; ivi trattar m'è dato le sorti della Scozia.

EDGARDO: I am setting sail for the friendly shores of France; there I am being sent to act for the fate of Scotland.

LUCIA: E me nel pianto abbandoni così?

LUCIA: And you are abandoning me, like this, to my tears?

EDGARDO: Pria di lasciarti Ashton mi vegga, io stenderò placato a lui la destra, e la tua destra pegno fra noi di pace—

EDGARDO: Ashton shall behold me before I leave you. I shall hold out my right hand to him in peace, and I shall ask for your right hand as a pledge of peace—

EDGARDO: —chiederò.

EDGARDO: —between us.

LUCIA: Che ascolto!

LUCIA: What do I hear!

LUCIA: Ah no, rimanga nel silenzio sepolto per or l'arcano affetto.

LUCIA: Ah, no, our secret love must remain buried in silence for now.

EDGARDO [*ironically*]: Intendo! Di mia stirpe il reo persecutor de' mali miei ancor pago non è! Mi tolse il padre, il mio

EDGARDO [*ironically*]: I understand! My sufferings still do not satisfy the infamous persecutor of my family! He caused my

* The Cammarano 1836 edition and many later editions of the libretto have two extra lines here: "Athol, riparator di mie sciagure, a tanto onor m'innalza" (Athol, the mender of my misfortunes, raises me to such a great honor).

Set for Act 1, Scene 2, with Lucia and Edgardo at the fountain. (*Courtesy New York City Opera; photo by Beth Bergman*)

Joan Sutherland as Lucia and Gianni Raimondi as Edgardo in
the fountain scene. Costumes by Giovanni Miglioli; set by
Alessandro Benois; staging by Margherita Wallmann. *(Courtesy
Teatro alla Scala, Milan; photo by E. Piccagliani)*

retaggio avito— Nè basta? Che brama ancor quel cor feroce e rio? la mia perdita intera? il sangue mio? Egli m'odia!

LUCIA: Ah no!

EDGARDO: M'abborre!

LUCIA: Calma, o ciel, quell'ira estrema!

EDGARDO: Fiamma ardente in sen mi corre! M'odi!

LUCIA: Edgardo!

EDGARDO: M'odi, e trema!

Sulla tomba che rinserra il tradito genitore, al tuo sangue eterna guerra io giurai nel mio furore;—

LUCIA [*crying out*]: Ah!

EDGARDO: —ma ti vidi, e in cor mi nacque altro affetto, e l'ira tacque. Pur quel voto non è infranto, io potrei, sì, sì, sì, sì, potrei compirlo ancor!

LUCIA: Deh! ti placa, deh! ti placa, deh! ti frena!

EDGARDO: Ah Lucia!

LUCIA: Può tradirne, può tradirne un solo accento! Non ti basta la mia pena? Vuoi ch'io mora di spavento?

EDGARDO: Ah! no, no, no, no!

---

father's death, he stole my ancestral inheritance: is it not enough? What else does that fierce and wicked heart desire? My total destruction? My blood? He hates me!

LUCIA: Ah, no!

EDGARDO: He detests me!

LUCIA: O heavens, subdue this violent rage!

EDGARDO: A searing flame runs through my breast! Listen to me!

LUCIA: Edgardo!

EDGARDO: Listen to me, and tremble!

On the tomb where my betrayed father lies buried, I swore eternal warfare, in my rage, against your line—

LUCIA [*crying out*]: Ah!

EDGARDO: —but I saw you, and another passion was born in my heart, and my wrath abated. Yet that vow is not broken, I can, yes, yes, yes, yes, I can still fulfill it!

LUCIA: Come, calm yourself! come, calm yourself! come, restrain yourself!

EDGARDO: Ah, Lucia!

LUCIA: A single word can betray us, can betray us! Is my suffering not enough for you? Do you want me to die of fright?

EDGARDO: Ah! no, no, no, no!

[handwritten: cedere — cede, give up / intrans — succumb]

LUCIA: Ceda, ceda ogn'altro affetto, solo amor t'infiammi il petto; un più nobile, più santo d'ogni—

LUCIA: —voto è un puro amor, ah, solo amore t'infiammi il petto, ah, solo, sì, solo amor, ah, solo amore t'infiammi il petto, ah, solo, sì, solo amor!

EDGARDO: Pur quel voto non è infranto, io potrei, sì, potrei compirlo ancor, no, non è infranto, io potrei, sì, potrei compirlo ancor,—

EDGARDO: —io potrei compirlo ancor,—

LUCIA: Cedi, cedi a me,—

EDGARDO: —sì, potrei compirlo ancor, ancor!

LUCIA: —cedi, cedi all'amor!

EDGARDO [*firmly*]: Qui di sposa eterna fede, qui mi giura al cielo innante. Dio ci ascolta, Dio ci vede; tempio ed ara è un core amante; al tuo fato unisco il mio: son tuo sposo.

[handwritten: ?]

LUCIA: Renounce, renounce all other feelings, let only love inflame your breast; pure love is more noble, more sacred—

LUCIA: —than any vow, ah, let only love inflame your breast, ah, only, yes, only love, ah, let only love inflame your breast, ah, only, yes, only love!

EDGARDO: Yet that vow is not broken, I can, yes, I can still fulfill it, no, it is not broken, I can, yes, I can still fulfill it—

EDGARDO: —I can still fulfill it—

LUCIA: Yield, yield to me—

EDGARDO: —yes, I can still fulfill it, still!

LUCIA: —yield, yield to love!

EDGARDO [*firmly*]: Here in the sight of Heaven, here, swear to me eternal faith as my wife. God hears us, God sees us; a loving heart is church and altar; I unite my fate with yours; I am your husband.

He places a ring on Lucia's finger; she in turn puts a ring on his finger.

LUCIA: E tua son io.

LUCIA, EDGARDO: Ah! soltanto il nostro foco spegnerà di morte il gel.

LUCIA: A' miei voti amore invoco, a' miei voti invoco il ciel, a' miei voti invoco il cielo, invoco il cielo, invoco il ciel.

LUCIA: And I am yours.

LUCIA, EDGARDO: Ah! Only the ice of death can extinguish our fire.

LUCIA: I invoke love to my vows, I invoke Heaven to my vows, to my vows I invoke Heaven, I invoke Heaven, I invoke Heaven.

EDGARDO: A' miei voti invoco il ciel, il ciel, invoco il ciel, a' miei voti invoco il ciel, invoco il ciel, invoco il ciel.

EDGARDO: To my vows I invoke Heaven, Heaven, I invoke Heaven, to my vows I invoke Heaven, I invoke Heaven, I invoke Heaven.

is appropriate

EDGARDO: Separarci omai conviene.

EDGARDO: Now we must part.

LUCIA: Oh parola a me funesta! Il mio cor con te ne viene.

LUCIA: Oh, saddest words. My heart goes with you.

EDGARDO: Il mio cor con te qui resta, il mio cor con te qui resta.

EDGARDO: My heart remains here with you, my heart remains here with you.

LUCIA: Ah! Edgardo! ah! Edgardo!

LUCIA: Ah! Edgardo! ah! Edgardo!

EDGARDO: Separarci omai convien.

EDGARDO: Now we must part.

sometimes

LUCIA: Ah! talor del tuo pensiero venga un foglio messagiero, e la vita fuggitiva di speranze nudrirò.

fugitive

LUCIA: Ah! Send a letter now and then as messenger of your thoughts, and I will maintain my fleeting life with hope.

EDGARDO: Io di te memoria viva sempre, o cara, serberò.

EDGARDO: I shall always keep the memory of you alive, O dear one.

pascere – pasture, graze (reflex)– feed self, live upon

LUCIA: Ah! Verranno a te sull'aure i miei sospiri ardenti, udrai nel mar che mormora l'eco de' miei lamenti. Pensando ch'io di gemiti mi pasco e di dolor, spargi un'amara lagrima su questo pegno allor, ah! su questo pegno allor, ah! su questo pegno allor, ah! su quel pegno allor.

spill / shed

LUCIA: Ah! My ardent sighs will be wafted to you on the breezes, in the murmuring of the sea you will hear the echo of my laments. When you remember that groans and sorrow are my fare, then shed a bitter tear on this pledge, ah! on this pledge then, ah! on this pledge then, ah! on this pledge then.

EDGARDO: Verranno a te sull'aure i miei sospiri ardenti, udrai nel mar che mormora l'eco de' miei

EDGARDO: My ardent sighs will be wafted to you on the breezes, in the murmuring of the sea

lamenti. Pensando ch'io di gemiti mi pasco e di dolor, spargi un'amara lagrima su questo pegno allor, ah! su questo pegno allor,—

LUCIA: Ah! sì, su quel pegno allor, Edgardo—

EDGARDO: —ah! su questo pegno allor, ah!—

EDGARDO: —su quel pegno allor.

LUCIA: Il tuo scritto sempre viva—

EDGARDO: Cara!

LUCIA: —la memoria in me terrà!

EDGARDO: Sì, sì, Lucia, sì, sì.

LUCIA, EDGARDO: Ah! Verranno a me sull'aure i tuoi sospiri ardenti, udrò nel mar che mormora l'eco de' miei lamenti.

LUCIA: Pensando che di gemiti mi pasco e di dolor,—

EDGARDO: Spargi un'amara lagrima—

LUCIA: —spargi—

LUCIA, EDGARDO: —su questo pegno allor, ah! su questo pegno allor, ah! su questo pegno allor, ah! questo pegno allor, sì, sì, allor, sì, sì, allor!

EDGARDO: Io parto.

you will hear the echo of my laments. When you remember that groans and sorrow are my fare, then shed a bitter tear on this pledge, ah! on this pledge then—

LUCIA: Ah! yes, on this pledge then, Edgardo—

EDGARDO: —ah! on this pledge then, ah—

EDGARDO: —on this pledge then.

LUCIA: Your letters will always keep—

EDGARDO: Dear one!

LUCIA: —remembrance alive within me.

EDGARDO: Yes, yes, Lucia, yes, yes.

LUCIA, EDGARDO: Ah! Your ardent sighs will be wafted to me on the breezes, in the murmuring of the sea I shall hear the echo of my laments.

LUCIA: When you remember that groans and sorrow are my fare—

EDGARDO: Shed a bitter tear—

LUCIA: —shed—

LUCIA, EDGARDO: —on this pledge then, ah! on this pledge then, ah! on this pledge then, ah! this pledge then, yes, yes, then, yes, yes, then!

EDGARDO: I am leaving.

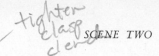

LUCIA: Addio.

LUCIA: Farewell.

EDGARDO: Rammentati, ne stringe il ciel!

EDGARDO: Remember, Heaven binds us together.

LUCIA: Edgardo!

LUCIA: Edgardo!

EDGARDO: Addio!

EDGARDO: Farewell!

They part—Lucia goes in the direction of the Castle, Edgardo the opposite way.

Act Two

Set design for Act 2, Scene 1, by Adriana Muojo. (*Courtesy Teatro di San Carlo, Naples*)

ACT TWO

Scene One

Some weeks or months have passed. The scene is laid in Lord Enrico Ashton's study or morning-room in Ravenswood Castle. Lord Enrico sits at a desk or table and converses with Normanno, who stands near him.

NORMANNO: Lucia fra poco a te verrà.

ENRICO: Tremante l'aspetto. A festeggiar le nozze illustri, già nel castello i nobili parenti giunser di mia famiglia; in breve Arturo qui volge. [*Rising in agitation from his chair:*] E s'ella pertinace osasse d'opporsi?

NORMANNO: Non temer: la lunga assenza del tuo nemico, i fogli da noi rapiti, e la bugiarda nuova ch'egli s'accese d'altra fiamma, in core di Lucia spegneranno il cieco amore.

ENRICO: Ella s'avvanza. Il simulato foglio porgimi.

NORMANNO: Lucia will come to you soon.

ENRICO: I await her with trembling. The noble kinsmen of my family have already arrived at the castle to celebrate this illustrious wedding; very soon Arturo will arrive. [*Rising in agitation from his chair:*] And if she stubbornly dares to oppose it?

NORMANNO: Do not fear; your enemy's long absence, the letters we have seized, and the false news that he is in love with another woman will extinguish this blind love in Lucia's heart.

ENRICO: She is coming. Give me the forged letter.

Normanno hands him a letter.

Ed esci sulla via che tragge alla città regina di Scozia, e qui fra plausi e liete grida conduci Arturo.

And go along the way that leads to Scotland's queenly city, and lead Arturo here amid cheers and shouts of joy.

Normanno leaves. A moment later Lucia enters hesitantly and stands by the doorway.

Appressati, Lucia.   Come here, Lucia.

Lucia moves nearer to him. She looks pale and haggard; her manner is listless.

Sperai più lieta in questo dì vederti, in questo dì, che d'Imeneo le faci s'accendono per te. Mi guardi, e taci?

I hoped to see you happier on this day, on this day when Hymen's torches are being lighted for you. You look at me and are silent?

LUCIA: Il pallor funesto, orrendo, che ricopre il volto mio, ti rimproverò tacendo il mio strazio, il mio dolore. Perdonare ti possa un Dio l'inumano tuo rigor, perdonarti possa Iddio, ah! l'inumano tuo rigor, l'inumano tuo rigor, il tuo rigor, il tuo rigor, e il mio dolor!

LUCIA: The awful, deathly pallor that covers my face has reproached you silently for my pain, my sorrow. May God pardon your inhuman harshness, may God pardon you, ah! your inhuman harshness, your inhuman harshness, your harshness, your harshness, and my sorrow!

ENRICO: A ragion mi fe' spietato, quel che t'arse indegno affetto; ma si taccia del passato; tuo fratello, tuo fratello sono ancor. Spenta è l'ira nel mio petto, spegni tu l'insano amor, spenta è l'ira nel mio petto, spegni tu l'insano amor, sì, spegni tu l'insano amor, ah, spegni tu l'insano amor, l'insano amor, l'insano amor, spegni tu l'insano amor.* Nobil sposo—

ENRICO: With right did that ignoble passion that burned in you make me cruel, but let us be silent about the past; I am still your brother, your brother. The wrath in my breast is spent, stifle your mad love, the wrath in my breast is spent, stifle your mad love, yes, stifle your mad love, ah, stifle your mad love, your mad love, your mad love, stifle your mad love. A noble husband—

* The Cammarano 1836 libretto inserts the following lines at this point: "LUCIA: La pietade è tardi omai! Il mio fin di già s'appressa! ENRICO: Viver lieta ancor potrai ... LUCIA: Lieta! e puoi tu dirlo a me?" (LUCIA: Mercy is too late by this time! My end is already approaching! ENRICO: You can still live happily ... LUCIA: Happily! How can you say that to me?). Donizetti started to write music for a variant of this text, then crossed it out, omitting this passage.

LUCIA: Cessa, cessa!

ENRICO: Come?

LUCIA: Ad altr'uom giurai mia fè.

ENRICO [*becoming angry*]: Nol potevi—

LUCIA: Enrico!

ENRICO: Nol potevi—

LUCIA: Ad altro giurai, ad altro giurai mia fè.

LUCIA: Stop, stop!

ENRICO: What?

LUCIA: I have pledged my faith to another man.

ENRICO [*becoming angry*]: Impossible—

LUCIA: Enrico!

ENRICO: Impossible—

LUCIA: I have pledged my faith to another man, to another man.

Enrico tries to restrain his anger.

ENRICO: Basti! Questo foglio appien ti dice qual crudel, qual empio amasti. Leggi.

ENRICO: Enough: This letter will tell clearly what a heartless scoundrel you loved. Read it.

Enrico hands to Lucia the letter which Normanno gave him earlier. As Lucia reads the letter, her dismay and horror become so intense that she appears to be on the point of swooning.

LUCIA: Ah! il core mi balzò!

LUCIA: Ah! my heart has burst!

Enrico rushes to her assistance.

ENRICO: Tu vacilli!

LUCIA: Me infelice! ahi! la folgore piombò!

Soffriva nel pianto, languia nel dolore, la speme, la vita riposi in un cor, l'istante di morte è giunto per me! quel core infedele ad altra, ad altra si diè!

ENRICO: Un folle t'accese, un perfido core, tradisti il tuo sangue per—

ENRICO: —vil seduttore,—

LUCIA: Oh Dio!

ENRICO: You seem faint!

LUCIA: Unhappy me! Woe! the thunderbolt has struck!

I suffered in tears, languished in sorrow, my hope, my life reposed in one heart. The moment of death is come for me! That faithless heart has vowed love to another, to another!

ENRICO: A mad, a treacherous heart set you afire, you betrayed your family for—

ENRICO: —a vile seducer—

LUCIA: Oh, Lord!

ENRICO: —ma degna del cielo ne avesti mercè: quel core infedele ad—

ENRICO: —altra si diè. Un folle t'accese, un perfido amore; tradisti il tuo sangue per vil seduttore, ma degna dal cielo ne avesti mercè: quel core infedele, quel core infedele ad altra si diè, ad altra si diè, sì, sì, si diè, ad altra, ad altra, ad altra si diè!

LUCIA: Ahimè! L'istante tremendo è giunto per me, sì, quel core infedele ad altra si diede, quel core infedele ad altra si diè, quel core infedele, quel core infedele ad altra si diè, ad altra si diè, ad altra, ad altra, ad altra si diè!

ENRICO: —but you have received a fitting reward from Heaven; that faithless heart—

ENRICO: —has vowed love to another. A mad, a treacherous love set you afire; you betrayed your family for a vile seducer, but you have received a fitting reward from Heaven; that faithless heart, that faithless heart has vowed love to another, has vowed love to another, yes, yes, has vowed love to another, to another, has vowed love to another!

LUCIA: Alas! The dreadful moment is come for me, yes, that faithless heart has vowed love to another, that faithless heart has vowed love to another, that faithless heart, that faithless heart has vowed love to another, has vowed love to another, to another, to another, has vowed love to another!

From the distance come sounds of music and rejoicing.

LUCIA: Che fia!

LUCIA: What is happening?

ENRICO: Suonar di giubilo odi la riva?

ENRICO: Do you hear the sounds of rejoicing on the shore?

LUCIA: Ebbene?

LUCIA: What does it mean?

ENRICO: Giunge il tuo sposo.

ENRICO: Your bridegroom is arriving.

LUCIA: Un brivido mi corse per le vene!

LUCIA: A chill ran through my veins.

ENRICO: A te s'appresta il talamo.

ENRICO: Your nuptials are being prepared.

Enrico (Piero Cappuccilli) shows Lucia (Joan Sutherland) the forged letter. Costumes by Giovanni Miglioli; set by Alessandro Benois; staging by Margherita Wallmann. (*Courtesy Teatro alla Scala, Milan; photo by E. Piccagliani*)

Enrico (Geraint Evans) persuades Lucia (Joan Sutherland) to marry Arturo. *(Courtesy Royal Opera House, Covent Garden, London; photo by Houston Rogers)*

LUCIA: La tomba, la tomba a me s'appresta!

ENRICO: Ora fatale è questa!

LUCIA: Ho sugl'occhi un vel!

ENRICO: M'odi! Però Guglielmo —ascendere vedremo il trono Maria— Prostrata è nella polvere la parte ch'io seguia—

LUCIA: Ah! io tremo!

ENRICO: Dal precipizio Arturo può sottrarmi, sol egli—

LUCIA: Ed io? ed io?

ENRICO: Salvarmi devi.

LUCIA: Enrico!

ENRICO: Vieni allo sposo.

LUCIA: Ad altri giurai.

ENRICO: Devi salvarmi.

He prepares to leave.

LUCIA: Ma—

ENRICO: Il devi.

LUCIA: Oh ciel! oh ciel!

Enrico changes his mind and addresses her with determination.

ENRICO: Se tradirmi tu potrai, la mia sorte è già compita; tu m'involi onore e vita, tu la scure appresti a me. Ne' tuoi sogni mi vedrai, ombra irata e minacciosa! quella scure sanguinosa starà sempre innanzi a te, starà sempre, starà sempre

LUCIA: My tomb, my tomb is being prepared for me.

ENRICO: A fateful hour is this!

LUCIA: A veil hangs before my eyes!

ENRICO: Listen to me! William is dead—we shall see Mary take the throne— The side which I have followed lies prostrate in the dust—

LUCIA: Ah! I tremble!

ENRICO: Arturo can save me from the precipice, he alone—

LUCIA: And I? and I?

ENRICO: You must save me.

LUCIA: Enrico!

ENRICO: Come to your bridegroom.

LUCIA: I am sworn to another.

ENRICO: You must save me.

LUCIA: But—

ENRICO: You must.

LUCIA: Oh heavens! oh heavens!

ENRICO: If you can betray me, my fate is already sealed; you rob me of honor and life, you make ready the executioner's axe for me. You will see me in your dreams, a wrathful and menacing shade! That bloodstained axe will always be

innanzi a te, starà sempre, sempre, sempre innanzi a te!

before you, will always be, will always be before you, will always, always, always be before you!

Lucia weeps and addresses Heaven.

LUCIA: Tu che vedi il pianto mio, tu che leggi in questo core, se rejetto il mio dolore, come in terra, in ciel non è; tu mi togli, eterno Iddio, questa vita disperata, io son tanto sventurata, che la morte è un ben per me, sì, la morte, sì, la morte è un ben per me, sì, la morte, sì, la morte è un ben per me.

LUCIA: You that see my tears, you that read my innermost heart, if Heaven, like earth, does not reject my sorrow; take away, eternal God, this life of despair; I am so wretched that death would be a blessing for me, yes, death, yes, death would be a blessing for me, yes, death, yes, death would be a blessing for me.

ENRICO: A te s'appresta il talamo!

ENRICO: Your nuptials are drawing near!

LUCIA: Ah! la tomba!

LUCIA: Ah! the tomb!

ENRICO: Salvar mi devi.

ENRICO: You must save me.

LUCIA: Ho sugl'occhi un vel!

LUCIA: A veil hangs before my eyes!

ENRICO: Ah! Se tradirmi tu potrai, la mia sorte è già compita, tu m'involi onore e vita, tu la scure appresti a me.

ENRICO: Ah, if you can betray me, my fate is already sealed; you rob me of honor and life, you make ready the executioner's axe for me.

LUCIA: Ah, mi togli, eterno Iddio,—

LUCIA: Ah, take away, eternal God—

LUCIA: —questa vita disperata, io son tanto sventurata, che la morte è un ben per me, sì, la morte, sì, la morte è un ben per me, sì, la morte, sì, la morte è un ben per me, la morte è un ben, è un ben per me, sì, sì, la morte, sì, la morte è un ben, è un ben per me, è un ben per

LUCIA: —this life of despair, I am so wretched that death would be a blessing for me, yes, death, yes, death would be a blessing for me, yes, death, yes, death would be a blessing for me, death would be a blessing, would be a blessing for me, yes, yes, death, yes, death would be

me, è un ben per me, è un ben,
è un ben, è un ben per me.

a blessing, would be a blessing
for me, would be a blessing for
me, would be a blessing for me,
would be a blessing, would be a
blessing, would be a blessing for
me.

ENRICO: Mi vedrai, ombra irata,
quella scure sanguinosa starà
sempre innanzi a te, sempre,
sempre, sempre, sempre innanzi a te, sempre, sempre,
sempre, sempre innanzi a te, sì,
sempre, sempre innanzi a te,
innanzi a te, a te, sì, sì, starà
sempre innanzi a te, innanzi a
te, innanzi a te, a te, a te, a te,
a te.

ENRICO: You will see me, a
wrathful shade, that bloodstained axe will always be
before you, always, always,
always, always before you,
always, always, always, always
before you, yes, always, always
before you, before you, you,
yes, yes, will always be before
you, before you, before you,
you, you, you, you.

Lucia collapses tearfully into a chair. Enrico strides out angrily.
Raimondo Bide-the-Bent enters, and Lucia runs to meet him.

LUCIA: Ebben?

LUCIA: Well?

RAIMONDO: Di tua speranza
l'ultimo raggio tramontò. Credei, al tuo sospetto, che il fratel
chiudesse tutte le strade onde
sul franco suolo, all'uom che
amar giurasti, non giungesser
tue nuove: io stesso un foglio da
te vergato per sicura mano
recar gli feci—invano! Tace
mai sempre. Quel silenzio assai
d'infedeltà ti parla!

RAIMONDO: The final glimmer of
your hopes has disappeared. I
believed, as you suspected, that
your brother had closed all the
routes so that in France no
news from you would reach the
man whom you swore to love;
I myself had a letter written by
you carried to him by a safe
hand—in vain. He keeps un-
varying silence. This silence
tells you enough of his faithlessness.

LUCIA: E me consigli?

LUCIA: And what do you counsel
me to do?

RAIMONDO: Di piegarti al destino.

RAIMONDO: To submit to fate.

LUCIA: E il giuramento?

LUCIA: And my vow?

RAIMONDO: Tu pur vaneggi! I nuziali voti che il ministro di Dio non benedice, nè il ciel, nè il mondo riconosce.

LUCIA: Ah! cede persuasa la mente, ma sordo alla ragion resiste il core!

RAIMONDO: Vincerlo è forza.

LUCIA: Oh sventurato amore!

RAIMONDO: Ah! cedi, cedi, o più sciagure ti sovrastan, ti sovrastano, infelice. Per le tenere mie cure, per l'estinta genitrice, il periglio, il periglio d'un fratello, il periglio d'un fratello, deh ti muova, e cangi il cor. O la madre, o la madre nell'avello fremerà, fremerà per te d'orror. Ah, cedi, cedi, il periglio d'un fratello ti commova e cangi, e cangi il cor.

LUCIA: Taci, taci!

RAIMONDO: No, no, cedi.

LUCIA: Ah! ah! taci.

RAIMONDO: La madre—

LUCIA: Ah!—

RAIMONDO: —il fratello.

LUCIA: —ah! taci. Deh! vincesti. Non son tanto snaturata.

RAIMONDO: Oh! qual gioja in me tu desti! oh qual nube hai dissipata! Ah! Qual gioja!

RAIMONDO: You are out of your mind. Neither Heaven nor earth acknowledges nuptial vows that a minister of God has not blessed.

LUCIA: Ah! my mind yields, convinced, but my heart resists, deaf to reason!

RAIMONDO: You must overcome it.

LUCIA: Oh miserable love!

RAIMONDO: Ah! yield, yield, or more misfortunes threaten you, threaten you, unhappy girl. By my compassionate ministrations, by your deceased mother, let the danger, the danger to your brother, the danger to your brother—come—move you and change your heart. Or your mother, or your mother will turn, will turn in her grave with horror for you. Ah, yield, yield, let the danger to your brother move you and change, and change your heart.

LUCIA: Be still, be still!

RAIMONDO: No, no, yield.

LUCIA: Ah! ah! be still.

RAIMONDO: Your mother—

LUCIA: Ah!—

RAIMONDO: —your brother.

LUCIA: Ah! be still. Ah! you have won. I am not so unnatural.

RAIMONDO: Oh! what joy you awaken within me, oh what clouds you have scattered! Ah! what joy!

Al ben de' tuoi qual vittima offri, Lucia, te stessa; e tanto sacrifizio scritto nel ciel sarà, nel ciel sarà. Offri, Lucia, te stessa, e tanto sacrifizio scritto nel ciel sarà. Se la pietà degli uomini a te non fia concessa, v'è un Dio, v'è un Dio che tergere il pianto tuo saprà. Se la pietà degli uomini a te non fia concessa, v'è un Dio, v'è un Dio, che tergere il pianto tuo saprà, il pianto tuo saprà, il pianto tuo saprà.

LUCIA: Guidami tu, tu reggimi, son fuori di me stessa! Lungo, crudel supplizio la vita a me sarà!

RAIMONDO: Sì, figlia, coraggio! Qual nube hai disgombrata!

RAIMONDO: Oh figlia mia, coraggio!

LUCIA: Sì, guidami, sì, sì.

RAIMONDO: Ah! Al ben de' tuoi qual vittima offri, Lucia, te stessa, e tanto sacrifizio scritto nel ciel sarà, nel ciel sarà.

LUCIA: Nel ciel sarà, sì.

RAIMONDO: Offri, Lucia, te stessa, e tanto sacrifizio scritto nel ciel sarà.

LUCIA: Ah!

You are offering yourself, Lucia, as victim for your family's good; and so great a sacrifice will be noted in Heaven, noted in Heaven. You are offering yourself, Lucia, and so great a sacrifice will be noted in Heaven. If human mercy is not granted to you, there is a God, there is a God who can dry your tears. If human mercy is not granted to you, there is a God, there is a God who can dry your tears, dry your tears, dry your tears.

LUCIA: Guide me, direct me, I am beside myself! A long, cruel punishment my life will be to me!

RAIMONDO: Yes, daughter, have courage! What clouds you have dispelled!

RAIMONDO: Oh my daughter, have courage!

LUCIA: Yes, guide me, yes, yes.

RAIMONDO: Ah! You are offering yourself, Lucia, as victim for your family's good, and so great a sacrifice will be noted in Heaven, noted in Heaven.

LUCIA: Noted in Heaven, yes.

RAIMONDO: You are offering yourself, Lucia, and so great a sacrifice will be noted in Heaven.

LUCIA: Ah!

RAIMONDO: Se la pietà degli uomini a te non fia concessa, v'è un Dio, v'è un Dio che tergere il pianto tuo saprà. Se la pietà—

LUCIA: Oh Dio! Son fuor di me! Ingrato! Edgardo ingrato! [*Begins to cry.*]

RAIMONDO: —degli uomini a te non fia concessa, v'è un Dio, v'è un Dio che tergere il pianto tuo saprà, il pianto tuo saprà, il pianto tuo saprà, il pianto tuo saprà, il pianto tuo saprà,—

RAIMONDO: —ah, sì, saprà, il pianto tuo saprà.

LUCIA: Guidami, vincesti, ah! ah! ah!

RAIMONDO: If human mercy is not granted to you, there is a God, there is a God who can dry your tears. If human mercy—

LUCIA: Oh God! I am beside myself! Ingrate! Ungrateful Edgardo! [*Begins to cry.*]

RAIMONDO: —is not granted to you, there is a God, there is a God who can dry your tears, dry your tears, dry your tears, dry your tears, dry your tears—

RAIMONDO: —ah, yes, can, can dry your tears.

LUCIA: Guide me, you have won, ah! ah! ah!

Scene Two

A few days have passed, and preparations for the wedding have been completed. The curtain rises on a large hall of Ravenswood Castle, which is festively arrayed for the ceremony. At the rear is a door; on one side of the hall is the table where the principals are to sign the marriage contract. A crowd of knights, ladies, retainers, soldiers, etc., most of them in holiday attire, are present, waiting for the wedding to begin.

CHORUS, ENRICO: Per te d'immenso giubilo, tutto s'avviva intorno, per te veggiam rinascere della speranza il giorno, qui l'amistà ti guida, qui ti conduce amore, tutto s'avviva intorno, qui ti conduce amor, qual astro in notte infida, qual riso nel dolor, qual astro in notte infida, qual riso nel dolor.

CHORUS, ENRICO: Through you there is great rejoicing all around, through you we see the day of hope reborn, friendship guides you here, love leads you here, everything takes heart all around, love leads you here, like a star on a treacherous night, like a smile in the midst of sorrow, like a star on a

ARTURO: Per poco fra le tenebre sparì la vostra stella: io la farò risorgere, più fulgida, più bella. La man mi porgi, Enrico, ti stringi a questo cor, a te ne vengo amico, fratello e difensor.

ARTURO: Your star almost vanished in the darkness. I shall make it rise again, more dazzling, more beautiful. Give me your hand, Enrico, press yourself to this heart, I come to you as friend, brother and defender.

CHORUS, ENRICO: Ah! Per te d'immenso giubilo tutto s'avviva intorno, per te veggiam rinascere della speranza il giorno, qui l'amistà ti guida, qui ti conduce amore, tutto ravviva intorno, qui ti conduce amor,—

CHORUS, ENRICO: Ah! Through you there is great rejoicing all around, through you we see the day of hope reborn; friendship guides you here, love leads you here, everything takes heart all around, love leads you here—

CHORUS, ENRICO: —qual astro in notte infida, qual riso nel dolor, qual astro in notte infida, qual riso nel dolor,—

CHORUS, ENRICO: —like a star on a treacherous night, like a smile in the midst of sorrow, like a star on a treacherous night, like a smile in the midst of sorrow—

ARTURO: A te ne vengo amico, fratello e difensore, a te ne vengo amico, fratello e difensor,—

ARTURO: I come to you as friend, brother and defender, I come to you as friend, brother and defender—

ARTURO: —fratello e difensor, fratello e difensor, difensor, difensor, fratello e difensor, a te ne vengo difensor.

ARTURO: —brother and defender, brother and defender, defender, defender, brother and defender, I come to you as defender.

TENORS, BASSES, ENRICO: —e difensor, fratello c difensor, difensor, difensor, fratello e difensor, e difensor, e difensor.

TENORS, BASSES, ENRICO: —and defender, brother and defender, defender, defender, brother and defender, and defender, and defender.

SOPRANOS: —e difensor, difensor, difensor, e difensor, e difensor, e difensor.

SOPRANOS: —and defender, defender, defender, and defender, and defender, and defender.

ARTURO: Dov'è Lucia!

ENRICO: Qui giungere or la vedrem.

He speaks confidentially to Arturo.

Se in lei soverchia è la mestizia, maravigliarti, no, no, non dêi. Dal duolo oppressa e vinta, piange la madre estinta.

ARTURO: M'è noto, sì, sì, m'è noto.

ENRICO: Soverchia è la mestizia, ma piange la madre.

ARTURO: Or solvi un dubbio. Fama, fama suonò ch'Edgardo sovr'essa, sovr'essa temerario alzare osò lo sguardo—temerario.

ENRICO: È vero, è vero, quel folle ardia, ma—

ARTURO: Ah!

CHORUS: S'avanza qui Lucia, s'avanza.

ENRICO [*to Arturo*]: Piange la madre estinta.

ARTURO: Where is Lucia?

ENRICO: We shall soon see her coming here.

If she seems overpowered by sadness, you must not wonder at it, no, no. She is subdued and oppressed by sorrow, she weeps for her late mother.

ARTURO: I am aware of it, yes, yes, I am aware of it.

ENRICO: Her sorrow is excessive, but she is weeping for her mother.

ARTURO: Resolve a doubt for me now. Rumor, rumor has claimed that Edgardo brashly dared to cast desirous eyes upon her, upon her brashly.

ENRICO: It is true, it is true, the madman dared, but—

ARTURO: Ah!

CHORUS: Lucia is approaching, approaching.

ENRICO [*to Arturo*]: She is weeping for her dead mother.

Lucia, pale and distraught, totters in, supported by Alisa and Raimondo.
Enrico presents her to Arturo; she recoils with repulsion.

Ecco il tuo sposo. [*Aside to Lucia:*] (Incauta! perdermi vuoi?)

LUCIA [*aside*]: (Gran Dio!)

ARTURO: Ti piaccia i voti accogliere del tenero amor mio.

Here is your husband. [*Aside to Lucia:*] (Heedless girl! Do you want to ruin me?)

LUCIA [*aside*]: (Great God!)

ARTURO: May it please you to accept the vows of my tender love.

Act 2, Scene 2: Enrico presents Lucia to Arturo. (*Courtesy Royal Opera House, Covent Garden, London; photo by Houston Rogers*)

Enrico (Richard Torigi) compels Lucia (Linda Newman) to sign
the marriage contract. *(Courtesy National Broadcasting Company)*

Arturo seems about to speak further, but Enrico cuts him short by walking over to the table where the marriage contract lies.

ENRICO [*aside to Lucia*]: (Incauta!) [*To the others:*] Omai si compia il rito.

LUCIA [*aside*]: (Gran Dio!)

ENRICO: T'appressa.

ARTURO: Oh dolce invito!

ENRICO [*aside to Lucia*]: (Heedless girl!) [*To the others:*] Now let the rite be celebrated.

LUCIA [*aside*]: (Great God!)

ENRICO: Come here.

ARTURO: Oh, sweet request!

Arturo bends over the table and signs the contract. Lucia, in a daze, is assisted to the table by Alisa and Raimondo, who indicate to her that it is her turn to sign.

RAIMONDO [*aside*]: (Reggi, buon Dio, l'afflitta.)

LUCIA [*aside*]: (Io vado al sacrifizio! me misera!)

ENRICO [*impatiently to Lucia*]: (Non esitar! Scrivi, scrivi!)

RAIMONDO [*aside*]: (Good Lord, sustain the suffering girl.)

LUCIA [*aside*]: (I am going to the sacrifice! Unhappy me!)

ENRICO [*impatiently to Lucia*]: (Do not hesitate! Sign, sign!)

Lucia signs the contract. When she is done, she clings trembling to Raimondo.

LUCIA [*aside*]: (La mia condanna ho scritta!)

ENRICO [*aside, with relief*]: (Respiro!)

LUCIA [*aside*]: (Io gelo ed ardo! io manco!)

LUCIA [*aside*]: (I have signed my death warrant!)

ENRICO [*aside, with relief*]: (I can breathe again!)

LUCIA [*aside*]: (I am freezing and burning! I feel faint!)

The door at the rear is flung open. Edgardo, shielding his face behind his cloak, strides into the hall. All turn and stare at him with dismay.

ALISA, ARTURO, ENRICO, RAIMONDO, CHORUS: Qual fragor! Chi giunge?

EDGARDO [*loudly, menacingly*]: Edgardo!

CHORUS: Ah!

ALISA, ARTURO, ENRICO, RAIMONDO, CHORUS: What a noise! Who has come?

EDGARDO [*loudly, menacingly*]: Edgardo!

CHORUS: Ah!

LUCIA: Edgardo! oh fulmine!

LUCIA: Edgardo! oh, a thunderbolt!

ALISA, ARTURO, ENRICO, RAIMONDO, CHORUS: Edgardo! Oh terror!

ALISA, ARTURO, ENRICO, RAIMONDO, CHORUS: Edgardo! Oh, horror!

Lucia faints. Amid the horrified confusion of the crowd, Alisa and other women attendants help her to a chair.

ALISA, SOPRANOS: Edgardo!

ALISA, SOPRANOS: Edgardo!

RAIMONDO, TENORS, BASSES: Oh terror!

RAIMONDO, TENORS, BASSES: Oh, horror!

EDGARDO [*to himself*]: Chi mi frena in tal momento? Chi troncò dell'ire il corso? Il suo duolo, il suo spavento son la prova, son la prova d'un rimorso! Ma qual rosa inaridita, ella sta fra morte e vita! Io son vinto, son commosso! t'amo, ingrata, t'amo, t'amo, ingrata, t'amo ancor!

EDGARDO [*to himself*]: Who restrains me at such a moment? Who cut short the outpouring of my wrath? Her anguish, her terror are proof, are proof of remorse! But like a wilting rose, she hovers between life and death! I am overcome, I am moved! I love you, thankless girl, I love you, I love you, thankless girl, I still love you!

ENRICO: Chi raffrena il mio furore, e la man che al brando corse? Della misera in favore nel mio petto un grido sorse! È mio sangue! l'ho tradita! Ella sta fra morte e vita! Ah! che spegnere non posso i rimorsi del mio core, del mio cor!

ENRICO: Who restrains my fury, and the hand that grasped for the sword? A cry of sympathy for the poor girl has sprung up in my breast! She is my blood! I have betrayed her! She hovers between life and death! Ah! that I cannot quench my heart's, my heart's remorse!

LUCIA: Io sperai che a me la vita tronca avesse il mio spavento, ma la morte non m'aita, vivo ancor per mio tormento! Da' miei lumi cadde il velo, mi tradì la terra e il cielo! Vorrei piangere e non posso, m'ab-

LUCIA: I hoped my terror would cut short my life, but death does not come to help me, I keep on living in my misery! The veil has fallen from my eyes, Heaven and earth have betrayed me! I would weep but I cannot,

to form

sg?

bandona, m'abbandona il pianto ancor;—

RAIMONDO: Qual terribile momento! più formar non sò parole! densa nube di spavento par che copra i rai del sole! Come rosa inaridita, ella sta fra morte e vita, chi per lei non è commosso ha di tigre in petto il cor.

ENRICO: È mio sangue! l'ho tradita! io l'ho tradita! ah! sì, sì! ella sta fra morte e vita, fra morte e vita! spegnere non posso i rimorsi!

EDGARDO: Chi mi frena in tal momento? ma chi? chi? Come rosa inaridita, ella sta fra morte e vita! Ingrata, t'amo ancor, sì, t'amo ancor!

ALISA: Come rosa inaridita, ella sta fra morte e vita, chi per lei non è commosso ha di tigre in petto il cor. Come rosa inaridita, ella sta fra morte e vita; chi per lei non è commosso, ha di tigre in petto il cor, ah! il cor, in petto il cor,—

ARTURO: Qual terribile momento, più formar non sò parole, denso velo di spavento par che copra i rai del sole. Come rosa inaridita, ella sta fra morte e vita, chi per lei non è commosso ha di tigre in petto il cor, ha di tigre in petto il cor,

even weeping forsakes me, forsakes me.

RAIMONDO: What a dreadful moment! I cannot find words for it. Thick clouds of terror seem to cut off the rays of the sun! Like a wilting rose, she hovers between life and death; whoever is not moved for her has a tiger's heart in his breast.

ENRICO: She is my blood! I have betrayed her! I have betrayed her! ah! yes, yes! she hovers between life and death, between life and death! I cannot quench my remorse!

EDGARDO: Who restrains me at such a moment? But who? who? Like a wilting rose, she hovers between life and death! Thankless girl, I still love you, yes, I still love you!

ALISA: Like a wilting rose, she hovers between life and death; whoever is not moved for her has a tiger's heart in his breast. Like a wilting rose, she hovers between life and death; whoever is not moved for her has a tiger's heart in his breast, ah! heart, heart in his breast—

ARTURO: What a dreadful moment, I cannot find words for it! A dense veil of terror seems to cut off the rays of the sun. Like a wilting rose, she hovers between life and death, whoever is not moved for her has a tiger's heart in his breast, has a

ha di tigre in petto il cor,—

ENRICO: Ah! è mio sangue, l'ho tradita! ella sta fra morte e vita, ah, che spegnere non posso i rimorsi del mio cor; ah! è mio sangue, l'ho tradita, ella sta fra morte e vita, ah, che spegnere non posso i rimorsi del mio cor, non posso i rimorsi del cor,—

TENORS, BASSES, THEN SOPRANOS: Come rosa inaridita, ella sta fra morte e vita. Chi per lei non è commosso ha di tigre in petto il core, in petto il cor, in petto il cor, il cor,—

LUCIA: —vorrei piangere, ah, vorrei piangere e non posso, m'abbandona il pianto ancor! Vorrei piangere, ah! vorrei piangere e non posso, m'abbandona il pianto ancor, il pianto ancor, il pianto—

RAIMONDO: Chi per lei non è commosso ha di tigre in petto il cor, il cor! chi per lei non è commosso ha di tigre in petto il cor, il cor, sì, di tigre, sì, il cor,—

EDGARDO: Ah! son vinto, son commosso, t'amo, ingrata, t'amo ancor! ah! son vinto, son commosso, t'amo, ingrata, t'amo ancor, t'amo ancor, sì, sì, t'amo ancor,—

tiger's heart in his breast, has a tiger's heart in his breast—

ENRICO: Ah! she is my blood, I have betrayed her! She hovers between life and death, ah, that I cannot quench my heart's remorse; ah! she is my blood, I have betrayed her, she hovers between life and death, ah, that I cannot quench my heart's remorse, cannot quench my heart's remorse—

TENORS, BASSES, THEN SOPRANOS: Like a wilting rose, she hovers between life and death. Whoever is not moved for her has a tiger's heart in his breast, heart in his breast, heart in his breast, heart—

LUCIA: —I would weep, ah, I would weep but I cannot, even weeping forsakes me! I would weep, ah! I would weep but I cannot, even weeping forsakes me, even weeping, weeping—

RAIMONDO: Whoever is not moved for her has a tiger's heart, heart in his breast! whoever is not moved for her has a tiger's heart in his breast, yes, a tiger's heart, yes, heart—

EDGARDO: Ah! I am overcome, I am moved, I love you, thankless girl, I still love you! ah! I am overcome, I am moved, I love you, thankless girl, I still love you, I still love you, yes, yes, I still love you—

The sextet scene as performed in Munich. Set by Herbert Jürgens; staging by Herbert List. Erika Köth is seen as Lucia and Richard Holm as Edgardo. *(Courtesy Bayerische Staatsoper, Munich; photo by Rudolf Betz)*

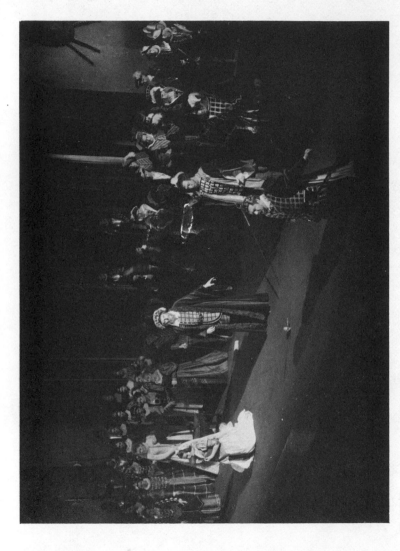

The sextet scene as performed in Milan. Costumes by Giovanni Miglioli; set by Alessandro Benois; staging by Margherita Wallmann. (Courtesy Teatro alla Scala, Milan; photo by E. Piccagliani)

EDGARDO: —ingrata, t'amo ancor, sì,—	EDGARDO: —thankless girl, I still love you, yes—
ENRICO: —ah spegner non li posso,—	ENRICO: —ah, I cannot quench it—
LUCIA: —ancor!	LUCIA: —even!
ALISA: —il cor!	ALISA: —heart!
EDGARDO: —ancor!	EDGARDO: —still!
ARTURO: —il cor!	ARTURO: —heart!
ENRICO: —ahimè!	ENRICO: —alas!
RAIMONDO: —il cor!	RAIMONDO: —heart!
CHORUS: —il cor!	CHORUS: —heart!

Arturo and Enrico draw their swords and rush toward Edgardo.

ARTURO, ENRICO: T'allontana, sciagurato, il tuo sangue fia versato!	ARTURO, ENRICO: Be gone, villain, your blood will flow!
TENORS, BASSES: T'allontana, sciagurato!	TENORS, BASSES: Be gone, villain!

Edgardo draws his sword.

EDGARDO: Morirò, ma insiem col mio altro sangue scorrerà.	EDGARDO: I shall die, but other blood will stream forth along with mine.

Raimondo commandingly steps between them.

RAIMONDO: Rispettate in me di Dio la tremenda maestà. In suo nome vel comando, deponete l'ira e il brando. Pace, pace, egli abborisce l'omicida, e scritto sta: "Chi di ferro altrui ferisce, pur di ferro perirà."	RAIMONDO: In my person respect God's tremendous majesty. I command you in His name, lay aside your anger and your swords. Peace, peace. He loathes killing, and it is written, "He that lives by the sword shall die by the sword."

The others sheathe their swords.

Pace, pace.

Peace, peace.

Enrico approaches Edgardo.

ENRICO: Sconsigliato! in queste porte chi ti guida?

ENRICO: Rash fellow! who leads you within this door?

EDGARDO [*proudly*]: La mia sorte, il mio dritto.

EDGARDO [*proudly*]: My destiny, my right.

ENRICO: Sciagurato!

ENRICO: Villain!

EDGARDO: Sì; Lucia la sua fede a me giurò!

EDGARDO: Yes; Lucia swore faith to me!

Raimondo again steps between them.

RAIMONDO: Ah! questo amor funesto obblia: ella è d'altri.

RAIMONDO: Ah! forget this fatal love: she belongs to another.

EDGARDO: D'altri! no!

EDGARDO: To another! no!

Raimondo gives him the marriage contract. Edgardo reads it and turns toward Lucia.

RAIMONDO: Mira.

RAIMONDO: Look.

EDGARDO: Tremi... ti confondi ... Son tue cifre? A me rispondi: son tue cifre? Rispondi!

EDGARDO: You tremble...you are confused....Is this your writing? Answer me: is this your writing? Answer!

LUCIA [*groaning*]: Sì!

LUCIA [*groaning*]: Yes!

In cold fury, Edgardo takes off his ring and returns it to Lucia.

EDGARDO: Riprendi il tuo pegno, infido cor ...

EDGARDO: Take back your pledge, false heart ...

LUCIA [*groaning*]: Ah!

LUCIA [*groaning*]: Ah!

EDGARDO: Il mio dammi.

EDGARDO: Give me mine.

LUCIA: Almen—

LUCIA: At least—

EDGARDO: Lo rendi!

EDGARDO: Give it back!

LUCIA: Edgardo! Edgardo!

LUCIA: Edgardo! Edgardo!

As if in a trance, Lucia takes off her ring; angrily, Edgardo snatches it from her, throws it down and stamps on it.

EDGARDO: Hai tradito il cielo e amor. Maledetto, maledetto sia l'istante che di te, sì, che di te mi rese amante, stirpe iniqua, abbominata, io dovea da te

EDGARDO: You have betrayed Heaven and love. Damned, damned be the moment when I became your, yes, your lover, loathsome, abominated race, I

fuggir, abbominata, maledetta,
io dovea da te fuggir.

LUCIA: Ah!

EDGARDO: Ah! ma di Dio la
mano irata vi disperda—

ENRICO, RAIMONDO, TENORS,
BASSES: Insano ardir!

CHORUS: Insano ardir! insano
ardir!

ENRICO: Esci! Esci!

RAIMONDO: Pace!

ARTURO, ENRICO, TENORS,
BASSES: Esci, fuggi, il furor che
m'accende solo un punto i suoi
colpi sospende, ma fra poco più
atroce, più fiero sul tuo capo
abborrito cadrà, ma fra poco
più atroce, più fiero sul tuo
capo abborrito cadrà.

RAIMONDO: Infelice, t'invola,
t'affretta, i tuoi giorni, il suo
stato rispetta, vivi e forse il tuo
duolo fia spento: tutto è lieve
all'eterna pietà; vivi e forse il
tuo duolo fia spento, tutto è
lieve all'eterna pietà.

should have fled from you,
abominated, damned race, I
should have fled from you.

LUCIA: Ah!

EDGARDO: Ah! may God's outraged hand shatter you—

ENRICO, RAIMONDO, TENORS,
BASSES: Insane boldness!

CHORUS: Insane boldness! insane
boldness!

ENRICO: Begone! Begone!

RAIMONDO: Peace!

ARTURO, ENRICO, TENORS, BASSES:
Begone, fly, the rage that inflames me delays its blows only
for an instant, but soon it will
fall more dreadfully, more
fiercely on your hated head, but
soon it will fall more dreadfully,
more fiercely on your hated
head.

RAIMONDO: Unhappy man, depart, make haste, respect your
life and her position, live on
and perhaps your sorrow will
be spent: everything is easy to
eternal mercy; live on and perhaps your sorrow will be spent,
everything is easy to eternal
mercy.

*Lucia falls to her knees. Edgardo tosses away his sword and offers his
breast for his enemies to stab.*

LUCIA: Dio, lo salva, in sì fiero
momento d'una misera ascolta
il lamento. È la prece d'immenso dolore, che più in terra
speranza non ha,—

LUCIA: God, save him, at such an
awful moment hear a wretched
girl's plea. It is the prayer of
great suffering that has no more
earthly hope—

(rite) – ritual ceremony   *massacre*   *ruination (litt – slaughter)*

EDGARDO: Trucidatemi e pronubo al rito sia lo scempio d'un core tradito. Del mio sangue coperta la soglia, dolce vista per l'empia sarà!

impious, pitiless, wicked

EDGARDO: Kill me and let the slaughter of a betrayed heart give away the bride at the ceremony. The threshold covered with my blood will be a pleasant sight for this vile woman!

RAIMONDO: Infelice! [*To Edgardo:*] Deh, ti salva!

RAIMONDO: Unhappy man! [*To Edgardo:*] Come, save yourself!

ARTURO, ENRICO, CHORUS: Esci! Va!

ARTURO, ENRICO, CHORUS: Begone! Go!

blow emanate die expire

LUCIA: —è l'estrema domanda del core che sul labbro spirando mi sta, è l'estrema domanda d'un core che spirando sul labbro mi sta, che spirando sul labbro mi sta, sul labbro mi sta, mi sta.

LUCIA: —it is the last request of my dying heart that rises to my lips, it is the last request of my dying heart that rises to my lips, that dying rises to my lips, that rises, rises to my lips.

trample   *bloodless, pale*

EDGARDO: Calpestando l'esangue mia spoglia all'altare più lieta ne andrà, calpestando l'esangue mia spoglia all'altare più lieta ne andrà, all'altare più lieta ne andrà, lieta ne andrà.

slough skin husk (litt – body)

EDGARDO: Trampling on my bloodless corpse, she will go more blithely to the altar, trampling on my bloodless corpse, she will go more blithely to the altar, she will go more blithely, go more blithely to the altar.

RAIMONDO: Vivi, forse il tuo duolo, il tuo duolo fia spento, tutto è lieve, tutto è lieve all'eterna pietà, tutto è lieve, tutto, all'eterna pietà.

RAIMONDO: Live on, perhaps your sorrow, your sorrow will be spent, everything is easy, everything is easy to eternal mercy, everything is easy, everything, to eternal mercy.

ALISA: Infelice! t'invola, t'affretta! Ah! il suo stato, i tuoi giorni rispetta, ah, va, va, va!

ALISA: Unhappy man! depart, make haste! Ah! respect her position, your life, ah, go, go, go!

ENRICO: T'invola, va, va, la macchia d'oltraggio sì nero, ah!

ENRICO: Depart, go, go, the stain of so black an outrage, ah! will

spot stain

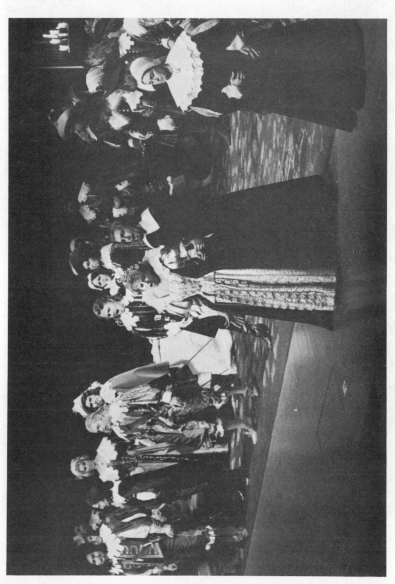

The sextet scene as performed at the New York State Theater, with Beverly Sills as Lucia. *(Courtesy New York City Opera; photo by Fred Fehl)*

Beverly Sills as Lucia in the sextet scene. (*Courtesy New York City Opera; photo by Fred Fehl*)

lavata col sangue, lavata sarà.

ARTURO: Va, col sangue tuo lavata sarà, sì, sì, sarà, va, va, va!

CHORUS: Va, col sangue tuo lavata sarà, sì, sì, sarà, va, va!

SOPRANOS: Infelice, t'invola, t'affretta, i tuoi giorni, il suo stato rispetta. Ah, vivi, e forse il tuo duolo fia spento, ah! sì, ah! sì, fuggi, esci, esci, tutto è lieve all'eterna pietà, tutto è lieve all'eterna pietà, sì, all'eterna pietà, sì, quante volte ad un solo tormento mille gioje, sì, quante volte ad un solo tormento mille apprestate non ha, apprestate non ha, apprestate non ha, ah, sì, non ha, sì, quante gioje apprestate non ha!

prepare, supply, provide

ALISA: Infelice, t'invola, t'affretta, i tuoi giorni, il suo stato rispetta, vivi, e forse il tuo duolo fia spento, tutto è lieve all'eterna pietà, ah, sì, ah, sì, Dio! Dio! fuggi, tutto è lieve all'eterna pietà, all'eterna pietà, all'eterna pietà, sì, quante volte ad un solo tormento mille gioje apprestate non ha, sì, quante volte ad un solo tormento quante gioje, ah! quante, quante gioje apprestate non ha, apprestate non ha, apprestate

be washed away, washed away with blood!

ARTURO: Go, it will be washed away, yes, yes, washed away with your blood, go, go, go!

CHORUS: Go, it will be washed away, yes, yes, washed away with your blood, go, go!

SOPRANOS: Unhappy man, depart, make haste, respect your life, her position. Ah, live, and perhaps your sorrow will be spent, ah, yes, ah, yes, fly, begone, begone; everything is easy to eternal mercy, everything is easy to eternal mercy, yes, to eternal mercy, yes; how many times has it not repaid a single pain with a thousand joys, yes, how many times has it not repaid a single pain with a thousand joys, has it not repaid, has it not repaid, ah, yes, has it not, yes, how many joys has it not repaid!

ALISA: Unhappy man, depart, make haste, respect your life, her position, live on and perhaps your sorrow will be spent; everything is easy to eternal mercy, ah, yes, ah yes; God! God! fly, everything is easy to eternal mercy, to eternal mercy, to eternal mercy, yes, how many times has it not repaid a single pain with a thousand joys, yes, how many times has it not repaid a single pain with a thousand joys, ah! how many,

non ha! Esci, fuggi, sì, tutto è lieve all'eterna pietà.

RAIMONDO: Ah, vivi, e forse il tuo duolo fia spento, tutto è lieve all'eterna pietà, sì, tutto, sì, tutto, sì, tutto, all'eterna pietà, tutto, sì, sì, infelice, t'invola, t'affretta, i tuoi giorni, il suo stato rispetta, vivi, e forse il tuo duolo fia spento, tutto è lieve all'eterna pietà, tutto è lieve all'eterna pietà, sì, tutto è lieve, sì, quante volte ad un solo tormento gioje apprestate non ha, sì, quante volte ad un solo tormento, ad un sol, quante gioje apprestate, sì, apprestate non ha, apprestate non ha, apprestate non ha! Esci, fuggi, sì, tutto è lieve all'eterna pietà.

LUCIA: Dio, lo salva! In sì fiero momento, ah, d'una misera ascolta l'accento, Dio, lo salva, Dio, Dio, è l'estrema, l'estrema domanda che sul labbro mi sta, ah, sì, che sul labbro mi sta, sul labbro mi sta, sì, è l'estrema domanda del core che spirando mi sta, sì, è l'estrema domanda del core che morendo sul labbro mi sta, sul labbro mi sta, sul labbro mi sta, sì, sì, mi sta, ahimè!

how many times has it not repaid, has it not repaid, not repaid! Begone, fly, yes, everything is easy to eternal mercy.

RAIMONDO: Ah, live on, and perhaps your sorrow will be spent; everything is easy to eternal mercy, yes, everything, yes, everything, yes, everything, to eternal mercy, everything, yes, yes, unhappy man, depart, make haste, respect your life, her position; live on, and perhaps your sorrow will be spent, everything is easy to eternal mercy, everything is easy to eternal mercy, yes, everything is easy, yes; how many times has it not repaid a single pain with a thousand joys, yes, how many times a single pain, a single one, with many joys repaid, yes, repaid, repaid, repaid! Begone, fly, yes, everything is easy to eternal mercy.

LUCIA: God, save him! At such a dreadful moment, ah, hear the words of a wretched girl, God, save him, God, God, it is the last, the last request that rises to my lips, ah, yes, that rises to my lips, that rises to my lips, yes, it is the last request of my dying heart, yes, it is the last request of my dying heart that rises to my lips, rises to my lips, rises to my lips, yes, yes, rises, alas!

ARTURO: Esci, fuggi! il furor che m'accende solo un punto i suoi colpi sospende, sì, sì, sì, sì, esci, fuggi, il furor che m'accende solo un punto i suoi colpi sospende, ma fra poco più atroce, più fiero sul tuo capo abborrito cadrà, sul tuo capo abborrito cadrà, sì, sul tuo capo cadrà, sì, sì, la macchia d'oltraggio sì nero col tuo sangue lavata sarà, sì, col tuo sangue lavata sarà, col tuo sangue, sol col tuo sangue lavata sarà, lavata sarà, lavata sarà! Esci, fuggi, o col tuo sangue lavata sarà.

ARTURO: Begone, fly! The rage that inflames me delays its blows only for an instant, yes, yes, yes, yes, begone, fly, the rage that inflames me delays its blows only for an instant, but soon it will fall more dreadfully, more fiercely on your hated head, it will fall on your hated head, yes, it will fall on your head, yes, yes, the stain of so black an outrage will be washed away with your blood, yes, will be washed away with your blood, with your blood, will only be washed away, washed away, washed away with your blood! Begone, fly, or it will be washed away with your blood.

ENRICO: Esci, fuggi! fuggi, vanne, la macchia lavata col sangue sarà, lavata col sangue, lavata sarà, sì, esci, fuggi, il furor che m'accende solo un punto i suoi colpi sospende, ma fra poco più atroce, più fiero sul tuo capo abborrito cadrà, sul tuo capo abborrito cadrà, sì, sul tuo capo cadrà, sì, sì, la macchia d'oltraggio sì nero col tuo sangue lavata sarà, sì, col tuo sangue lavata sarà, sì, col tuo sangue lavata sarà, sì, sol col tuo sangue lavata sarà, lavata sarà, lavata sarà! Esci, fuggi, o col tuo sangue lavata sarà.

ENRICO: Begone, fly! fly, go away, the stain will be washed away with blood, will be washed away, washed away with blood, yes, begone, fly, the rage that inflames me delays its blows only for an instant, but soon it will fall more dreadfully, more fiercely on your hated head, it will fall on your hated head, yes, it will fall on your head, yes, yes, the stain of so black an outrage will be washed away with your blood, yes, will be washed away with your blood, yes, will be washed away with your blood, yes, will only be washed away, washed away, washed away with your

TENORS: Esci, fuggi, il furor che n'accende solo un punto i suoi colpi sospende, sì, sì, sì, sì, esci, fuggi, il furor che n'accende solo un punto i suoi colpi sospende, ma fra poco più atroce, più fiero sul tuo capo abborrito cadrà, sul tuo capo abborrito cadrà, sì, sul tuo capo cadrà, sì, sì, la macchia d'oltraggio sì nero lavata sarà, sì, col tuo sangue lavata sarà, col tuo sangue lavata sarà, lavata sarà, lavata sarà! Esci, fuggi, o col tuo sangue lavata sarà.

BASSES: Esci, fuggi, il furor che n'accende solo un punto i suoi colpi sospende, sì, sì, sì, sì, esci, fuggi, il furor che n'accende solo un punto i suoi colpi sospende, ma fra poco più atroce, più fiero sul tuo capo abborrito cadrà, sul tuo capo abborrito cadrà, sì, sul tuo capo cadrà, sì, sì, la macchia d'oltraggio sì nero col tuo sangue lavata sarà, sì, col tuo sangue lavata sarà, col tuo sangue lavata sarà, lavata sarà, lavata sarà! Esci, fuggi, o col tuo sangue lavata sarà.

EDGARDO: No, no, no, truci-

TENORS: Begone, fly, the rage that inflames us delays its blows only for an instant, yes, yes, yes, yes, begone, fly, the rage that inflames us delays its blows only for an instant, but soon more dreadfully, more fiercely it will fall on your hated head, it will fall on your hated head, yes, it will fall on your head, yes, yes, the stain of so black an outrage will be washed away, yes, will be washed away with your blood, will be washed away, washed away, washed away with your blood! Begone, fly, or it will be washed away with your blood.

BASSES: Begone, fly, the rage that inflames us delays its blows only for an instant, yes, yes, yes, yes, begone, fly, the rage that inflames us delays its blows only for an instant, but soon it will fall more dreadfully, more fiercely on your hated head, it will fall on your hated head, yes, it will fall on your head, yes, yes, the stain of so black an outrage will be washed away with your blood, yes, will be washed away with your blood, will be washed away, washed away, washed away with your blood! Begone, fly, or it will be washed away with your blood.

EDGARDO: No, no, no, kill me.

datemi. No, no, no, no, calpe-
statemi, sì, del mio sangue
coperta la soglia, la soglia, dolce
vista sarà, trucidate, trucidate,
calpestate, calpestate, all'altare
più lieta ne andrà, più lieta ne
andrà, sì, calpestando l'esangue
mia spoglia, sì, più lieta n'andrà,
sì, calpestando l'esangue mia
spoglia, all'altare più lieta, più
lieta ne andrà, più lieta ne
andrà, più lieta ne andrà, sì, sì,
ne andrà, sì, sì, più lieta ne
andrà.

No, no, no, no, trample on me,
yes, the threshold, the threshold
covered with my blood will be a
pleasant sight, kill, kill, trample,
trample, she will go more
blithely to the altar, she will go
more blithely, yes, trampling
on my bloodless corpse, yes,
she will go more blithely, yes,
trampling on my bloodless
corpse, she will go more blithely, more blithely to the altar,
she will go more blithely, she
will go more blithely, yes, yes,
she will go, yes, yes, she will go
more blithely.

Act 3, Scene 2: Raimondo informs the wedding guests of the tragedy. Costumes by Ebe Colciaghi; set by Gianni Ratto; staging by Herbert von Karajan. (*Courtesy Teatro alla Scala, Milan; photo by E. Piccagliani*)

Act Three

Act 3, Scene 2: Lucia's mad scene, with Joan Sutherland. Costumes, set and staging by Franco Zeffirelli. *(Courtesy Lyric Opera of Chicago; photo by Nancy Sorenson)*

ACT THREE

Scene One

(This scene is frequently omitted in performance.) A few hours have passed; it is a wild and stormy night. Edgardo has retired and taken refuge in a rudely furnished room of the Tower which is all that remains of the Ravenswoods' former holdings. At the rear is a door; on one side a window is open to the stormy night outside. Edgardo sits gloomily at a rough table. Presently, he rises and looks out of the window.

EDGARDO: Orrida è questa notte come il destino mio!

EDGARDO: This night is as horrid as my destiny!

A thunderclap is heard.

Sì, tuona, o cielo, imperversate, o fulmini—sconvolto sia l'ordin di natura, e pera il mondo! Ma non m'inganno! Scalpitar d'appresso odo un destrier! S'arresta! Chi mai della tempesta fra le minacce e l'ira, chi puote a me venire?

Yes, thunder, O heavens, rage forth, O lightning-bolts—let the laws of nature be overturned, and let the world perish! But I am not mistaken! I hear the hoofbeats of a horse close by! It is stopping! Who can be coming to me in the midst of the storm's dangers and wrath?

Enrico enters and throws back his cloak.

ENRICO: Io!

ENRICO: I!

EDGARDO: Quale ardire! Ashton!

EDGARDO: What bold insolence! Ashton!

ENRICO: Sì!

ENRICO: Yes!

EDGARDO: Fra queste mura osi offrirti al mio cospetto!

EDGARDO: You dare to present yourself to me within these walls!

ENRICO: Io vi sto per tua sciagura.

EDGARDO: Per mia?

ENRICO: Non venisti nel mio tetto?

EDGARDO: Qui del padre ancor respira l'ombra inulta, e par che frema! morte ogn'aura a te qui spira! Il terren, il terren per te qui trema! Nel varcar la soglia orrenda ben dovresti palpitar, come un uom che vivo scenda la sua tomba ad alber-gar, nel varcar la soglia or-renda, nel varcar la soglia orrenda ben dovresti palpitar, come un uom che vivo scenda, come un uom che vivo scenda la sua tomba ad albergar, ad albergar, ad albergar, la sua tomba, la sua tomba ad albergar!

ENRICO: Fu condotta al sacro rito quindi al talamo Lucia.

EDGARDO [to himself]: (Ei più squarcia il cor ferito! Oh tormento! gelosia!)

ENRICO: Ella è al talamo.

EDGARDO [to himself]: (Oh gelo-sia!) [Aloud:] Ebben? ebben?

ENRICO: Ascolta! Di letizia il mio soggiorno e di plausi rim-bombava; ma più forte al cor d'intorno la vendetta, la ven-detta mi parlava! Qui mi trassi,

ENRICO: It is to your misfortune that I stand here.

EDGARDO: To mine?

ENRICO: Did you not come under my roof?

EDGARDO: The spirit of my un-avenged father still breathes here, and seems to rage! every breeze here whispers death to you! The earth, the earth here trembles for you! You ought well to have quaked at crossing this fearful threshold, like a living man who has gone to dwell in his tomb, in crossing this fearful threshold, in crossing this fearful threshold you ought well to have quaked, like a living man who has gone, like a living man who has gone to dwell in his tomb, to dwell, to dwell, to dwell in his tomb, in his tomb.

ENRICO: Lucia has gone through the holy ceremony and thence to her nuptial bed.

EDGARDO [to himself]: (He further rends my wounded heart! Oh, torture! jealousy!)

ENRICO: She is in her nuptial bed.

EDGARDO [to himself]: (Oh, jea-lousy!) [Aloud:] Well? well?

ENRICO: Listen! My residence was resounding with gaiety and cheers; but round about me vengeance, vengeance spoke more loudly to my heart! I be-in mezzo ai venti, la sua voce udia tuttor, e il furor degl'elementi rispondeva al mio furor, il furor degli elementi, il furor degli elementi rispondeva al mio furor,—

EDGARDO [*to himself*]: (Oh tormento, oh gelosia!)

ENRICO: —il furor degli elementi,—

ENRICO: —il furor degli elementi rispondeva al mio furor, al mio furor, al mio furor, il furor degli elementi rispondeva, rispondeva al mio furor!

EDGARDO [*icily*]: Da me che brami?

ENRICO: Ascoltami! Onde punir l'offesa, de' miei, de' miei la spada vindice pende su te sospesa, onde punir l'offesa, ma ch'altri ti spenga, mai—chi dee svenarti il sai!

EDGARDO: Sò che al paterno cenere giurai strapparti il core.

ENRICO: Tu!

EDGARDO: Sì.

ENRICO: Tu!

EDGARDO [*haughtily*]: Quando?

ENRICO: Al primo sorgere del mattutino albore.

EDGARDO: Ove?

ENRICO: Fra l'urne gelide di Ravenswood.

took myself here, in the midst of the gale I heard its voice continually, and the rage of the elements gave reply to my rage, the rage of the elements, the rage of the elements gave reply to my rage—

EDGARDO [*to himself*]: (Oh, torture, oh, jealousy!)

ENRICO: —the rage of the elements—

ENRICO: —the rage of the elements gave reply to my rage, to my rage, to my rage, the rage of the elements gave reply, gave reply to my rage!

EDGARDO [*icily*]: What would you have of me?

ENRICO: Listen to me! To punish your offense, my people's, my people's avenging sword hangs suspended over you, to punish your offense, but should another kill you?—never—you know who must take your life!

EDGARDO: I know that I swore by my father's remains to tear out your heart.

ENRICO: You!

EDGARDO: Yes.

ENRICO: You!

EDGARDO [*haughtily*]: When?

ENRICO: At the first glimmer of dawn.

EDGARDO: Where?

ENRICO: Among the chilly tombs of Ravenswood.

EDGARDO: Verrò. Sì, verrò, sì, sì.

EDGARDO: I shall come. Yes, I shall come, yes, yes.

ENRICO: Ivi a restar preparati.

ENRICO: Be prepared to remain there.

EDGARDO: Ivi t'ucciderò.

EDGARDO: I shall kill you there.

ENRICO: Al primo albore.

ENRICO: At the first rays of dawn.

EDGARDO: Al primo albore.

EDGARDO: At the first rays of dawn.

EDGARDO, ENRICO: Ah! O sole più ratto a sorger t'appresta, ti cinga di sangue ghirlanda funesta, con quella rischiara l'orribile gara d'un odio mortale, d'un cieco furore, o sole più ratto risorgi e rischiara d'un odio mortale il cieco, il cieco furor.

EDGARDO, ENRICO: Ah! O sun, make haste to rise more quickly, may a funeral wreath encircle you with blood, and with it illumine the dreadful strife of a deadly hate, of a blind fury, O sun, rise more quickly and illumine the blind, blind fury of a deadly hate.

EDGARDO: Giurai strapparti il core.

EDGARDO: I swore to tear out your heart.

ENRICO: La spada pende su te.

ENRICO: The sword hangs over you.

EDGARDO: Fra l'urne di Ravenswood—

EDGARDO: Among the tombs of Ravenswood—

ENRICO: All'alba verrò.

ENRICO: I shall come at the dawn.

The storm increases in intensity.

EDGARDO, ENRICO: Ah! Farà di nostr'alme atroce governo gridando vendetta lo spirto d'Averno. Del tuono che mugge, del nembo che rugge, più l'ira è tremenda che m'arde nel core. O sole, più ratto risorgi e rischiara d'un odio mortale il cieco, il cieco furor,—

EDGARDO, ENRICO: Ah! The spirit of Hell, shrieking vengeance, will become fierce ruler of our souls. The wrath that smolders in my heart is greater than the thunder that roars, than the storm that howls. O sun, rise more quickly and illumine the blind, blind fury of a deadly hate—

ENRICO: —con quella rischiara—

ENRICO: —and with it illumine—

EDGARDO: —l'orribile gara—

EDGARDO, ENRICO: —d'un odio mortale, d'un cieco furor, d'un cieco furor, d'un cieco furor, d'un cieco furor, d'un cieco furor, d'un cieco furor, d'un cieco furor, d'un cieco furor!

EDGARDO: —the dreadful strife—

EDGARDO, ENRICO: —of a deadly hate, of a blind fury, of a blind fury, of a blind fury, of a blind fury, of a blind fury, of a blind fury, of a blind fury.

Scene Two

The same night, Lucia's wedding-night. In a hall of Ravenswood Castle, the assembled guests continue to celebrate the wedding which has just taken place. At rear center stage a wide staircase descends from a gallery into the actual hall. Cheerful dance-music can be heard from adjoining rooms. The wedding guests move about, conversing animatedly.

CHORUS: D'immenso giubilo s'innalzi un grido, d'immenso giubilo s'innalzi un grido: corra la Scozia di lido in lido, e avverta i perfidi nostri nemici che a noi sorridono le stelle ancor, e avverta i perfidi nostri nemici che a noi sorridono le stelle ancor.

BASSES: Che più terribili, che più felici, ne rende l'aura d'alto favor—

CHORUS: —d'alto favor, d'alto favor, e avverta i perfidi nostri nemici che a noi sorridono le stelle ancor, avverta i perfidi nostri nemici che a noi sorridono le stelle, le stelle ancor, le stelle ancor, le stelle ancor!

CHORUS: Raise a shout of great rejoicing, raise a shout of great rejoicing: let it sweep over Scotland from shore to shore, and warn our treacherous enemies that the stars smile on us again, and warn our treacherous enemies that the stars smile on us again.

BASSES: That the aura of high favor makes us more awesome, more fortunate—

CHORUS: —of high favor, of high favor, and let it warn our treacherous enemies that the stars smile on us again, let it warn our treacherous enemies that the stars, the stars smile on us again, the stars again, the stars again!

Raimondo enters; he is obviously greatly upset.

RAIMONDO: Cessi, ah cessi quel contento!

RAIMONDO: Stop, ah, stop your merrymaking!

TENORS, BASSES: Sei cosparso di pallor!

TENORS, BASSES: You are white and shaken!

RAIMONDO: Cessi, cessi!

RAIMONDO: Stop, stop!

TENORS, BASSES: Ciel! che rechi?

TENORS, BASSES: Heavens! What is the matter?

RAIMONDO: Un fiero evento!

RAIMONDO: A dreadful happening!

CHORUS: Tu ne agghiacci di terror!

CHORUS: You turn us cold with fear!

Raimondo signals the guests to come near and listen.

RAIMONDO: Ah! Dalle stanze ove Lucia tratta avea col suo consorte, un lamento, un grido uscia, come d'uom vicino a morte! Corsi ratto in quelle mura— Dio! ahi! terribile sciagura! Steso Arturo al suol giaceva, muto, freddo, insanguinato! e Lucia l'acciar stringeva, che fu già del trucidato! Ella in me le luci affisse— "Il mio sposo, ov'è?" mi disse, e nel volto suo pallente un sorriso balenò! Infelice! della mente la virtude a lei mancò, a lei, a lei, infelice, infelice! della mente la virtude a lei mancò! ah!

RAIMONDO: Ah! From the rooms where I had led Lucia and her husband, a wail, a shriek rang out, as of a man in the throes of death! I ran quickly into those apartments—God! woe! a dreadful catastrophe! Arturo lay sprawling on the floor, silent, cold, weltering in blood! and Lucia was clutching the blade which was the dead man's. She fixed her eyes on me—"My husband, where is he?" she said to me, and a smile lit up her ashen face! Unhappy girl! her mind has failed her, her, her, unhappy, unhappy girl! her mind has failed her! ah!

CHORUS: Oh! qual funesto avvenimento! tutti ne ingombra cupo spavento! Notte, ricopri la ria sventura, col tenebroso tuo denso vel.

CHORUS: Oh! what a frightful happening! dark fear engulfs us all! Night, conceal the criminal tragedy with your dense, impenetrable veil.

RAIMONDO: Ah! quella destra di sangue impura l'ira non chiami su noi del ciel.

RAIMONDO: Ah! may that right hand, unclean with blood, not call down the wrath of Heaven on us.

RAIMONDO, CHORUS: Ah! quella destra di sangue impura l'ira non chiami su noi del ciel.

RAIMONDO, CHORUS: Ah! may that right hand, unclean with blood, not call down the wrath of Heaven on us.

RAIMONDO: Ella in me le luci affisse, e l'acciar, l'acciar stringeva!

RAIMONDO: She fixed her eyes on me, and clutched the blade, the blade!

CHORUS: E l'acciar, l'acciar stringeva!

CHORUS: And clutched the blade, the blade!

TENORS: L'acciar!

TENORS: The blade!

BASSES: L'acciar!

BASSES: The blade!

RAIMONDO: Ah!

RAIMONDO: Ah!

RAIMONDO, CHORUS: Ah! quella destra di sangue impura l'ira non chiami su noi del ciel,—

RAIMONDO, CHORUS: Ah! may that right hand, unclean with blood, not call down the wrath of Heaven on us—

TENORS, BASSES: —l'ira non chiami su noi del ciel, l'ira non chiami su noi del ciel,—

TENORS, BASSES: —may it not call down the wrath of Heaven on us, may it not call down the wrath of Heaven on us—

RAIMONDO, SOPRANOS: —non chiami l'ira su noi del ciel, non chiami l'ira su noi del ciel,—

RAIMONDO, SOPRANOS: —may it not call down the wrath of Heaven on us, may it not call down the wrath of Heaven on us—

RAIMONDO, CHORUS: —l'ira del ciel, sì, sì, l'ira del ciel, sì, sì, l'ira del ciel.

RAIMONDO, CHORUS: —the wrath of Heaven, yes, yes, the wrath of Heaven, yes, yes, the wrath of Heaven.

Lucia enters. She is dressed in a flowing white gown, and her hair streams loosely down over her shoulders. She has gone mad and is quite oblivious of her surroundings.

RAIMONDO: Eccola!

CHORUS: Oh giusto cielo! Par dalla tomba uscita!

LUCIA: Il dolce suono mi colpì di sua voce! Ah! quella voce m'è qui nel cor discesa! Edgardo! io ti son resa, Edgardo! ah! Edgardo mio! sì, ti son resa; fuggita io son da' tuoi nemici, da' tuoi nemici. Un gelo mi serpeggia nel sen! trema ogni fibra! vacilla il piè! Presso la fonte meco t'assidi alquanto, sì, presso la fonte meco t'assidi! Ohimè! sorge il tremendo fantasma e ne separa! Ohimè! ohimè! Edgardo! Edgardo! ah! [*As if in terror:*] il fantasma! il fantasma ne separa! Qui ricovriamo, Edgardo, a piè dell'ara. Sparsa è di rose! Un'armonia celeste, di', non ascolti? Ah! l'inno suona di nozze! Ah, ah, ah! l'inno di nozze! Il rito per noi s'appresta! Oh me felice! Edgardo! Edgardo! Oh! me felice! Oh gioja che si sente, oh gioja che si sente, e non si dice! Ardon gl'incensi— Splendon le sacre faci, splendon intorno! Ecco il ministro! Porgimi la destra! Oh lieto giorno! oh lieto! Alfin son tua, alfin sei mio, a me ti dona, a me ti dona un Dio.

RAIMONDO: There she is!

CHORUS: Oh, good heavens! Like someone risen from the tomb!

LUCIA: The sweet sound of his voice struck me! Ah! that voice has sunk into my heart here! Edgardo! I am yours again, Edgardo! ah! my Edgardo! Yes, I am yours again; I have escaped from your enemies, from your enemies. A chill is crawling through my breast! every nerve quivers! I am unsteady on my feet! Sit near the fountain with me for a while, yes, sit near the fountain with me! Alas! the awful phantom emerges and separates us! Alas! alas! Edgardo! Edgardo! ah! [*As if in terror:*] the phantom! the phantom separates us! Let us take refuge here, Edgardo, at the foot of the altar. It is strewn with roses! Tell me, do you not hear heavenly music? Ah! the wedding-hymn sounds forth! Ah, ah, ah! the wedding-hymn! The ceremony is being prepared for us! Oh, happy me! Edgardo! Edgardo! Oh! happy me! Oh, joy that I feel, oh, joy that I feel and cannot express! The incense is burning— The sacred torches are shining, shining everywhere! Here is the minister! Give me your right hand! Oh, blissful day! oh, bliss! At last I am yours, at last you are mine, God bestows you on me, bestows you on me.

The mad scene. *(Courtesy New York City Opera; photo by Beth Bergman)*

The mad scene, with Linda Newman as Lucia, Chester Watson as Raimondo and Richard Torigi as Enrico. *(Courtesy National Broadcasting Company)*

NORMANNO, RAIMONDO, CHORUS: Abbi in sì crudo stato, di lei, Signore, di lei pietà.

LUCIA: Ogni piacer più grato, sì, ogni piacere mi fia con te diviso,—

LUCIA: —con te, con te.

SOPRANOS: Signor, pietà.

TENORS, BASSES: Signor, Signor, pietà.

LUCIA: Del ciel clemente, del ciel clemente un riso la vita a noi sarà, la vita a noi, a noi sarà, del ciel clemente, clemente un riso la vita a noi, a noi sarà, la vita a noi sarà, a noi sarà,—

LUCIA: —sarà.

NORMANNO, RAIMONDO, CHORUS: Pietà!

RAIMONDO: S'avanza Enrico!

NORMANNO, RAIMONDO, CHORUS: In such a cruel state, Lord have mercy on her, on her.

LUCIA: Every most pleasurable delight, yes, every delight I shall share with you—

LUCIA: —with you, with you.

SOPRANOS: Lord, mercy.

TENORS, BASSES: Lord, Lord, mercy.

LUCIA: Kindly Heaven, kindly Heaven will smile upon our life, upon our, our life, kindly, kindly Heaven will smile upon our, our life, upon our life, upon our—

LUCIA: —life.

NORMANNO, RAIMONDO, CHORUS: Mercy!

RAIMONDO: Enrico is coming!

Enrico rushes in.

ENRICO: Ditemi: vera è l'atroce scena?

RAIMONDO: Vera, pur troppo!

ENRICO: Ah perfida! ne avrai condegna pena!

ENRICO: Tell me: is this terrible story true?

RAIMONDO: All too true!

ENRICO: Ah, treacherous girl! you shall suffer for it as you deserve!

He hurries toward Lucia.

CHORUS: T'arresta!

RAIMONDO: Oh ciel! Non vedi lo stato suo?

LUCIA [*still delirious*]: Che chiedi?

ENRICO [*staring at her*]: Oh!

ENRICO: Qual pallor!

CHORUS: Stop!

RAIMONDO: Oh, heavens! Don't you see her condition?

LUCIA [*still delirious*]: What are you asking?

ENRICO [*staring at her*]: Oh!

ENRICO: How pale she is!

LUCIA: Che chiedi!

RAIMONDO: Ha la region smar-
rita.

ENRICO: Gran Dio!

RAIMONDO: Tremare, o barbaro,
tu dêi per la sua vita.

LUCIA: Ah, me misera!

LUCIA: Non mi guardar sì fiero,
segnai quel foglio, è vero, sì, sì,
sì, è vero.

LUCIA: What are you asking!

RAIMONDO: She has lost her
reason.

ENRICO: Great God!

RAIMONDO: You ought to fear for
her life, O cruel man!

LUCIA: Ah, wretched me!

LUCIA: Do not glare at me so
fiercely, I signed that paper, it
is true, yes, yes, yes, it is true.

She continues as if in a trance.

Nell'ira sua terribile calpesta,
oh Dio, l'anello! mi maledice!
Ah! vittima fui d'un crudel
fratello: ma ognor, ognor
t'amai, ognora, Edgardo, sì,
ognor, ognor t'amai, ah! e
t'amo ancor,—

In his fearful rage he tramples,
oh God, upon the ring! he
curses me! Ah! I was the victim
of a cruel brother: but I always
loved you, Edgardo, always,
always, yes, I always, always
loved you, ah! and I love you
still—

LUCIA: —Edgardo mio, sì, te lo
giuro, ognor t'amai, e t'amo
ancor, ognor, ognor t'amai, ah!
e t'amo ancor, ah! t'amo,
t'amo ancor, ah! t'amo ancor,
t'amo, t'amo ancor!

LUCIA: —my Edgardo, yes, I
swear it to you, I always loved
you, and I love you still, I
always, always loved you, ah!
and I love you still, ah! I love
you, I love you still, ah! I love
you still, I love you, I love you
still!

ENRICO: Ah! di lei, Signor,
pietà! Ah sì, di lei, Signor,
pietà, pietà, pietà, di lei pietà!
ah Signor, pietà, Signor, pietà,
ah pietà!

ENRICO: Ah! Lord, mercy on
her! Ah, yes, Lord, mercy,
mercy, mercy on her, mercy on
her! ah, Lord, mercy, Lord,
mercy, ah, mercy!

RAIMONDO: Pietà di lei, Signor,
pietà, pietà! ah Signor, pietà,
Signor, pietà, ah pietà!

RAIMONDO: Mercy on her, Lord,
mercy, mercy! ah, Lord, mercy,
Lord, mercy, ah, mercy!

LUCIA: Chi mi nomasti? Arturo! Tu nomasti. Arturo! Ah! non fuggir! Ah, per pietà!—

LUCIA: —no, non fuggir! ah perdon! ah perdon, perdon!

ENRICO, RAIMONDO, CHORUS: Infelice! Ah, pietà, Signor, pietà!

ENRICO: Lucia! gran Dio! Ah Lucia!

RAIMONDO, TENORS, BASSES: Qual notte di terror, di terror, di terror!

SOPRANOS: Qual notte di terror, oh notte di terror!

LUCIA: Ah!

spread shed spill

Lucia falls to her knees.

veil, coating, skin

LUCIA: Ah! no, non fuggir, Edgardo!*

Spargi d'amaro pianto il mio terrestre velo, mentre lassù nel cielo io pregherò, pregherò per te. Al giunger tuo soltanto fia bello il ciel per me! ah sì, ah sì, ah sì, per me, fia bello il ciel, il ciel per me, ah sì, ah sì, ah sì, per me, sì, per me, per me, per me.

LUCIA: Whom did you mention? Arturo! You mentioned him. Arturo! Ah! do not flee! Ah, for pity's sake!—

LUCIA: —no, do not flee! ah, forgive me! ah, forgive me, forgive me!

ENRICO, RAIMONDO, CHORUS: Unhappy girl! Ah, mercy, Lord, mercy!

ENRICO: Lucia! great God! Ah, Lucia!

RAIMONDO, TENORS, BASSES: What a night of dread, of dread, of dread!

SOPRANOS: What a night of dread, oh, night of dread!

LUCIA: Ah!

LUCIA: Ah! no, do not flee, Edgardo!

Sprinkle my earthly substance with bitter tears, while up there in Heaven I shall pray, I shall pray for you. Not until you join me will Heaven be beautiful for me! ah, yes, ah, yes, ah, yes, for me, will Heaven, Heaven be beautiful for me, ah, yes, ah, yes, ah, yes, for me, yes, for me, for me, for me.

* The 1836 Cammarano libretto inserts the following lines at this point: "Presso alla tomba io sono ... Odi una prece ancor,—Deh! Tanto almen t'arresta, ch'io spiri a te d'appresso ... Già dall'affanno oppresso, gelido langue il cor! Un palpito gli resta, è un palpito d'amor" (I am almost at the tomb ... Hear yet one more prayer— Come! Stop long enough for me to die near you ... Already, oppressed by sorrow, my cold heart languishes! One throb remains, it is a throb of love). Donizetti started to write music for a variant of this text, then crossed it out, omitting this passage.

ENRICO: Giorni d'amaro pianto serba il rimorso a me, sì, serba il rimorso a me, ah sì, a me.

RAIMONDO: Più raffrenare il pianto possibile non è, possibile non è, ah no, non è.

TENORS: Più raffrenare il pianto possibile non è, no, no, possibile non è, ah no, non è.

BASSES: Più raffrenare il pianto possibile non è, possibile non è, ah no, non è.

SOPRANOS: Ah, più raffrenare il pianto possibile non è, ah no, non è.

LUCIA: Ah! Spargi d'amaro pianto il mio terrestre velo, mentre lassù nel cielo io pregherò, pregherò per te; al giunger tuo soltanto fia bello il ciel per me! ah sì, ah sì, ah sì, per me, fia bello il ciel, il ciel per me, ah sì, ah sì, ah sì, per me, sì, per me, per me, per me.

ENRICO: Ah, vita d'amaro, d'amaro pianto serba il rimorso a me, il rimorso a me, vita d'amaro, d'amaro pianto serba il rimorso a me, sì, sì, a me, sì, sì, a me, sì, sì, a me, a me!

RAIMONDO, CHORUS: Ah, più raffrenare il pianto, no, no, possibile non è, no, no, non è, più raffrenare il pianto, no, no, possibile non è, no, no, non è,

ENRICO: Days of bitter tears my remorse holds for me, yes, my remorse holds for me, ah, yes, for me.

RAIMONDO: To refrain any longer from weeping is not possible, is not possible, ah, no, it is not.

TENORS: To refrain any longer from weeping is not possible, no, no, is not possible, ah, no, it is not.

BASSES: To refrain any longer from weeping is not possible, is not possible, ah, no, it is not.

SOPRANOS: Ah, to refrain any longer from weeping is not possible, ah, no, it is not.

LUCIA: Ah! Sprinkle my earthly substance with bitter tears, while up there in Heaven I shall pray, I shall pray for you; not until you join me there will Heaven be beautiful for me! ah, yes, ah, yes, ah, yes, for me, will Heaven, Heaven be beautiful for me, ah, yes, ah, yes, ah, yes, for me, yes, for me, for me, for me.

ENRICO: Ah, a life of bitter, bitter tears my remorse holds for me, my remorse for me, a life of bitter, bitter tears, my remorse holds for me, yes, yes, for me, yes, yes, for me, yes, yes, for me, for me!

RAIMONDO, CHORUS: Ah, to refrain any longer from weeping, no, no, it is not possible, no, no, it is not, to refrain any longer from weeping no, no, it is not pos-

Anna Moffo as Lucia in the mad scene. *(Courtesy San Francisco Opera Company; photo by Carolyn Mason Jones)*

Beverly Sills as Lucia in the mad scene. *(Courtesy New York City Opera; photo by Fred Fehl)*

no, no, non è, no, no, non è, no, non è!

LUCIA: Ah! ch'io spiri accanto a te, accanto a te! Ah! ch'io spiri accanto a te, accanto a te, appresso a te, appresso a te, a te!

sible, no, no, it is not, no, no, it is not, no, no, it is not, no, it is not!

LUCIA: Ah! may I die at your side, at your side! Ah! may I die at your side, at your side, near you, near you, you!

Lucia faints into the arms of Alisa.

ENRICO: Si tragga altrove. Alisa— [*To Raimondo:*] Uom del Signor, deh! voi la misera vegliate— Io più me stesso in me non trovo.

ENRICO: Carry her to another place. Alisa— [*To Raimondo:*] Man of God, come! attend the unhappy girl— I am no longer myself.

Lucia is taken away by Alisa and other ladies of the entourage. Enrico follows.

RAIMONDO [*to Normanno*]: Delator! gioisci dell'opra tua!

NORMANNO: Che parli?

RAIMONDO: Sì, dell'incendio che divampa e strugge questa casa infelice, hai tu destata la primiera scintilla!

NORMANNO: Io non credei—

RAIMONDO: Tu del versato sangue, empio, tu sei la ria cagion! Quel sangue al ciel t'accusa, e già la man suprema segna la tua sentenza! Or vanne, e trema!

RAIMONDO [*to Normanno*]: Informer! rejoice over your work!

NORMANNO: What are you saying?

RAIMONDO: Yes, you struck the first spark of the holocaust that is blazing and consuming this unhappy house!

NORMANNO: I did not think—

RAIMONDO: You, wicked man, you are the guilty cause of this blood that has been spilled! That blood condemns you to Heaven, and already the supreme hand is signing your sentence! Now go, and tremble!

Raimondo hastily follows Lucia; Normanno leaves in the opposite direction.

Scene Three

A short time later in the burial ground of the Ravenswoods. Far away, lights can be seen in Ravenswood Castle. It is still dim, and Edgardo broods among the tombs of his ancestors.

EDGARDO: Tombe degl'avi miei, l'ultimo avanzo d'una stirpe infelice, deh! raccogliete voi! Cessò dell'ira il breve foco; sul nemico acciaro abbandonar mi vo'. Per me la vita è orrendo peso! l'universo intero è deserto per me senza Lucia! Di faci tuttavia splende il castello— Ah! scarsa fu la notte al tripudio! Ingrata donna! mentr'io mi struggo in disperato pianto, tu ridi, esulti accanto al felice consorte! Tu delle gioje in seno, tu delle gioje in seno, io della morte!

Fra poco a me ricovero darà negletto avello, una pietosa lagrima non scenderà su quello! ah! fin degli estinti, ahi misero! manca il conforto a me. Tu pur, tu pur dimentica quel marmo dispregiato: mai non passarvi, o barbara, del tuo consorte a lato. Ah! rispetta almen le ceneri di chi moria per te, rispetta almen le ceneri di chi moria per te! Mai non passarvi, tu lo dimentica, rispetta almeno chi muore per te, mai non passarvi, tu lo dimentica, rispetta almeno chi

EDGARDO: Tombs of my forebears, come, give shelter to the last remnant of an ill-fated line! The brief fire of my wrath is out; I will give myself up to my enemy's sword. Life is a horrid burden to me! Without Lucia, the whole universe is a wasteland for me! The castle is still aglow with lights— Ah! the night was too brief for their merrymaking! Thankless woman! while I waste away with hopeless weeping, you are laughing, rejoicing at your fortunate husband's side. You in the bosom of joy, you in the bosom of joy, I in death's!

Soon a neglected grave will give me shelter, no pitying tear will fall on it! ah! even the comforts of the dead, alas, wretched man! are denied to me. Do you, even you, forget this despised monument: never pass through here, O cruel woman, at your husband's side. Ah! at least respect the remains of the one who died for you, at least respect the remains of the one who died for you! Never pass through here, forget this place, at least respect the one

muore, chi muore per te, o barbara, io moro per te!

who is dying for you, never pass through here, forget this place, at least respect the one who is dying, who is dying for you, O cruel woman, I die for you.

A somber group is seen coming from the direction of the castle.

TENORS, BASSES: Oh meschina! Oh fato orrendo! più sperar non giova omai, omai! Questo dì che sta sorgendo tramontar più non vedrà!

TENORS, BASSES: Oh, wretched girl! Oh, dreadful fate! From now on, from now on it is useless to hope any more! She will not see the end of this day which is now dawning!

EDGARDO [*appalled*]: Giusto cielo! rispondete, rispondete—ah!

EDGARDO [*appalled*]: Great heavens! answer, answer—ah!

TENORS, BASSES: Oh meschina!

TENORS, BASSES: Oh, wretched girl!

EDGARDO: Di chi mai, di chi piangete? Rispondete, rispondete per pietà!

EDGARDO: Who, who is it you are weeping for? Answer, answer, for pity's sake!

TENORS, BASSES: Di Lucia.

TENORS, BASSES: For Lucia.

EDGARDO [*terrified*]: Lucia diceste!

EDGARDO [*terrified*]: You said Lucia!

TENORS, BASSES: La meschina—

TENORS, BASSES: The wretched girl—

EDGARDO: Su parlate.

EDGARDO: Go on, speak.

TENORS, BASSES: Sì; la misera sen muore.

TENORS, BASSES: Yes; the poor girl is dying.

EDGARDO: Ah!

EDGARDO: Ah!

TENORS, BASSES: Fur le nozze a lei funeste, di ragion la trasse amore, s'avvicina all'ore estreme, e te chiede, per te geme—

TENORS, BASSES: Her nuptials were fatal to her, love deprived her of her senses, she is nearing her last hours, and asks for you, moans for you—

EDGARDO: Ah, Lucia! muore! Lucia! ah!

TENORS, BASSES: Questo dì che sta sorgendo tramontar più non vedrà!

TENORS, BASSES: Di ragion la trasse amore, e te chiede, per te geme.

EDGARDO: Questo dì che sta sorgendo tramontar più non vedrà la mia Lucia?

TENORS, BASSES: Di ragion la trasse amore, per te, sì, sì, per te.

EDGARDO: Ah!

thunder boom

TENORS, BASSES: Rimbomba già la squilla in suon di morte.

? ring ringing

The passing-bell is heard tolling mournfully in the distance.

EDGARDO: Quel suono in cor mi piomba! È decisa la mia sorte!

Fall swoop down

He makes an effort to leave, but the mourners block his way.

TENORS, BASSES: Oh Dio!

EDGARDO: Rivederla ancor vogl'io,—

EDGARDO: —rivederla e poscia—

TENORS, BASSES: Qual trasporto, sconsigliato! ah desisti, ah riedi in te, in te.

Edgardo breaks away, but is again halted by Raimondo.

RAIMONDO: Dove corri, sventurato? Ella in terra più non è.

EDGARDO: Lucia!

EDGARDO: Ah, Lucia! she is dying! Lucia! Ah!

TENORS, BASSES: She will not see the end of this day which is now dawning!

TENORS, BASSES: Love deprived her of her senses, and she is asking for you, moaning for you.

EDGARDO: My Lucia will not see the end of this day which is now dawning?

TENORS, BASSES: Love for you, yes, yes, for you, deprived her of her senses.

EDGARDO: Ah!

TENORS, BASSES: Already the bell is echoing the tones of death.

The passing-bell is heard tolling mournfully in the distance.

EDGARDO: That sound sinks into my heart! My fate is settled!

He makes an effort to leave, but the mourners block his way.

TENORS, BASSES: Oh, God!

EDGARDO: I want to see her again—

EDGARDO: —to see her, and then—

TENORS, BASSES: What passion, misguided fellow! ah stop, ah compose yourself, yourself.

Edgardo breaks away, but is again halted by Raimondo.

RAIMONDO: Where are you rushing, wretched man? She is no longer on earth.

EDGARDO: Lucia!

unfold, unfurl, spread (wings)

RAIMONDO: Sventurato!

EDGARDO: In terra più non è? Ella dunque—

turn again *(re)turn* *turn around*

RAIMONDO: È in cielo.

EDGARDO: Lucia più non è!

TENORS, BASSES: Sventurato! Sventurato!

EDGARDO [*calming*]: Tu che a Dio spiegasti l'ali, o bell'alma innamorata, ti rivolgi a me placata, teco ascenda, teco ascenda il tuo fedel. Ah! se l'ira dei mortali fece a noi sì cruda guerra, se divisi fummo in terra, ne congiunga il Nume in ciel, o bell'alma innamorata, bell'alma innamorata, ne congiunga il Nume in ciel, o bell'alma innamorata, bell'alma innamorata, ne congiunga il Nume in ciel! Io ti seguo—

mad, insane (n)—lunatic

RAIMONDO: Forsennato! forsennato!

RAIMONDO, TENORS, BASSES: Ah! che fai? Ah! che fai?

EDGARDO: Morir voglio, morir voglio.

RAIMONDO, TENORS, BASSES: Ritorna in te, ritorna in te, ritorna in te.

EDGARDO: No, no, no!

He stabs himself.

RAIMONDO, TENORS, BASSES: Ah!

RAIMONDO: Che facesti!

RAIMONDO: Wretched man!

EDGARDO: She is no longer on earth? Then she—

RAIMONDO: She is in Heaven.

EDGARDO: Lucia is no more!

TENORS, BASSES: Wretched man! Wretched man!

EDGARDO [*calming*]: You that have spread your wings to God, O beautiful, loving spirit, return to me in peace, let your faithful lover ascend to Heaven with you, ascend to Heaven with you. Ah! if the wrath of mortals waged so cruel a war against us, if we were divided on earth, let God unite us in Heaven, O beautiful, loving spirit, O beautiful, loving spirit, let God unite us in Heaven, O beautiful, loving spirit, beautiful, loving spirit, let God unite us in Heaven! I shall follow you—

RAIMONDO: Madman! madman!

RAIMONDO, TENORS, BASSES: Ah! what are you doing? Ah! what are you doing?

EDGARDO: I want to die, I want to die.

RAIMONDO, TENORS, BASSES: Come to your senses, come to your senses, come to your senses.

EDGARDO: No, no, no!

RAIMONDO, TENORS, BASSES: Ah!

RAIMONDO: What have you done!

EDGARDO [*dying*]: A te vengo— o bell'alma,—

{ RAIMONDO: Sciagurato!

EDGARDO: —ti rivolgi, ah!—

EDGARDO: —al tuo fedel.

RAIMONDO: Pensa al ciel.

{ EDGARDO: Ah se l'ira dei mortali—

TENORS, BASSES: Quale orror! Quale orror!

EDGARDO: —sì cruda guerra,—

RAIMONDO: Oh Dio, perdona,—

EDGARDO: —o bell'alma, ne—

RAIMONDO: Pensa al ciel.

EDGARDO: —congiunga il Nume in ciel,—

{ EDGARDO: —o bell'alma inna- morata, bell'alma innamorata, ne congiunga il Nume in ciel, o bell'alma innamorata, bell'alma innamorata, ne congiunga il Nume in ciel!

TENORS, BASSES: Oh tremendo, oh nero fato! Dio, perdona tanto error!*

RAIMONDO: Pensa al ciel, al ciel, al ciel, ah sciagurato, pensa al ciel.

EDGARDO [*dying*]: I am coming to you— O beautiful spirit—

RAIMONDO: Wretched man!

EDGARDO: —return to me, ah!—

EDGARDO: —to your faithful lover.

RAIMONDO: Reflect upon Heaven.

EDGARDO: Ah, since the wrath of mortals—

TENORS, BASSES: How horrible! how horrible!

EDGARDO: —so cruel a war—

RAIMONDO: Oh, God, forgive,—

EDGARDO: —O beautiful spirit—

RAIMONDO: Reflect upon Heaven.

EDGARDO: —let God unite us in Heaven—

EDGARDO: —O beautiful, loving spirit, O beautiful, loving spirit, let God unite us in Heaven, O beautiful, loving spirit, O beauti- ful, loving spirit, let God unite us in Heaven!

TENORS, BASSES: Oh, terrible, oh, black doom! God, forgive such a crime!

RAIMONDO: Reflect upon Heaven, upon Heaven, upon Heaven, ah, wretched man, reflect upon Heaven.

---

* Although many modern texts give " orror " (horror), the manuscript clearly indicates " error."

EDGARDO: Se divisi fummo in terra, ne congiunga il Nume in ciel, ne congiunga il Nume in ciel, il Nume in ciel, il Nume in ciel, il Nume in ciel!

RAIMONDO, TENORS, BASSES: Dio, perdona, perdona tanto error, tanto error, perdon, perdon, perdona tanto error!

EDGARDO: If we were divided on earth, let God unite us in Heaven, let God unite us in Heaven, God in Heaven, God in Heaven, God in Heaven!

RAIMONDO, TENORS, BASSES: God, forgive, forgive such a crime, such a crime, forgive, forgive, forgive such a crime!

Edgardo falls dead.

Michele Carafa, composer of *Le Nozze di Lammermoor*. Lithograph by Maurin. *(Courtesy Bibliothèque et Musée de l'Opéra, Paris)*

CARAFA AND
"LE NOZZE DI LAMMERMOOR"

Michele Carafa (1787–1872), son of Prince Giovanni di Colobrano, was a Neapolitan musician who settled in Paris. After studying music with Cherubini, he served during the Napoleonic wars as a lieutenant in the Huszars and became equerry to Joachim Murat, the Napoleonic king of Naples. He took part in the invasions of Sicily and of Russia. After Napoleon's collapse Carafa resumed his musical studies. He made his operatic début at the Opéra-Comique in Paris in 1821 with *Jeanne d'Arc*. He became naturalized in 1834, was elected to the Académie in 1837, and in 1840 became professor of composition at the Conservatoire. He was an intimate friend of Rossini's, and was practically a fixture at Rossini's soirées.

Carafa was not a great composer, although he was praised during his lifetime for his melodies and his orchestration. He was, however, a competent musician who could be counted upon to provide a reasonable evening's entertainment. In all, he wrote some thirty-five operas, many of which were very popular, including *Le Solitaire*, *Gabriella di Vergy* (Donizetti later wrote an opera of the same name to the same libretto) and *Le Nozze di Lammermoor*. It is very doubtful if any of his operas are currently known or performed.

Le Nozze di Lammermoor was first performed at the Théâtre-Italien on December 12, 1829. The libretto was by Giuseppe Luigi Balochi (1766–1832), who also wrote the libretto for Rossini's *Mosè in Egitto*. *Le Nozze di Lammermoor* held the stage for a few performances, and then was dropped, even though the well-known soprano Henrietta Sontag starred as Lucia. As far as can be determined, it has never been revived.

Carafa's opera has now been so completely forgotten that it has never been described; indeed, a full score does not seem ever to have been published. The only surviving evidence of its nature is a piano transcription by V. Rifaut, with vocal score, which probably appeared in 1830. This piano and vocal score does not provide stage directions, which have had to be postulated from context.

Le Nozze di Lammermoor is an *opera semiseria*; that is to say, comic scenes are intermingled with the tragic scenes of the drama. It is divided into numbers, as was customary, in which recitative carried part of the action, while the arias simply reported emotional attitudes of the singers. There is considerable repetition in the libretto, with most lines being worked twice musically.

On the whole it seems to be derivative music. The general musical approach is Rossinian, with occasional melodic reminiscences of individual Rossini operas. The buffo bass arias, for example, recall material from *La Cenerentola*. The other strong resemblance, surprisingly enough, is to the music of Carl Maria von Weber; many melodies scattered throughout the opera echo parts of *Der Freischütz* and *Oberon*.

It is a fast-moving opera, with little of the languid charm of Donizetti's work, and it is very florid in all ranges, with ornaments and cadenzas written out. The melodies are Italian in style, and occasionally interesting, but much inferior to Donizetti's.

A plot summary follows.

ACT ONE

PART ONE

Setting: the wooded hills of Scotland. In a forest glade is gathered a troop of huntsmen, captained by Donaldo. To one side are the ruins of a tower, the sole patrimony of Edgardo Ravensvud. Caleb Balderston (Edgardo's loyal retainer) and Misia (the cook) are lurking within the ruins watching the huntsmen.

The chorus sings: "The ferocious bull is hiding in the wood, but it has no place to take refuge. The fleet greyhounds have followed its trail, and tomorrow it will fall to the beloved master, the Chancellor [Asthon]." The chorus of huntsmen troops off the stage.

Caleb and Misia emerge from their hiding places, Caleb bewailing the fact that there is no food and drink in the tower, yet he still must save the honor of the family if he is asked for hospitality. Misia declares that Caleb is driving himself to distraction with this worry.

The huntsmen are heard again in the distance, approaching the tower, and Caleb frantically says that he will lock the door, hide the key, and swear he cannot enter.

The huntsmen reappear, shouting loudly, "Edgardo, Edgardo, why are you hiding? The hero saved the lovable damsel from a horrible fate. Where is Edgardo?" Caleb replies that he does not know. The chorus then tells that the bull charged at Lucia, but Edgardo saved her life and then rushed away before he could be thanked. Caleb wishes the huntsmen would leave, and the chorus, shouting "Edgardo, Edgardo," disappears into the forest.

Edgardo now enters, complaining bitterly at the irony of fate: love and desire for revenge are battling within him. He had sworn revenge on the Asthons, by his father's tomb, and yet he fell in love with Lucia the moment he saw her. Torn between his hatred and his amorous passion, he calls alternately for revenge and for love.

A storm has now arisen, and it is dark. Thunder, lightning and a torrential rain batter the forest. Chancellor Asthon, Lucia and their retainers come to Edgardo's tower. The Chancellor declares that he will invoke hospitality; Lucia says that she is terribly frightened; and Caleb and Misia, who are looking out, warn that the Asthons are in peril because of their *faux pas* in applying to Ravensvud for hospitality.

Edgardo has heard the pounding on his door, comes forward, and then staggers back, overcome with fury. Edgardo, Lucia, the Chancellor, Caleb, and Misia sing a quintet: Edgardo declares that he can hardly believe his eyes at this affront; Lucia exclaims in terror at the flames that dart from Edgardo's eyes; the Chancellor wishes that Edgardo's heart could be softened; and the servants comment on the dangerous situation.

Edgardo asks the Chancellor how he dare approach the tower, since the Chancellor is the author of the misfortunes that have bowed the Ravensvuds. The Chancellor calmly replies that he has come to thank Edgardo for having saved Lucia's life. Edgardo rages, but when Lucia urges him to curb his wrath, he becomes quieter. The quintet then resumes.

When Edgardo has become less excited, the Chancellor urges him to visit the Castle. Edgardo again refuses bitterly, but yields when Lucia begs him. The Chancellor offers him his hand in friendship. In an aside the Chancellor states that this is the politic thing to do, since he does not know which way the wind will blow.

By now the storm has abated, and all, including the huntsmen, troop off to Lammermoor Castle, singing that there is great cause for rejoicing.

PART TWO

Setting: chambers in Lammermoor Castle. Lords and ladies wander through the large rooms.

A chorus of cavaliers proclaims that the intrepid Lady Asthon will soon return from the royal camp, and will be home within an hour. Lucia's bridegroom, who is rich and of good family, will also arrive very shortly.

Bucklaw enters, and in an *allegretto* buffo aria declares that he has his family tree with him, that he has come like the wind in a six-wheeled coach, that he is rich and powerful, and anxious to approach his bride; that his aunt has gone to the Elysian Fields and has left him money and power. He demands his bride. Donaldo and the chorus reply that Lucia is with her mother. Bucklaw and the others leave the stage.

Edgardo enters, bewailing the fact that he is still torn between hatred and love. He reveals that the ghost of his father has appeared to him in a dream, and has urged him to remember his oath to avenge the Ravens-vuds. Edgardo decides to leave the Castle.

Lucia enters and calls to Edgardo, who first says that he is leaving, and then in a duet tells Lucia that though he is madly in love with her, his duty forces him to leave. Lucia reveals that she, in turn, is in love with him. Lucia says that the Chancellor will not object, but that she is afraid of her mother's reaction. Edgardo and Lucia take each other's right hand and swear to the heavens to be true to each other. When Lucia balks a little, Edgardo bids her remember the ancient custom in Scotland which permits such marriage vows. Edgardo then breaks his ring in half, giving one part to Lucia and keeping the other. Begging Heaven to protect them, they leave separately.

Lady Asthon enters, followed by the chorus of lords and ladies. She announces that she has good news, that there have been victories, and their star is rising. The chorus leaves and the Chancellor enters.

Lady Asthon is furious at Ravensvud's presence in the castle, and she upbraids the Chancellor for having admitted him. To the Chancellor's reply that Edgardo saved their daughter, Lady Asthon opposes the fact that Edgardo is their mortal enemy and has sworn to kill them. She demands that Edgardo be immediately expelled. In a duet husband and wife argue, Lady Asthon demanding action, the Chancellor claiming that it would be impolitic and dishonorable to ask Edgardo to leave.

Their argument is interrupted by the appearance of Bucklaw, Donaldo, and the guests. Bucklaw again announces himself eager to have his bride, and Lady Asthon promises that his desires will be fulfilled. Donaldo then informs the Asthons that Edgardo is leaving and wishes to pay his respects. Lady Asthon does not wish to receive him, but the Chancellor insists. Edgardo enters and declares that he is leaving since his presence embarrasses the Asthons, but that he has abandoned his hatred. The Asthons, their servants and their guests are all somewhat bewildered.

The situation is saved for them by the appearance of Caleb Balderston, who jostles his way to the front and declares that he has an important message: Edgardo's cousin, Athol, is waiting for him. The shrewish Lady Asthon immediately screams that Edgardo should leave so that he can betray his honor and his country. In an octet, in which all the major characters join, Edgardo in fury shouts threats at the Asthons, while Lady Asthon and Bucklaw reply in kind; the politic Chancellor tries to soothe everyone; while Lucia and her maid Elisa urge Edgardo to escape before he is killed.

It is revealed that Lucia and Edgardo have become engaged, and Lady Asthon's fury becomes even greater. While Edgardo in manly fashion defies her, she screams insults, Bucklaw declares that Lucia is his, and the Chancellor tries to persuade everyone that a compromise can be reached. As they all cry that they have never known such rage, the chorus recognizes the implacability of fate and the impending tragedy. Edgardo and Caleb eventually leave.

ACT TWO

PART ONE

Setting: the tombs of the noble family of Ravensvud. It is apparently the anniversary of the death of Edgardo's father, Allan, and memorial services are being performed. Edgardo has left the country with Athol, and although months seem to have passed, he has not yet returned.

After the chorus, with Caleb and Misia, have sung a hymn to the dead Lord Ravensvud, informing him of the vendetta against the Asthons, the Minister enters and abjures them to let love govern them instead of hatred. Let the dead rest in peace, he says, and the chorus joins in.

Edgardo enters, travel-stained and tired. He laments that he has arrived too late for his father's rites. Caleb recognizes his voice, and the two greet each other. Caleb renders thanks that his prayers have been recognized and that Edgardo is alive, but Edgardo, overcome with sadness, replies that he is sorry to be alive. He announces that he is going to the usurped seat of his ancestors. He believes that Lucia has abandoned him. Caleb tries to dissuade him, and calls to mind an ancient prophecy, that when a Ravensvud brashly returns to his usurped castle, the line will become extinct. But prophecy or not, Edgardo declares he will go; he cannot resist fate.

Part Two

Setting: chambers in Lammermoor Castle. Lucia sadly contemplates her lot. She has heard nothing from Edgardo, and she is now convinced that he has been untrue to her. Still, she has made a vow to Edgardo and she will keep it. Her spirit will triumph over death.

As she leaves, Bucklaw and the Chancellor enter the apartments, quarreling noisily and foolishly, in a buffo patter duet. Bucklaw accuses the Chancellor of trying to lead him by the nose and make a fool of him, and scolds the Chancellor for having invited his mortal enemy, Edgardo, to the castle. The Chancellor pleads political necessities and gratiutde, but Bucklaw will not listen. The two bicker back and forth, eventually leaving without having reached any decision.

Lady Asthon and Lucia enter, Lady Asthon commenting upon Lucia's pallor. To Lady Asthon's plea to be trusted, since she has Lucia's good at heart, Lucia replies bitterly that she is a victim for sacrifice, and that one day Lady Asthon will weep at her fate. Lady Asthon urges Lucia to trust her, and promises that the wedding will put an end to her troubles, to which Lucia replies that she trusts only death.

Part Three

Setting: the large banquet hall in Lammermoor Castle. Guests in splendid costumes are rejoicing; it is the moment for signing the marriage contract. Lucia totters in with her mother. Her father and Bucklaw await her. Bucklaw comments on her pallor, but Lady Asthon passes it off as something to be expected. Bucklaw, with surprising frankness, asks Lucia if she is really willing to marry him and is acting of her own free will. Lucia replies that she can delay no longer, and must obey her mother. Bucklaw promises to do everything possible to make her happy. The minister and the chorus beg God to stretch His protecting hand over the couple, and they sign the contract.

Lucia is near collapse when an uproar breaks forth. It is Edgardo, forcing his way through the crowd. In an octet with chorus, all bemoan the horrible situation. Lady Asthon demands to know how Edgardo dared to set foot in the Castle, while Bucklaw vows vengeance. Edgardo challenges them all, and invokes his sacred rights. The Minister proposes a solution: Edgardo shall speak to him and Lady Asthon and Lucia in private. The Chancellor is against it, but Lady Asthon shouts that violence is meaningless, since Lucia is married. The others draw aside while Edgardo, the Minister, Lady Asthon and Lucia parley.

Edgardo implores Lucia to listen to him, but she merely stands in a daze. He reminds her of her oath, but Lady Asthon and the Minister interrupt them. Edgardo declares that he has been betrayed, that his love was pure and eternal; perhaps, he adds sarcastically, her love for her second husband will be so. Lucia murmurs that Edgardo is too harsh with her, and when Edgardo demands his ring back, she reveals that she has taken poison.

All exclaim in horror as Lucia collapses. Lucia reveals that she believed Edgardo had betrayed her, and that death was her last resort. As Lucia lies dying, Edgardo curses her mother for her barbarous spite, her cruelty and her ambition. Bucklaw and Edgardo are about to quarrel when Lucia calls to them and tells Edgardo that she had been faithful to him, and now wishes to die near him. Lucia promises that they will be united one day in Heaven. Lucia dies, and Edgardo, crying, "Wife, I cannot resist my sorrows," stabs himself* as the chorus comments upon the barbarous scene.

* The vocal score indicates that Edgardo dies, but does not actually state that he stabs himself. This seems the obvious action to accompany the events.

THÉATRE DE LA RENAISSANCE.

LUCIE DE LAMERMOOR.

Opéra en 4 Actes.

N:

Hancké f.ᵗ d'après F.Grenier.   Lith Formentin & Cⁱᵉ

Musique de

G. DONIZETTI.

Paroles de Mᴹˢ Alphonse Royer & Gustave Vaëz.

From the original edition of *Lucie de Lammermoor.* Lithograph
by Hancké after a picture by F. Grenier. *(Courtesy Bibliothèque
et Musée de l'Opéra, Paris)*

TRANSLATION OF THE FRENCH LIBRETTO "LUCIE DE LAMMERMOOR" *

ACT ONE

The stage represents a place in the woods where two paths cross; at the left is a fountain shaded by an oak.

SCENE I

Gilbert; nobility in hunting costume; peasants.

CHORUS: Let us crown the crest of the mountains, let us sweep through the green meadows of the countryside. Sounds of the hunting horn, may echo prolong you; golden sun, ah, shine yet a long while! Dart breathlessly down on the plain, skilled dogs, on the stag at bay; may evening call you back under your roofs, fine hunters, tired and victorious.

The hunt disappears in the distance.

SCENE II

Gilbert and Asthon enter.

GILBERT: How gloomy you look. Would you need the aid of my sword?
ASTHON: Perhaps.
GILBERT: Good! Use my arm, your servant Gilbert will not fail you.
ASTHON: Gilbert—enveloped in black despair, my soul bemoans my sister's crime; this Edgard Ravenswood, the enemy of my race, the worthless ravisher of my Lucie's heart ... she loves him!

* For the background of the French version see pages 39 and 84.

GILBERT: A single word, a sign, and I shall immediately set out on his trail and I shall answer for him.

ASTHON: To have placed so much hope on this girl! You know the powerful Lord Athol would once again have become the support of my family, which is presently out of favor with the King. Lucie was about to give her hand to young Arthur, the minister's nephew.... O sinister passion! Edgard has upset everything!

GILBERT: Master, a blow from this sword will get rid of this infernal Edgard!

ASTHON: A crime like that? Oh! Never!

GILBERT: As you wish, Excellency. Edgard and your sister, defying your ban, are nevertheless coming this morning like two turtledoves to this dismal place, near the fountain, where troubled Scottish lovers come by custom to exchange rings plighting their faith.

ASTHON: Are you telling the truth?

GILBERT: My lord, I carried the message. I am paid by the lover to be silent, and by you to talk. I serve both of you.

ASTHON: Very well! His blood shall quench my rage! I must break the ties of this love which defies me; my blood, like a flow of lava, kindles my fury. Shall I be your slave, concern about empty honor? A curse on the man who defies me! Edgard, a curse on you! Too long have I been forgiving, at last my hatred is growing weary; the day of forgiveness is past; no, nothing can acquit you, like a thunderbolt my arm will force your mad pride into the dust.

GILBERT: My sword hangs idle at my side; it is ready to spring forth to serve you.

Chorus is heard drawing near.

The hunt is coming toward us. There it is.

ASTHON: Not a word more. Silence.

SCENE III

Asthon, Gilbert; hunters reenter.

CHORUS: The sun drove us out of the plain, to seek shelter by the cool air of the fountain, on that sweet flowering mead.

Advancing toward Asthon.

In a shaded byway your hated enemy came into our view. He took flight on his steed, and we instantly flung ourselves in pursuit of him. But far from the heat of the plain, fatigue leads us back.

ASTHON: An enemy! Who was it?

CHORUS: Edgard.

ASTHON: Again? O rage that devours me! It is settled, he must die.

GILBERT: Yes, that is the wisest course. [*Aside:*] (And suiting me best. This will make me rich.)

ASTHON: Angel of Evil, come to me, open thy wings, I invoke thee, come serve my deadly rage, arm your fatal hand for me. Edgard, my vengeance shall reach you. This love which makes you feared, since nothing can extinguish it, I shall crush in your heart.

CHORUS: This vengeance will reach him, for hatred is in his heart, and nothing can extinguish it. I foresee a day of horror.

GILBERT [*aside*]: (For the same price, without any pretense, I would gladly save him.)

The hunt is stopped for a time. The nobles recline beneath the trees, their servants distribute refreshments carried in baskets.

Scene IV

The same, Arthur.

ARTHUR: I am the last to arrive at the gathering place for the hunt. Greetings, Henri.

ASTHON: Arthur, greetings to you; your dreams of love have carried you far from us ...

ARTHUR: Reassure me, I beg you; I love Lucie and I believe myself loved in return; but I cannot dispel a suspicion that obsesses me.

ASTHON: A suspicion?

ARTHUR: A single word will restore peace to my calmed spirit.

ASTHON: Speak.

ARTHUR: Help me. Is Lucie really coming to me of her own free will?

ASTHON: Do you doubt it?

ARTHUR: Edgard ...

ASTHON: At one time, that insolent wretch, forgetting the hatred between us and braving my anger, dared to protest his love to my sister, I believe; she rejected him.

ARTHUR: She did herself? Ah! Brother, thank you, I am happy now and have hope. I knew about Edgard's deluded passion, I was jealous of him; but my uncle, Lord Athol, is sending him on a mission to the French court.

ASTHON [*with joy*]: He is leaving ...

ARTHUR: That has been promised to me.

ASTHON: And soon?

ARTHUR: I believe so.

ASTHON [*aside*]: (I breathe again.)

GILBERT [*sotto voce to Asthon*]: I am to meet him in a moment.

ASTHON [*sotto voce to Gilbert*]: Since he is about to leave, no.

GILBERT [*sotto voce to Asthon*]: Still, dead men tell no tales.

ASTHON: Let the hunt begin!

Huntsmen arise and leave.

CHORUS: Let the hunt begin! Now is the hour when we set the hounds on the weeping stag. The horn resounds afar and the forest shakes under the hooves of the horses.

SCENE V

Gilbert, alone.

GILBERT: He is leaving, I am being robbed! I would have had a nice enough sum from my master for killing our lover. The Devil take these scruples! With a man like that there is no way to make an honest living. Ah, along that dark path down there I see our charming Lucie coming. Softly, Sir Gilbert, each role in its turn. Let us now assume the sympathetic air of love's confidant.

SCENE VI

Gilbert, Lucie.

LUCIE: Gilbert ...

GILBERT: Yes, mademoiselle.

LUCIE: Edgard ...

GILBERT: He is going to come. I shall stand guard for you.

LUCIE [*giving him her purse*]: Here is something for your zeal. Go! If anyone chances to come, be sure to warn us.

Gilbert leaves.

Scene VII

Lucie, alone.

LUCIE: O fountain, O pure spring! Beneath the foam your murmur sings and sighs like a sweet voice. It was here that I first saw Edgard, Edgard! O height of misery!

This name which is so sweet to me, alas, must it, for my brother, be the name of a bitter enemy? The hatred we have inherited from our ancestors stands like an unappeased ghost between us. Why do we not have wings? Carried far away by them, out of mortal paths, to the golden stars, our two faithful spirits would unite their soaring flight. When barbarous hatred here on Earth separates us, let us lift up our eyes; a beacon gleams at the eternal haven; those who are separated here are joined in Heaven. You, through whom my heart is radiant, your God-given love makes happiness shine from my visage, a chaste corona. The thought of our ecstasies perfumes the past and plants hope, like a flower, in a soul which is still bewildered and numb.

Scene VIII

Lucie, Edgard.

EDGARD: Here I am, Lucie. I wanted to talk to you here, without witnesses.... A cruel fate is withering my life. It is horrible! O my God! Dearest, before tomorrow I shall be far from our Scotland.

LUCIE: O Heaven!

EDGARD: I am leaving for France. The order is definite; my country calls on me, tomorrow, tomorrow, without delay.

LUCIE: Abandoning me, alone, in my misery!

EDGARD: I will go and meet my enemy, and beseech him to forget our hatred. And with my hand in his, ask to marry you.

LUCIE: Edgard, O Heaven! What do I hear? Fatal love! Ah! You will die, you will be obliterated from our hearts.

EDGARD: I can anticipate it, a refusal. O strange destiny! What! His plans for revenge have been carried through, my father is dead, my property has been wrested from me ... this is still too little. He still pursues me with his rage. My blood, my complete destruction—this is his vow. He hates me.

LUCIE: Edgard!

EDGARD: Great God!

LUCIE: Have mercy, do not blaspheme!

EDGARD: A curse on your brother, let him tremble ...

LUCIE: Edgard!

EDGARD: Judge for yourself. On my father's tomb, in my rage, I swore vengeance and warfare upon your race. I swore death in return for death. Then I saw you, and God sent a ray of love into my soul, but my oath again claims me; one day I shall fulfill it.

LUCIE: Leave me some hope! You see my heart's anguish. I am the sister of the man you are cursing in your revenge. Extinguish the flames in your eyes, look at mine filling with tears. Oh! Your revenge is base, Edgard, if it causes my death.

EDGARD: Come in the shade of this oak where you have sworn faith to me. Bear witness, holy fountain, and you, Heaven. She is mine. [*To Lucie:*] Take this ring ...

He gives her his ring and takes in exchange the ring which she had on her finger.

Yours is a pledge to me. Preserve my pledge.

LUCIE: To the tomb!

EDGARD, LUCIE: Ah, may only God dissolve you, bonds fashioned upon this altar; yes, my soul devotes itself to you; may my pact be inscribed in Heaven.

EDGARD: Let us part, my Lucie.

LUCIE: Beloved Edgard, I shall die of terror; my life is going away with you.

EDGARD: And my heart remains with you.

LUCIE: Let a letter come to console me at least in my misery, and rebind to this Earth a soul ready to breathe away.

EDGARD: My thoughts and my prayers will fly to you from afar.

LUCIE: My hopeful dreams will always fly to you; the sound of the waves will be for you the echo of my suffering. If my poor desolated heart succumbs to its sorrow, pick a single flower in this lonely wood for my tomb. Farewell, all my happiness. Death is in my heart.

EDGARD: My hopeful dreams will always fly to you; the sound of the waves will be for you the echo of my suffering; and if your desolated lover succumbs to his sorrow, shed a tear for this exile; let your heart be his tomb. Farewell, all my happiness. Death is in my heart. I am leaving ...

LUCIE: Farewell.

EDGARD: We are one in the eyes of God.

LUCIE, EDGARD: Farewell.

ACT TWO

A Gothic hall in Asthon's castle.

SCENE I

*As the curtain rises, Asthon is seated, elbow resting on a table. Gilbert,
in traveling clothes, enters, hat in hand.*

ASTHON: So you are back from France?

GILBERT: Yes, master; I have just arrived.

ASTHON: And what is that detested Edgard doing?

GILBERT: He is despondent and believes that Lucie has been unfaithful.

ASTHON: Wonderful!

GILBERT: And doubtless she still loves him and still insists upon disobey-
ing you?

ASTHON [*getting up*]: Gilbert, if you help me, today is the day when
instead of loving Edgard she will hate him.

GILBERT: Tell me! According to your order and good pleasure, I have
already suppressed their letters. Total silence is a good remedy for the
sorrows of love. What is to be done now?

ASTHON: The engagement ring which my sister gave Ravenswood in the
forest one day ...

GILBERT: While Edgard slept, soul benumbed by love, I slipped off his
pledge; for a few pieces of gold a clever workman, a man of very bad
reputation (but otherwise a good fellow), made me an imitation that
would deceive a jeweler's eye. Here it is.

ASTHON: Splendid!

GILBERT: But we must make haste. Edgard is going to return ...

ASTHON: What does it matter? By tomorrow Lucie will have given her
hand to Lord Arthur. I hear her—she is coming. Stay ready behind
this door, my dear Gilbert, and when I call, come in with the ring ...

GILBERT: I shall show it to her.

Exit Gilbert.

Scene II

Asthon, Lucie; later, Gilbert.

ASTHON: I have been waiting for you; come here. I hoped to find you more cheerful on this day which is to consecrate the love of an illustrious husband. You remain silent?

LUCIE: When my heart is in despair, consuming its bitter pain, can you, my brother, see my pangs without being horrified? May God in His wrath not avenge them on you!

ASTHON: Your Edgard has abandoned you; you are no longer betrothed to him; this love has degraded you, but your fate is not bound to his. I ought to be pitiless about your mad passion. A noble husband ...

LUCIE: Never, never!

ASTHON: Lucie!

LUCIE: Edgard has received my promise.

ASTHON: He has forgotten you.

LUCIE: He loves me; I have faith in his vow; we are one before God.

ASTHON: May the traitor's last gift finally let you know him for what he is. [*Calling:*] Gilbert!

Gilbert, without saying a word, reenters and shows the ring to Lucie, who screams.

LUCIE: My blood is frozen with horror!

ASTHON: Do you believe me?

LUCIE [*in consternation*]: My ring ... Death is descending upon me!... I wept over his absence, but beneath my suffering there lay the hope that he would return soon; perhaps, I would say to myself, yes, perhaps tomorrow! Alas! Farewell, belief. A fine dream. I hoped in vain.

Gilbert leaves, exchanging signs with Asthon.

ASTHON: The ungrateful scoundrel has abandoned you; his base heart laughs at the feebleness of the vow that deceived you. Realize your offense. Let indifference be our revenge; scorn for scorn.

LUCIE: The ingrate has abandoned me! To betray my love, his faith, his promise, vows written in Heaven! Farewell, hope! Oh! For my constancy, his indifference—that, then, is the reward.

Fanfares outside.

What do I hear?

ASTHON: Cries of joy resounding from afar.

LUCIE: For what?

ASTHON: Your husband.

LUCIE: Great God! The chill of terror seizes me.

ASTHON: The altar is being readied for you.

LUCIE: Say the tomb instead of the celebration ... terror freezes my heart.

ASTHON: Look, my life is at stake in this. You know how greatly the star of my fortunes has been eclipsed; I wish to elevate once again the splendor of my humbled glory: only Arthur can save me from ruin.

LUCIE: And I?

ASTHON: Only he.

LUCIE: I!

ASTHON: You must save me.

LUCIE: My brother!

ASTHON: To the altar!

LUCIE: I am going to leave this Earth.

ASTHON: Come, you must save me.

LUCIE: No.

ASTHON: You must.

LUCIE: O Heaven!

ASTHON: Do you hear these festive songs? It is your wedding that is being prepared. Go, adorn your head with flowers; you can still be happy. Yield to my wishes, Lucie. It is your brother who entreats you; give me back my lost splendor; you hold my fate in your hands.

LUCIE: Ah! Weeping instead of celebration! Let sorrow veil my head. It is my tomb that is being made ready; misery is my lot. God! I bow beneath my sorrow, hear my supplicating voice; come and snatch me away from life; I await death as a blessing.

Lucie staggers out weakly.

SCENE III

Asthon, lords and ladies, clansmen; a little later, Arthur.

CHORUS: Let us follow the lover who leads us to a beloved queen, to the bride of his choice, the perfumed flower of the woods. All who can sing, join our chorus, our concord; the clamoring festivities must tire out even Echo.

ARTHUR [*to Asthon*]: Envy wished to tarnish the gleam of your banner, but we shall see it shine again more brilliantly and more proudly. Your hand. — Come to my heart, let us swear sincere faith; I come to you as a brother, as a brother, a champion.

CHORUS [*repeats previous stanzas*]: Let us follow, etc.

ARTHUR [*to Asthon*]: And now! Lucie.

ASTHON: Joyful, she is making ready; perhaps a last care holds her back. She is adorning herself proudly, but she has just stopped mourning for her beloved mother.

ARTHUR: Her memory is sacred to me.

ASTHON: We are repaid for her loss by a marriage which makes us all happy.

ARTHUR: Brother, I have doubts.... Is she listening to her own heart ... Lucie?

ASTHON: What?

ARTHUR: What can I say? In her eyes I have often seen hidden tears.

ASTHON: Dispel your fears. Her heart glories in your love.

LORDS AND LADIES: She is coming, it is she!

ASTHON [*aside*]: (What deathly pallor!)

Scene IV

The same, Lucie led in by the Minister [Raimond].

ASTHON [*going to Lucie*]: Here is your groom....[*Sotto voce:*] (Cruel girl, do you want to destroy me?)

LUCIE [*aside*]: (Oh torment!)

ARTHUR [*to Lucie*]: I place the most loving heart at the feet of the most beautiful woman.

ASTHON [*going to the table*]: Before going to the chapel we must sign. [*To Arthur:*] Step over here.

ARTHUR [*signing*]: O sweet moment!

Asthon leads Lucie by the hand to the table.

LUCIE: I go to the sacrifice ...

ASTHON [*handing her the pen, sotto voce*]: (Do not falter, sign ...)

LUCIE [*aside*]: O anguish! [*She signs.*] Hope, precede me to Heaven!

MINISTER: She seems to be tottering ...

ASTHON [*aside*]: (I breathe again ...)

LUCIE [*holding herself erect with difficulty*] : I am ... weak ... I am ... dying ...
CHORUS: What is that noise?
ALL: Heavens! Edgard!
LUCIE [*hurling herself toward her brother*]: Lies!
CHORUS: O horrible day!

SCENE V

*Edgard appears, and stops at the back of the stage. He is pale; his
clothing indicates that he has made his journey without stopping on the
way. Lucie has fallen in a faint near the table. General consternation.
A long period of silence.*

EDGARD: My right, my sword are on my side; my arm is raised to strike
if I must lose my beautiful dream, her love, my treasure. I have here
the pledge of her vow, but the horror on her face is a forewarning of
broken faith; thankless woman, I still love you.

ASTHON: Fate suspends my sword over his upraised head; may this day,
at last, see my revenge completed with his death. My amazement (a
bad omen) is the calm before the storm ... [*To Edgard:*] Your return,
the last outrage, will trace your fate in blood.

LUCIE [*emerging from her swoon*]: He is faithful to his love! Everything
crushes me in my distress; the angel of remorse looms like an avenging
shade. A terrible scheme is bared, the veil of destiny is parted. There
are no longer any more stars in my night, there is no longer any haven
in the abyss.

MINISTER: The cry of distress follows songs of intoxicated joy; I seem to
see death hovering like a looming shade. God, let Thy hand be
revealed, let the star of hope shine in the shadow that enveils us, open
a haven for this afflicted woman.

ARTHUR: The veil is falling from my eyes, yes, the plot is being revealed;
the star of my happiness is waning; they had linked their fates. It is all
over, farewell, beautiful dream! But this outrage demands the sword;
yes, her love, which he has stolen from me, will cost him his life.

CHORUS: The cry of distress follows songs of intoxicated joy; I seem to see
death hovering like a looming shade.

ASTHON, ARTHUR [*drawing their swords*]: Away from us! I command it as
master of the house. Or this sword will destroy you here.

EDGARD [*drawing his sword*]: Sword for sword. A traitor's blood will also
redden the earth.

MINISTER [*throwing himself between them*]: Emulate the clemency and kindness of a forgiving God; my voice commands it in His name. Cast aside your swords. Divine grace is lost for the murderer. It is written, "He who lives by the sword shall die by the sword."

ASTHON [*sheathing his sword*]: Ravenswood, what brings you here again?

EDGARD: My Lucie, my just cause. She vowed to join her life to mine.

MINISTER: Remove any such vow from your memory, because another ...

EDGARD: Another ... Oh, no!

MINISTER [*showing Edgard the document which Lucie has signed*]: See ...

EDGARD [*snatching the paper from his hands, to Lucie*]: You are trembling ... shall I believe ... tell me that he is lying ... is this your signature?... Answer me with one word!

LUCIE [*weakly*]: Yes.

EDGARD [*wrenching from his finger the ring which he received from Lucie, and throwing it at her feet*]: Take back your pledge; give me back mine ... give it to me!

He tears the ring from Lucie's finger.

LUCIE: Listen, for Heaven's sake!

EDGARD: Get away from me; you have betrayed your oath. A curse upon this vile plot that transformed me from an avenger into a sacrilegious slave! Cursed be your witchcraft! Cursed the hour when I first saw you! Reptile-hearted, infamous race, Hell vomited you forth. May you be exterminated by poison and fire and sword ...

CHORUS: I tremble ...

ASTHON [*in a fury*]: Tremble, tremble! Tremble, madman! My terrible rage will crush you like a worm in the earth. Outspeeding thunder my arm will fall from the sky upon this blasphemer. Ah, better ask mercy from the tiger in his den than from my heart!

MINISTER: In the name of Heaven! Listen to my prayer. Forswear, all of you, vengeance and war. No more curses, God alone wields the thunder. Let pity descend into your hearts. If you refuse to forgive upon Earth, how can you hope for forgiveness from the Lord?

LUCIE: Lord, quench this rage in their hearts; do not add his death to my misery. This is the only wish, the last prayer of a loving heart which is shattered by sorrow, the last wish of a heart which can hope for no more happiness for itself upon Earth.

EDGARD: Here is my breast; strike! For there no longer remains a shelter for my misery on Earth. Cowards, villains, thirsting for vengeance, make my blood flow with my tears, and to hide the stains strew flowers on the stone floors of your festivities.

Asthon tries to hurl himself on Edgard; the minister holds them apart. All the lords have their swords in their hands. Edgard defies them and leaves, casting a last look at Lucie, who falls to her knees.

ACT THREE

A hallway connecting the apartments in Asthon's castle. Below, illuminated gardens.

SCENE I

CHORUS [*behind the scenes*]: Let us envelop the young bride with our prayers; Night, be envious of the ardor in their eyes. Night, enclose happy Arthur in your veil, and extinguish the stars on your azure brow.

Gilbert comes on the stage during the chorus, crossing, entering a room at the side, and emerging with Asthon.

SCENE II

Asthon, Gilbert.

GILBERT: Yes, my lord, a man is waiting for you at the little gate to your park.

ASTHON: Indeed! What does he want of me?

GILBERT: He answered my question in a very forbidding tone: "What does it matter? Is Lord Asthon afraid?" If you ask me, I think the stranger is in a sombre mood.

ASTHON: You did not recognize him?

GILBERT: What with the folds of his cape and a large hat, I could not see his face.

ASTHON: Let him enter. [*Aside:*] (An uncertain hope ...)

A man, wrapped in a cloak, appears, hat pulled down over his eyes. He stops at the back of the stage.

GILBERT: He followed me! There he is!

ASTHON [*to Gilbert*]: Leave us, but do not go far.

Scene III

Asthon; Edgard, who throws off his cloak.

ASTHON: Edgard!

EDGARD: Yes, it is I, also your judge; you must have expected to see me.

ASTHON: You have come to cast yourself on my mercy?

EDGARD: Perhaps ...

ASTHON: What brings you here?

EDGARD: Recollect that in this domain, from which your hatred still excludes me, I was once master, and gave orders. The arms of your family have been placed above mine and shine forth, but my right has not been yielded, and my slumbering vengeance is at last going to be fulfilled.

ASTHON: I cannot. I must take Lucie to her husband without delay.

EDGARD [*aside*]: (Each word is a dagger; O torture, O jealousy!)

ASTHON: To her husband ...

EDGARD: Be quiet! Be quiet!

ASTHON: Listen to me! This morning, beautiful and happy in her glorious destiny, she prayed at the altar. Now the young bride, the envy of every woman here, turns her glance gratefully to Heaven. Go! It is folly for your jealous rage to appeal to the sword!

EDGARD: I will have your blood!

ASTHON: Vain threats; to put an end to our hatred, I accept your challenge. May the memory of you and may your race be obliterated with your name. Go! die on Earth, disappear into oblivion.

EDGARD: Tremble! To avenge my father I shall lay you in the dust.

ASTHON: You!

EDGARD: I! At what hour?

ASTHON: All right! A moment before dawn blazes forth.

EDGARD: Where?

ASTHON: Near the tombs where your family lies.

EDGARD: I shall be there.

ASTHON: Select a tomb to your taste.

EDGARD: Yes, but I shall cast you into it.

EDGARD, ASTHON: Sun! Rise up and bring forth your disc of fire over the arena where hatred will take up arms. Livid phantom of a father! Come, guide my sword, preside at God's judgment.

EDGARD: I shall stretch you at my feet.

ASTHON: The day will be your death.

EDGARD: Don't keep me waiting.

ASTHON: I shall not attend the ball.

EDGARD, ASTHON: Blood-covered ground, serve him as a shroud; without crucifix, without prayers, let him die beneath my foot. If the sword fails, let the dagger do its work, without quarter. No forgiveness, no mercy!

Exeunt.

SCENE IV

Lords and ladies, coming from the garden and neighboring rooms.

CHORUS: The young bride has left; Night, be envious of the stars in their eyes. Night, enclose happy Arthur in your veil; and extinguish the stars on your brow. The sky is already growing pale, let us dance again; for us the dawn will come too soon.

SCENE V

Same, Minister.

MINISTER: A tragedy, a tragedy, a terrible fate.

CHORUS: Why are you shouting "tragedy"?

MINISTER: Lucie ...

CHORUS: Go on!

MINISTER: A horrible night!

CHORUS: Dispel our dread!

MINISTER: She had hardly retired to her apartments when, completely mad, she seized a dagger and struck her husband a mortal blow. Arthur died stretching out his arms toward us.

CHORUS: A frightful wedding! What a horrible fate! Rejoicing is already changing to mourning. A wicked angel, Hell itself, was jealous of their joy.

MINISTER: Hatred dug the abyss which is swallowing this house.

CHORUS: Hatred, alas, dug the abyss which is swallowing this house.

MINISTER: Heaven! Forgive Lucie for a crime which sanity has not committed.

CHORUS: Unhappiness destroyed her reason; God will pardon her for her crime.

MINISTER: She is coming, alas. Poor victim!

Scene VI

Same; Lucie, who comes in rapidly, hair disheveled, eyes haggard.

LUCIE: I heard my name amid your songs. It was his voice, so beloved and so well-known ... Edgard! I am yours again. Come, I have escaped the power of the evil ones. Come sit by the fountain, alone with me.

She believes she has taken Edgard's hand and is moving toward the fountain, when suddenly she stops, terrified.

O Heaven! Over there ... there ... a ghost is billowing toward us; it is coming between us! Alas! Let us fly, fly, Edgard.

She forgets her terror; a pleasant thought is depicted in her eyes.

The song of the wood warbler echoes through the forest. Let us plait my hair ... what sweet harmony! It is coming from the sky ... it is a wedding-hymn ... The altar is being prepared for us ... O delights! My soul overflows with happiness. The altar glows with light ... a sweet incense fills the air. Here is the priest. Yours is my life and all my being. Take me by the hand, O my Edgard so beloved!

MINISTER, CHORUS: May her good angel assuage the wrath of a vengeful God.

LUCIE: Days of unclouded azure sky, shine for us; an angel in Heaven might envy my happiness.

MINISTER: Asthon is coming.

Scene VII

As before, Asthon.

ASTHON: Tell me ... this terrible news ...

MINISTER: It is only too true.

ASTHON: Oh night of horror!... my sister ... you a murderess!...

MINISTER: Have pity on her. You can see in what a pitiful state ...

LUCIE [*believing she sees Edgard*]: He is speaking ... he is asking me something, and I, I must keep silence. Do not look so stern! It is true, I signed the contract, but ... but ... [*Clapping her hand to her forehead with anguish:*] My head ... O Heavens! In his rage he is dashing my ring on the floor ... He is cursing me! Brother, it was you who were my executioner. I am not forsworn, Edgard, I swear it to you, no, I have always loved you, always, and I still love you. My soul is pure of all bad faith. I still love you.

ASTHON: It is I, Lucie, your brother ...

LUCIE: Guard your life, my treasure. I am going far from Earth, to the dwelling place of light, where prayer mounts, where faith leads us. There, weeping stars, my eyes, will shine upon you, will pierce the veils of night and will smile on you from the skies.

ASTHON: Cruel disaster! I have lost everything.

LUCIE: My mother calls me to the heavens. Wait! I am coming to you! I am going far from Earth, etc.

After finishing Lucie falls unconscious into the arms of her women. Asthon speaks to certain gentlemen, who indicate by signs and gestures that they understand. They leave.

ACT FOUR

A melancholy, moonlit place. Tombs stand among trees. In the distance can be seen the lighted castle.

Scene I

EDGARD [*entering with slow pace*]: Tombs of my ancestors, receive the last member, the wretched ruin of an extinct family! No more anger, no more lamenting! This harsh and ungrateful world no longer is of any worth to me. Asthon, to you I yield my blood, since I can no longer live, Lucie, alas, after all your scorn. I see you at the ball, adorned with flowers, laughingly moving through the loathsome crowd, ungrateful girl. And I, burdened by my woes, to which I am succumbing, I vainly turn my pallid brow toward you. You seek pleasure, Lucie, and I seek the tomb.

Soon the weeds will grow upon my isolated gravestone, and not a tear will moisten my sad tomb. My soul will fly to the sky, withered and ruined. If one day your Arthur leads you, Lucie, to this sad place, pass in silence; a word of love would awaken my shade. Faithless woman, at least respect the lover who died for you.

Scene II

Edgard, the gentlemen sent by Asthon.

CHORUS: Ravenswood, Asthon must disappoint you; his duty keeps him at the side of his dying sister.

EDGARD: Great God! What do I hear? Who is dying at this time?

CHORUS: Weep, weep.

EDGARD: But for whom should I weep? Tell me who is dying.

CHORUS: Lucie!

EDGARD: Heaven!

CHORUS: Within an hour she will suffer no more. Yes, her last day is about to dawn; hope no more, she is dying.

EDGARD: Oh, God, do not say so.

CHORUS: Sanity no longer reigns in her broken heart, and her unsmiling lips still hurl your name toward the skies.

EDGARD [*in despair*]: You are dying, dying faithful? And I cursed you, alas!

CHORUS: On her deathbed she is calling you, holding out her arms to you.

A bell sounds in the distance.

Do you hear the death knell?

EDGARD: It has thundered upon my head! Wait for me, Lucie!

CHORUS: Stop!

EDGARD: No, I will see her again!

CHORUS [*holding him back*]: Let prudence restrain you. Remain here and regain your senses.

EDGARD [*breaking loose from their arms*]: I will see her again!

Scene III

Same, Minister.

MINISTER: May prayers escort her to the heavens; regret can do nothing.

EDGARD: I shall see her no more! Lucie!

MINISTER: She is dead.

EDGARD: Lost!

MINISTER: She is in Heaven.

EDGARD: Lost for ever.

CHORUS: Cruel fate!

EDGARD: O beautiful angel, whose wings, flying from our mortal sorrows, have borne away my hope to the eternal spheres; perfumed flower of my life, I follow you, my well-beloved; the earth has closed on us, come to the heavens to receive me. [*Seizing his dagger:*] I shall rejoin you.

MINISTER [*grasping his arm*]: Madman, this is lunacy!

EDGARD: I will die.

CHORUS: Come to your senses, come, Edgard!

EDGARD: No, no!

He stabs himself.

CHORUS: Ah!

Edgard falls into the arms of the Minister.

SCENE VI

Same, Asthon, Gilbert bearing two swords.

ASTHON: Here I am.

EDGARD: I am dying ... Henri, you come too late. [*In a broken voice:*] In the other life ... Lucie awaits me ... it is no longer in your power ... to take her away from me ... God gives her ... to my love.

MINISTER: Forgive him!

CHORUS: Forgive him!

EDGARD: Henri ... I forgive you ... come, my Lucie ... receive me in Heaven, O beautiful angel. My Lucie, I shall join you in the other life ... come to the skies to receive me. [*Dies.*]

ASTHON: Remorse shall be my lot. Alas, everything is collapsing under me.

CHORUS: All these evils are your work; may their blood be on your head!

BIBLIOGRAPHY

Alborghetti, Federico, and Galli, Michelangelo, *Gaetano Donizetti e G. Simone Mayr, Notizie e documenti*. Bergamo, 1875.

Arditi, Luigi, *My Reminiscences, with numerous illustrations, facsimiles, etc.* Second edition, London, 1896.

Barblan, Guglielmo, *L'Opera di Donizetti nell'età romantica*. Bergamo, 1948. [Excellent musicological study, opera by opera.]

Byron, Henry J., *Lucia di Lammermoor: or, The Laird, the Lady, and the Lover, A New and Original Operatic Burlesque Extravaganza, Founded on Donizetti's popular opera, and consequently very unlike the Romance*. London, [n.d., 1865?].

Calcraft, John William [pseud. of Cole, John William], *The Bride of Lammermoor. A drama in five acts*. French's Standard Drama, The Acting Edition, No. 179, New York, [186-?].

Carafa, Michele, and Balochi, Giuseppe L., *Le Nozze di Lammermoor*. Paris, [1830?]. [Piano transcription and vocal score.]

Cenni biografici di Donizetti e Mayr, raccolti dalle memorie di un vecchio ottuagenario dilettante di musica. Bergamo, 1875.

Clemente, Verzino Edgardo, *Le opere di Gaetano Donizetti. Contributo alla loro storia*. Bergamo, 1897.

Crockett, William S., *The Scott Originals*. London & Edinburgh, 1912.

Donizetti, Gaetano, and Cammarano, Salvatore, *Lucia di Lammermoor*. [Milan, 1941?] [Photographic facsimile of Donizetti's manuscript.]

———, *Lucia di Lammermoor. (The Bride of Lammermoor), Opera in Three Acts*. New York (Schirmer), [n.d.]. [Piano transcription and vocal score.]

———, *An English Version of Lucia di Lammermoor, a Grand Opera in Three Acts*. London (T. H. Lacy), [n.d., circa 1845]. [Princess Royal version.] [Libretto only.]

———, *Lucia di Lammermoor, Dramma Tragico in due parti ... da rappresentarsi al Teatro Carlo Felice, la primavera del 1836*. Genova, [n.d., 1836?]. [Libretto only.]

————, *Lucía de Lammermoor, drama trágico en dos partes.* Mexico, 1841. [Libretto only.]

————, *Lucie de Lammermoor, Grand Opéra en deux actes et en quatre parties, représenté pour la première fois, à Paris ... Paroles de MM. Alphonse Royer et Gustave Vaëz.* Paris, 1839.

————, *Lucie de Lammermoor. Paroles de M.M. Alphonse Royer et Gustave Vaëz, opéra en quatre actes.* Paris, [n.d.]. [Piano and vocal score.]

Ducange, Victor, *La Fiancée de Lammermoor. Pièce héroique en ·trois actes; imitée du roman de Sir Walter-Scott.* Paris, 1828.

Gell, Sir William, *Reminiscences of Sir Walter Scott's Residence in Italy, 1832.* London, 1957.

Graham, John Murray, *Annals and Correspondence of the Viscount and the First and Second Earls of Stair.* Two volumes, Edinburgh, 1875.

Grout, Donald Jay, *A Short History of Opera.* Two volumes, New York, 1947.

Klein, Herman, *The Reign of Patti.* New York, 1920.

————, *Thirty Years of Musical Life in London.* New York, 1903.

Lockhart, John Gibson, *The Life of Sir Walter Scott.* Boston, [1902–3].

Loewenberg, Alfred, *Annals of Opera, 1597–1940.* Second edition, two volumes, Geneva, [1955].

[Maidment, James, editor], *A Book of Scotish Pasquils, 1568–1715.* Edinburgh, 1868.

Mapleson, J. H., *The Mapleson Memoirs, 1848–1888.* Second edition, London, 1888.

Odell, George C. D., *Annals of the New York Stage.* New York, 1927–1949.

Scott, Sir Walter, *The Bride of Lammermoor.* Andrew Lang edition, with Introductory Essay and Notes by Andrew Lang, Boston, 1893.

Weinstock, Herbert, *Donizetti and the World of Opera in Italy, Paris, and Vienna in the First Half of the Nineteenth Century.* New York, 1963. [Very rich biographical and cultural study, but with little musical data; the standard English-language biography.]

White, Henry Adalbert, *Sir Walter Scott's Novels on the Stage.* Yale Studies in English, Vol. 76, New Haven, 1927.

Zavadini, Guido, *Donizetti: Vita, Musiche, Epistolario.* Bergamo, [1948]. [The indispensable book for the study of Donizetti, with listings of all music, all Donizetti's known letters, etc.]

A CATALOGUE OF SELECTED DOVER BOOKS
IN ALL FIELDS OF INTEREST

A CATALOGUE OF SELECTED DOVER BOOKS
IN ALL FIELDS OF INTEREST

AMERICA'S OLD MASTERS, James T. Flexner. Four men emerged unexpectedly from provincial 18th century America to leadership in European art: Benjamin West, J. S. Copley, C. R. Peale, Gilbert Stuart. Brilliant coverage of lives and contributions. Revised, 1967 edition. 69 plates. 365pp. of text.

21806-6 Paperbound $3.00

FIRST FLOWERS OF OUR WILDERNESS: AMERICAN PAINTING, THE COLONIAL PERIOD, James T. Flexner. Painters, and regional painting traditions from earliest Colonial times up to the emergence of Copley, West and Peale Sr., Foster, Gustavus Hesselius, Feke, John Smibert and many anonymous painters in the primitive manner. Engaging presentation, with 162 illustrations. xxii + 368pp.

22180-6 Paperbound $3.50

THE LIGHT OF DISTANT SKIES: AMERICAN PAINTING, 1760-1835, James T. Flexner. The great generation of early American painters goes to Europe to learn and to teach: West, Copley, Gilbert Stuart and others. Allston, Trumbull, Morse; also contemporary American painters—primitives, derivatives, academics—who remained in America. 102 illustrations. xiii + 306pp. 22179-2 Paperbound $3.00

A HISTORY OF THE RISE AND PROGRESS OF THE ARTS OF DESIGN IN THE UNITED STATES, William Dunlap. Much the richest mine of information on early American painters, sculptors, architects, engravers, miniaturists, etc. The only source of information for scores of artists, the major primary source for many others. Unabridged reprint of rare original 1834 edition, with new introduction by James T. Flexner, and 394 new illustrations. Edited by Rita Weiss. 6⅝ x 9⅝.

21695-0, 21696-9, 21697-7 Three volumes, Paperbound $13.50

EPOCHS OF CHINESE AND JAPANESE ART, Ernest F. Fenollosa. From primitive Chinese art to the 20th century, thorough history, explanation of every important art period and form, including Japanese woodcuts; main stress on China and Japan, but Tibet, Korea also included. Still unexcelled for its detailed, rich coverage of cultural background, aesthetic elements, diffusion studies, particularly of the historical period. 2nd, 1913 edition. 242 illustrations. lii + 439pp. of text.

20364-6, 20365-4 Two volumes, Paperbound $6.00

THE GENTLE ART OF MAKING ENEMIES, James A. M. Whistler. Greatest wit of his day deflates Oscar Wilde, Ruskin, Swinburne; strikes back at inane critics, exhibitions, art journalism; aesthetics of impressionist revolution in most striking form. Highly readable classic by great painter. Reproduction of edition designed by Whistler. Introduction by Alfred Werner. xxxvi + 334pp.

21875-9 Paperbound $2.50

VISUAL ILLUSIONS: THEIR CAUSES, CHARACTERISTICS, AND APPLICATIONS, Matthew Luckiesh. Thorough description and discussion of optical illusion, geometric and perspective, particularly; size and shape distortions, illusions of color, of motion; natural illusions; use of illusion in art and magic, industry, etc. Most useful today with op art, also for classical art. Scores of effects illustrated. Introduction by William H. Ittleson. 100 illustrations. xxi + 252pp.
21530-X Paperbound $2.00

A HANDBOOK OF ANATOMY FOR ART STUDENTS, Arthur Thomson. Thorough, virtually exhaustive coverage of skeletal structure, musculature, etc. Full text, supplemented by anatomical diagrams and drawings and by photographs of undraped figures. Unique in its comparison of male and female forms, pointing out differences of contour, texture, form. 211 figures, 40 drawings, 86 photographs. xx + 459pp.
5⅜ x 8⅜. 21163-0 Paperbound $3.50

150 MASTERPIECES OF DRAWING, Selected by Anthony Toney. Full page reproductions of drawings from the early 16th to the end of the 18th century, all beautifully reproduced: Rembrandt, Michelangelo, Dürer, Fragonard, Urs, Graf, Wouwerman, many others. First-rate browsing book, model book for artists. xviii + 150pp.
8⅜ x 11¼. 21032-4 Paperbound $2.50

THE LATER WORK OF AUBREY BEARDSLEY, Aubrey Beardsley. Exotic, erotic, ironic masterpieces in full maturity: Comedy Ballet, Venus and Tannhauser, Pierrot, Lysistrata, Rape of the Lock, Savoy material, Ali Baba, Volpone, etc. This material revolutionized the art world, and is still powerful, fresh, brilliant. With *The Early Work,* all Beardsley's finest work. 174 plates, 2 in color. xiv + 176pp. 8⅛ x 11.
21817-1 Paperbound $3.00

DRAWINGS OF REMBRANDT, Rembrandt van Rijn. Complete reproduction of fabulously rare edition by Lippmann and Hofstede de Groot, completely reedited, updated, improved by Prof. Seymour Slive, Fogg Museum. Portraits, Biblical sketches, landscapes, Oriental types, nudes, episodes from classical mythology—All Rembrandt's fertile genius. Also selection of drawings by his pupils and followers. "Stunning volumes," *Saturday Review.* 550 illustrations. lxxviii + 552pp.
9⅛ x 12¼. 21485-0, 21486-9 Two volumes, Paperbound $7.00

THE DISASTERS OF WAR, Francisco Goya. One of the masterpieces of Western civilization—83 etchings that record Goya's shattering, bitter reaction to the Napoleonic war that swept through Spain after the insurrection of 1808 and to war in general. Reprint of the first edition, with three additional plates from Boston's Museum of Fine Arts. All plates facsimile size. Introduction by Philip Hofer, Fogg Museum.
v + 97pp. 9⅜ x 8¼. 21872-4 Paperbound $2.00

GRAPHIC WORKS OF ODILON REDON. Largest collection of Redon's graphic works ever assembled: 172 lithographs, 28 etchings and engravings, 9 drawings. These include some of his most famous works. All the plates from *Odilon Redon: oeuvre graphique complet,* plus additional plates. New introduction and caption translations by Alfred Werner. 209 illustrations. xxvii + 209pp. 9⅛ x 12¼.
21966-8 Paperbound $4.00

DESIGN BY ACCIDENT; A BOOK OF "ACCIDENTAL EFFECTS" FOR ARTISTS AND DESIGNERS, James F. O'Brien. Create your own unique, striking, imaginative effects by "controlled accident" interaction of materials: paints and lacquers, oil and water based paints, splatter, crackling materials, shatter, similar items. Everything you do will be different; first book on this limitless art, so useful to both fine artist and commercial artist. Full instructions. 192 plates showing "accidents," 8 in color. viii + 215pp. 8⅜ x 11¼. 21942-9 Paperbound $3.50

THE BOOK OF SIGNS, Rudolf Koch. Famed German type designer draws 493 beautiful symbols: religious, mystical, alchemical, imperial, property marks, runes, etc. Remarkable fusion of traditional and modern. Good for suggestions of timelessness, smartness, modernity. Text. vi + 104pp. 6⅛ x 9¼.
20162-7 Paperbound $1.25

HISTORY OF INDIAN AND INDONESIAN ART, Ananda K. Coomaraswamy. An unabridged republication of one of the finest books by a great scholar in Eastern art. Rich in descriptive material, history, social backgrounds; Sunga reliefs, Rajput paintings, Gupta temples, Burmese frescoes, textiles, jewelry, sculpture, etc. 400 photos. viii + 423pp. 6⅜ x 9¾. 21436-2 Paperbound $4.00

PRIMITIVE ART, Franz Boas. America's foremost anthropologist surveys textiles, ceramics, woodcarving, basketry, metalwork, etc.; patterns, technology, creation of symbols, style origins. All areas of world, but very full on Northwest Coast Indians. More than 350 illustrations of baskets, boxes, totem poles, weapons, etc. 378 pp.
20025-6 Paperbound $3.00

THE GENTLEMAN AND CABINET MAKER'S DIRECTOR, Thomas Chippendale. Full reprint (third edition, 1762) of most influential furniture book of all time, by master cabinetmaker. 200 plates, illustrating chairs, sofas, mirrors, tables, cabinets, plus 24 photographs of surviving pieces. Biographical introduction by N. Bienenstock. vi + 249pp. 9⅞ x 12¾. 21601-2 Paperbound $4.00

AMERICAN ANTIQUE FURNITURE, Edgar G. Miller, Jr. The basic coverage of all American furniture before 1840. Individual chapters cover type of furniture—clocks, tables, sideboards, etc.—chronologically, with inexhaustible wealth of data. More than 2100 photographs, all identified, commented on. Essential to all early American collectors. Introduction by H. E. Keyes. vi + 1106pp. 7⅞ x 10¾.
21599-7, 21600-4 Two volumes, Paperbound $11.00

PENNSYLVANIA DUTCH AMERICAN FOLK ART, Henry J. Kauffman. 279 photos, 28 drawings of tulipware, Fraktur script, painted tinware, toys, flowered furniture, quilts, samplers, hex signs, house interiors, etc. Full descriptive text. Excellent for tourist, rewarding for designer, collector. Map. 146pp. 7⅞ x 10¾.
21205-X Paperbound $2.50

EARLY NEW ENGLAND GRAVESTONE RUBBINGS, Edmund V. Gillon, Jr. 43 photographs, 226 carefully reproduced rubbings show heavily symbolic, sometimes macabre early gravestones, up to early 19th century. Remarkable early American primitive art, occasionally strikingly beautiful; always powerful. Text. xxvi + 207pp. 8⅜ x 11¼. 21380-3 Paperbound $3.50

ALPHABETS AND ORNAMENTS, Ernst Lehner. Well-known pictorial source for decorative alphabets, script examples, cartouches, frames, decorative title pages, calligraphic initials, borders, similar material. 14th to 19th century, mostly European. Useful in almost any graphic arts designing, varied styles. 750 illustrations. 256pp. 7 x 10.   21905-4 Paperbound $4.00

PAINTING: A CREATIVE APPROACH, Norman Colquhoun. For the beginner simple guide provides an instructive approach to painting: major stumbling blocks for beginner; overcoming them, technical points; paints and pigments; oil painting; watercolor and other media and color. New section on "plastic" paints. Glossary. Formerly *Paint Your Own Pictures*. 221pp.   22000-1 Paperbound $1.75

THE ENJOYMENT AND USE OF COLOR, Walter Sargent. Explanation of the relations between colors themselves and between colors in nature and art, including hundreds of little-known facts about color values, intensities, effects of high and low illumination, complementary colors. Many practical hints for painters, references to great masters. 7 color plates, 29 illustrations. x + 274pp.
20944-X Paperbound $2.75

THE NOTEBOOKS OF LEONARDO DA VINCI, compiled and edited by Jean Paul Richter. 1566 extracts from original manuscripts reveal the full range of Leonardo's versatile genius: all his writings on painting, sculpture, architecture, anatomy, astronomy, geography, topography, physiology, mining, music, etc., in both Italian and English, with 186 plates of manuscript pages and more than 500 additional drawings. Includes studies for the Last Supper, the lost Sforza monument, and other works. Total of xlvii + 866pp. 7⅞ x 10¾.
22572-0, 22573-9 Two volumes, Paperbound $10.00

MONTGOMERY WARD CATALOGUE OF 1895. Tea gowns, yards of flannel and pillow-case lace, stereoscopes, books of gospel hymns, the New Improved Singer Sewing Machine, side saddles, milk skimmers, straight-edged razors, high-button shoes, spittoons, and on and on . . . listing some 25,000 items, practically all illustrated. Essential to the shoppers of the 1890's, it is our truest record of the spirit of the period. Unaltered reprint of Issue No. 57, Spring and Summer 1895. Introduction by Boris Emmet. Innumerable illustrations. xiii + 624pp. 8½ x 11⅝.
22377-9 Paperbound $6.95

THE CRYSTAL PALACE EXHIBITION ILLUSTRATED CATALOGUE (LONDON, 1851). One of the wonders of the modern world—the Crystal Palace Exhibition in which all the nations of the civilized world exhibited their achievements in the arts and sciences—presented in an equally important illustrated catalogue. More than 1700 items pictured with accompanying text—ceramics, textiles, cast-iron work, carpets, pianos, sleds, razors, wall-papers, billiard tables, beehives, silverware and hundreds of other artifacts—represent the focal point of Victorian culture in the Western World. Probably the largest collection of Victorian decorative art ever assembled— indispensable for antiquarians and designers. Unabridged republication of the Art-Journal Catalogue of the Great Exhibition of 1851, with all terminal essays. New introduction by John Gloag, F.S.A. xxxiv + 426pp. 9 x 12.
22503-8 Paperbound $4.50

A History of Costume, Carl Köhler. Definitive history, based on surviving pieces of clothing primarily, and paintings, statues, etc. secondarily. Highly readable text, supplemented by 594 illustrations of costumes of the ancient Mediterranean peoples, Greece and Rome, the Teutonic prehistoric period; costumes of the Middle Ages, Renaissance, Baroque, 18th and 19th centuries. Clear, measured patterns are provided for many clothing articles. Approach is practical throughout. Enlarged by Emma von Sichart. 464pp.   21030-8 Paperbound $3.50

Oriental Rugs, Antique and Modern, Walter A. Hawley. A complete and authoritative treatise on the Oriental rug—where they are made, by whom and how, designs and symbols, characteristics in detail of the six major groups, how to distinguish them and how to buy them. Detailed technical data is provided on periods, weaves, warps, wefts, textures, sides, ends and knots, although no technical background is required for an understanding. 11 color plates, 80 halftones, 4 maps. vi + 320pp. 6⅛ x 9⅛.   22366-3 Paperbound $5.00

Ten Books on Architecture, Vitruvius. By any standards the most important book on architecture ever written. Early Roman discussion of aesthetics of building, construction methods, orders, sites, and every other aspect of architecture has inspired, instructed architecture for about 2,000 years. Stands behind Palladio, Michelangelo, Bramante, Wren, countless others. Definitive Morris H. Morgan translation. 68 illustrations. xii + 331pp.   20645-9 Paperbound $2.50

The Four Books of Architecture, Andrea Palladio. Translated into every major Western European language in the two centuries following its publication in 1570, this has been one of the most influential books in the history of architecture. Complete reprint of the 1738 Isaac Ware edition. New introduction by Adolf Placzek, Columbia Univ. 216 plates. xxii + 110pp. of text. 9½ x 12¾.
                    21308-0 Clothbound $10.00

Sticks and Stones: A Study of American Architecture and Civilization, Lewis Mumford.One of the great classics of American cultural history. American architecture from the medieval-inspired earliest forms to the early 20th century; evolution of structure and style, and reciprocal influences on environment. 21 photographic illustrations. 238pp.   20202-X Paperbound $2.00

The American Builder's Companion, Asher Benjamin. The most widely used early 19th century architectural style and source book, for colonial up into Greek Revival periods. Extensive development of geometry of carpentering, construction of sashes, frames, doors, stairs; plans and elevations of domestic and other buildings. Hundreds of thousands of houses were built according to this book, now invaluable to historians, architects, restorers, etc. 1827 edition. 59 plates. 114pp. 7⅞ x 10¾.
                    22236-5 Paperbound $3.00

Dutch Houses in the Hudson Valley Before 1776, Helen Wilkinson Reynolds. The standard survey of the Dutch colonial house and outbuildings, with constructional features, decoration, and local history associated with individual homesteads. Introduction by Franklin D. Roosevelt. Map. 150 illustrations. 469pp. 6⅝ x 9¼.   21469-9 Paperbound $4.00

THE ARCHITECTURE OF COUNTRY HOUSES, Andrew J. Downing. Together with Vaux's *Villas and Cottages* this is the basic book for Hudson River Gothic architecture of the middle Victorian period. Full, sound discussions of general aspects of housing, architecture, style, decoration, furnishing, together with scores of detailed house plans, illustrations of specific buildings, accompanied by full text. Perhaps the most influential single American architectural book. 1850 edition. Introduction by J. Stewart Johnson. 321 figures, 34 architectural designs. xvi + 560pp.
22003-6 Paperbound $4.00

LOST EXAMPLES OF COLONIAL ARCHITECTURE, John Mead Howells. Full-page photographs of buildings that have disappeared or been so altered as to be denatured, including many designed by major early American architects. 245 plates. xvii + 248pp. 7⅞ x 10¾.
21143-6 Paperbound $3.50

DOMESTIC ARCHITECTURE OF THE AMERICAN COLONIES AND OF THE EARLY REPUBLIC, Fiske Kimball. Foremost architect and restorer of Williamsburg and Monticello covers nearly 200 homes between 1620-1825. Architectural details, construction, style features, special fixtures, floor plans, etc. Generally considered finest work in its area. 219 illustrations of houses, doorways, windows, capital mantels. xx + 314pp. 7⅞ x 10¾.
21743-4 Paperbound $4.00

EARLY AMERICAN ROOMS: 1650-1858, edited by Russell Hawes Kettell. Tour of 12 rooms, each representative of a different era in American history and each furnished, decorated, designed and occupied in the style of the era. 72 plans and elevations, 8-page color section, etc., show fabrics, wall papers, arrangements, etc. Full descriptive text. xvii + 200pp. of text. 8⅜ x 11¼.
21633-0 Paperbound $5.00

THE FITZWILLIAM VIRGINAL BOOK, edited by J. Fuller Maitland and W. B. Squire. Full modern printing of famous early 17th-century ms. volume of 300 works by Morley, Byrd, Bull, Gibbons, etc. For piano or other modern keyboard instrument; easy to read format. xxxvi + 938pp. 8⅜ x 11.
21068-5, 21069-3 Two volumes, Paperbound $10.00

KEYBOARD MUSIC, Johann Sebastian Bach. Bach Gesellschaft edition. A rich selection of Bach's masterpieces for the harpsichord: the six English Suites, six French Suites, the six Partitas (Clavierübung part I), the Goldberg Variations (Clavierübung part IV), the fifteen Two-Part Inventions and the fifteen Three-Part Sinfonias. Clearly reproduced on large sheets with ample margins; eminently playable. vi + 312pp. 8⅛ x 11.
22360-4 Paperbound $5.00

THE MUSIC OF BACH: AN INTRODUCTION, Charles Sanford Terry. A fine, non-technical introduction to Bach's music, both instrumental and vocal. Covers organ music, chamber music, passion music, other types. Analyzes themes, developments, innovations. x + 114pp.
21075-8 Paperbound $1.25

BEETHOVEN AND HIS NINE SYMPHONIES, Sir George Grove. Noted British musicologist provides best history, analysis, commentary on symphonies. Very thorough, rigorously accurate; necessary to both advanced student and amateur music lover. 436 musical passages. vii + 407 pp.
20334-4 Paperbound $2.75

JOHANN SEBASTIAN BACH, Philipp Spitta. One of the great classics of musicology, this definitive analysis of Bach's music (and life) has never been surpassed. Lucid, nontechnical analyses of hundreds of pieces (30 pages devoted to St. Matthew Passion, 26 to B Minor Mass). Also includes major analysis of 18th-century music. 450 musical examples. 40-page musical supplement. Total of xx + 1799pp.
(EUK) 22278-0, 22279-9 Two volumes, Clothbound $17.50

MOZART AND HIS PIANO CONCERTOS, Cuthbert Girdlestone. The only full-length study of an important area of Mozart's creativity. Provides detailed analyses of all 23 concertos, traces inspirational sources. 417 musical examples. Second edition. 509pp.
(USO) 21271-8 Paperbound $3.50

THE PERFECT WAGNERITE: A COMMENTARY ON THE NIBLUNG'S RING, George Bernard Shaw. Brilliant and still relevant criticism in remarkable essays on Wagner's Ring cycle, Shaw's ideas on political and social ideology behind the plots, role of Leitmotifs, vocal requisites, etc. Prefaces. xxi + 136pp.
21707-8 Paperbound $1.50

DON GIOVANNI, W. A. Mozart. Complete libretto, modern English translation; biographies of composer and librettist; accounts of early performances and critical reaction. Lavishly illustrated. All the material you need to understand and appreciate this great work. Dover Opera Guide and Libretto Series; translated and introduced by Ellen Bleiler. 92 illustrations. 209pp.
21134-7 Paperbound $1:50

HIGH FIDELITY SYSTEMS: A LAYMAN'S GUIDE, Roy F. Allison. All the basic information you need for setting up your own audio system: high fidelity and stereo record players, tape records, F.M. Connections, adjusting tone arm, cartridge, checking needle alignment, positioning speakers, phasing speakers, adjusting hums, trouble-shooting, maintenance, and similar topics. Enlarged 1965 edition. More than 50 charts, diagrams, photos. iv + 91pp.
21514-8 Paperbound $1.25

REPRODUCTION OF SOUND, Edgar Villchur. Thorough coverage for laymen of high fidelity systems, reproducing systems in general, needles, amplifiers, preamps, loudspeakers, feedback, explaining physical background. "A rare talent for making technicalities vividly comprehensible," R. Darrell, *High Fidelity*. 69 figures. iv + 92pp.
21515-6 Paperbound $1.25

HEAR ME TALKIN' TO YA: THE STORY OF JAZZ AS TOLD BY THE MEN WHO MADE IT, Nat Shapiro and Nat Hentoff. Louis Armstrong, Fats Waller, Jo Jones, Clarence Williams, Billy Holiday, Duke Ellington, Jelly Roll Morton and dozens of other jazz greats tell how it was in Chicago's South Side, New Orleans, depression Harlem and the modern West Coast as jazz was born and grew. xvi + 429pp.
21726-4 Paperbound $2.50

FABLES OF AESOP, translated by Sir Roger L'Estrange. A reproduction of the very rare 1931 Paris edition; a selection of the most interesting fables, together with 50 imaginative drawings by Alexander Calder. v + 128pp. 6½x9¼.
21780-9 Paperbound $1.50

AGAINST THE GRAIN (A REBOURS), Joris K. Huysmans. Filled with weird images, evidences of a bizarre imagination, exotic experiments with hallucinatory drugs, rich tastes and smells and the diversions of its sybarite hero Duc Jean des Esseintes, this classic novel pushed 19th-century literary decadence to its limits. Full unabridged edition. Do not confuse this with abridged editions generally sold. Introduction by Havelock Ellis. xlix + 206pp.   22190-3 Paperbound $2.00

VARIORUM SHAKESPEARE: HAMLET. Edited by Horace H. Furness; a landmark of American scholarship. Exhaustive footnotes and appendices treat all doubtful words and phrases, as well as suggested critical emendations throughout the play's history. First volume contains editor's own text, collated with all Quartos and Folios. Second volume contains full first Quarto, translations of Shakespeare's sources (Belleforest, and Saxo Grammaticus), Der Bestrafte Brudermord, and many essays on critical and historical points of interest by major authorities of past and present. Includes details of staging and costuming over the years. By far the best edition available for serious students of Shakespeare. Total of xx + 905pp.
21004-9, 21005-7, 2 volumes, Paperbound $7.00

A LIFE OF WILLIAM SHAKESPEARE, Sir Sidney Lee. This is the standard life of Shakespeare, summarizing everything known about Shakespeare and his plays. Incredibly rich in material, broad in coverage, clear and judicious, it has served thousands as the best introduction to Shakespeare. 1931 edition. 9 plates. xxix + 792pp.   (USO) 21967-4 Paperbound $3.75

MASTERS OF THE DRAMA, John Gassner. Most comprehensive history of the drama in print, covering every tradition from Greeks to modern Europe and America, including India, Far East, etc. Covers more than 800 dramatists, 2000 plays, with biographical material, plot summaries, theatre history, criticism, etc. "Best of its kind in English," *New Republic*. 77 illustrations. xxii + 890pp.
20100-7 Clothbound $8.50

THE EVOLUTION OF THE ENGLISH LANGUAGE, George McKnight. The growth of English, from the 14th century to the present. Unusual, non-technical account presents basic information in very interesting form: sound shifts, change in grammar and syntax, vocabulary growth, similar topics. Abundantly illustrated with quotations. Formerly *Modern English in the Making*. xii + 590pp.
21932-1 Paperbound $3.50

AN ETYMOLOGICAL DICTIONARY OF MODERN ENGLISH, Ernest Weekley. Fullest, richest work of its sort, by foremost British lexicographer. Detailed word histories, including many colloquial and archaic words; extensive quotations. Do not confuse this with the Concise Etymological Dictionary, which is much abridged. Total of xxvii + 830pp. 6½ x 9¼.
21873-2, 21874-0 Two volumes, Paperbound $6.00

FLATLAND: A ROMANCE OF MANY DIMENSIONS, E. A. Abbott. Classic of science-fiction explores ramifications of life in a two-dimensional world, and what happens when a three-dimensional being intrudes. Amusing reading, but also useful as introduction to thought about hyperspace. Introduction by Banesh Hoffmann. 16 illustrations. xx + 103pp.   20001-9 Paperbound $1.00

POEMS OF ANNE BRADSTREET, edited with an introduction by Robert Hutchinson. A new selection of poems by America's first poet and perhaps the first significant woman poet in the English language. 48 poems display her development in works of considerable variety—love poems, domestic poems, religious meditations, formal elegies, "quaternions," etc. Notes, bibliography. viii + 222pp.
22160-1 Paperbound $2.00

THREE GOTHIC NOVELS: THE CASTLE OF OTRANTO BY HORACE WALPOLE; VATHEK BY WILLIAM BECKFORD; THE VAMPYRE BY JOHN POLIDORI, WITH FRAGMENT OF A NOVEL BY LORD BYRON, edited by E. F. Bleiler. The first Gothic novel, by Walpole; the finest Oriental tale in English, by Beckford; powerful Romantic supernatural story in versions by Polidori and Byron. All extremely important in history of literature; all still exciting, packed with supernatural thrills, ghosts, haunted castles, magic, etc. xl + 291pp.
21232-7 Paperbound $2.00

THE BEST TALES OF HOFFMANN, E. T. A. Hoffmann. 10 of Hoffmann's most important stories, in modern re-editings of standard translations: Nutcracker and the King of Mice, Signor Formica, Automata, The Sandman, Rath Krespel, The Golden Flowerpot, Master Martin the Cooper, The Mines of Falun, The King's Betrothed, A New Year's Eve Adventure. 7 illustrations by Hoffmann. Edited by E. F. Bleiler. xxxix + 419pp.
21793-0 Paperbound $2.50

GHOST AND HORROR STORIES OF AMBROSE BIERCE, Ambrose Bierce. 23 strikingly modern stories of the horrors latent in the human mind: The Eyes of the Panther, The Damned Thing, An Occurrence at Owl Creek Bridge, An Inhabitant of Carcosa, etc., plus the dream-essay, Visions of the Night. Edited by E. F. Bleiler. xxii + 199pp.
20767-6 Paperbound $1.50

BEST GHOST STORIES OF J. S. LEFANU, J. Sheridan LeFanu. Finest stories by Victorian master often considered greatest supernatural writer of all. Carmilla, Green Tea, The Haunted Baronet, The Familiar, and 12 others. Most never before available in the U. S. A. Edited by E. F. Bleiler. 8 illustrations from Victorian publications. xvii + 467pp.
20415-4 Paperbound $3.00

THE TIME STREAM, THE GREATEST ADVENTURE, AND THE PURPLE SAPPHIRE— THREE SCIENCE FICTION NOVELS, John Taine (Eric Temple Bell). Great American mathematician was also foremost science fiction novelist of the 1920's. The Time Stream, one of all-time classics, uses concepts of circular time; The Greatest Adventure, incredibly ancient biological experiments from Antarctica threaten to escape; The Purple Sapphire, superscience, lost races in Central Tibet, survivors of the Great Race. 4 illustrations by Frank R. Paul. v + 532pp.
21180-0 Paperbound $3.00

SEVEN SCIENCE FICTION NOVELS, H. G. Wells. The standard collection of the great novels. Complete, unabridged. First Men in the Moon, Island of Dr. Moreau, War of the Worlds, Food of the Gods, Invisible Man, Time Machine, In the Days of the Comet. Not only science fiction fans, but every educated person owes it to himself to read these novels. 1015pp.
20264-X Clothbound $5.00

LAST AND FIRST MEN AND STAR MAKER, TWO SCIENCE FICTION NOVELS, Olaf Stapledon. Greatest future histories in science fiction. In the first, human intelligence is the "hero," through strange paths of evolution, interplanetary invasions, incredible technologies, near extinctions and reemergences. Star Maker describes the quest of a band of star rovers for intelligence itself, through time and space: weird inhuman civilizations, crustacean minds, symbiotic worlds, etc. Complete, unabridged. v + 438pp.   21962-3 Paperbound $2.50

THREE PROPHETIC NOVELS, H. G. WELLS. Stages of a consistently planned future for mankind. *When the Sleeper Wakes,* and *A Story of the Days to Come,* anticipate *Brave New World* and *1984,* in the 21st Century; *The Time Machine,* only complete version in print, shows farther future and the end of mankind. All show Wells's greatest gifts as storyteller and novelist. Edited by E. F. Bleiler. x + 335pp.   (USO) 20605-X Paperbound $2.25

THE DEVIL'S DICTIONARY, Ambrose Bierce. America's own Oscar Wilde— Ambrose Bierce—offers his barbed iconoclastic wisdom in over 1,000 definitions hailed by H. L. Mencken as "some of the most gorgeous witticisms in the English language." 145pp.   20487-1 Paperbound $1.25

MAX AND MORITZ, Wilhelm Busch. Great children's classic, father of comic strip, of two bad boys, Max and Moritz. Also Ker and Plunk (Plisch und Plumm), Cat and Mouse, Deceitful Henry, Ice-Peter, The Boy and the Pipe, and five other pieces. Original German, with English translation. Edited by H. Arthur Klein; translations by various hands and H. Arthur Klein. vi + 216pp.
                    20181-3 Paperbound $2.00

PIGS IS PIGS AND OTHER FAVORITES, Ellis Parker Butler. The title story is one of the best humor short stories, as Mike Flannery obfuscates biology and English. Also included, That Pup of Murchison's, The Great American Pie Company, and Perkins of Portland. 14 illustrations. v + 109pp.   21532-6 Paperbound $1.00

THE PETERKIN PAPERS, Lucretia P. Hale. It takes genius to be as stupidly mad as the Peterkins, as they decide to become wise, celebrate the "Fourth," keep a cow, and otherwise strain the resources of the Lady from Philadelphia. Basic book of American humor. 153 illustrations. 219pp.   20794-3 Paperbound $1.50

PERRAULT'S FAIRY TALES, translated by A. E. Johnson and S. R. Littlewood, with 34 full-page illustrations by Gustave Doré. All the original Perrault stories— Cinderella, Sleeping Beauty, Bluebeard, Little Red Riding Hood, Puss in Boots, Tom Thumb, etc.—with their witty verse morals and the magnificent illustrations of Doré. One of the five or six great books of European fairy tales. viii + 117pp. 8⅛ x 11.   22311-6 Paperbound $2.00

OLD HUNGARIAN FAIRY TALES, Baroness Orczy. Favorites translated and adapted by author of the *Scarlet Pimpernel.* Eight fairy tales include "The Suitors of Princess Fire-Fly," "The Twin Hunchbacks," "Mr. Cuttlefish's Love Story," and "The Enchanted Cat." This little volume of magic and adventure will captivate children as it has for generations. 90 drawings by Montagu Barstow. 96pp.
                    (USO) 22293-4 Paperbound $1.95

THE RED FAIRY BOOK, Andrew Lang. Lang's color fairy books have long been children's favorites. This volume includes Rapunzel, Jack and the Bean-stalk and 35 other stories, familiar and unfamiliar. 4 plates, 93 illustrations x + 367pp.
21673-X Paperbound $2.50

THE BLUE FAIRY BOOK, Andrew Lang. Lang's tales come from all countries and all times. Here are 37 tales from Grimm, the Arabian Nights, Greek Mythology, and other fascinating sources. 8 plates, 130 illustrations. xi + 390pp.
21437-0 Paperbound $2.50

HOUSEHOLD STORIES BY THE BROTHERS GRIMM. Classic English-language edition of the well-known tales — Rumpelstiltskin, Snow White, Hansel and Gretel, The Twelve Brothers, Faithful John, Rapunzel, Tom Thumb (52 stories in all). Translated into simple, straightforward English by Lucy Crane. Ornamented with head-pieces, vignettes, elaborate decorative initials and a dozen full-page illustrations by Walter Crane. x + 269pp. 21080-4 Paperbound $2.50

THE MERRY ADVENTURES OF ROBIN HOOD, Howard Pyle. The finest modern versions of the traditional ballads and tales about the great English outlaw. Howard Pyle's complete prose version, with every word, every illustration of the first edition. Do not confuse this facsimile of the original (1883) with modern editions that change text or illustrations. 23 plates plus many page decorations. xxii + 296pp.
22043-5 Paperbound $2.50

THE STORY OF KING ARTHUR AND HIS KNIGHTS, Howard Pyle. The finest children's version of the life of King Arthur; brilliantly retold by Pyle, with 48 of his most imaginative illustrations. xviii + 313pp. 6⅛ x 9¼.
21445-1 Paperbound $2.50

THE WONDERFUL WIZARD OF OZ, L. Frank Baum. America's finest children's book in facsimile of first edition with all Denslow illustrations in full color. The edition a child should have. Introduction by Martin Gardner. 23 color plates, scores of drawings. iv + 267pp. 20691-2 Paperbound $2.25

THE MARVELOUS LAND OF OZ, L. Frank Baum. The second Oz book, every bit as imaginative as the Wizard. The hero is a boy named Tip, but the Scarecrow and the Tin Woodman are back, as is the Oz magic. 16 color plates, 120 drawings by John R. Neill. 287pp. 20692-0 Paperbound $2.50

THE MAGICAL MONARCH OF MO, L. Frank Baum. Remarkable adventures in a land even stranger than Oz. The best of Baum's books not in the Oz series. 15 color plates and dozens of drawings by Frank Verbeck. xviii + 237pp.
21892-9 Paperbound $2.00

THE BAD CHILD'S BOOK OF BEASTS, MORE BEASTS FOR WORSE CHILDREN, A MORAL ALPHABET, Hilaire Belloc. Three complete humor classics in one volume. Be kind to the frog, and do not call him names . . . and 28 other whimsical animals. Familiar favorites and some not so well known. Illustrated by Basil Blackwell. 156pp. (USO) 20749-8 Paperbound $1.25

EAST O' THE SUN AND WEST O' THE MOON, George W. Dasent. Considered the best of all translations of these Norwegian folk tales, this collection has been enjoyed by generations of children (and folklorists too). Includes True and Untrue, Why the Sea is Salt, East O' the Sun and West O' the Moon, Why the Bear is Stumpy-Tailed, Boots and the Troll, The Cock and the Hen, Rich Peter the Pedlar, and 52 more. The only edition with all 59 tales. 77 illustrations by Erik Werenskiold and Theodor Kittelsen. xv + 418pp. 22521-6 Paperbound $3.00

GOOPS AND HOW TO BE THEM, Gelett Burgess. Classic of tongue-in-cheek humor, masquerading as etiquette book. 87 verses, twice as many cartoons, show mischievous Goops as they demonstrate to children virtues of table manners, neatness, courtesy, etc. Favorite for generations. viii + 88pp. 6½ x 9¼.
22233-0 Paperbound $1.25

ALICE'S ADVENTURES UNDER GROUND, Lewis Carroll. The first version, quite different from the final Alice in Wonderland, printed out by Carroll himself with his own illustrations. Complete facsimile of the "million dollar" manuscript Carroll gave to Alice Liddell in 1864. Introduction by Martin Gardner. viii + 96pp. Title and dedication pages in color. 21482-6 Paperbound $1.25

THE BROWNIES, THEIR BOOK, Palmer Cox. Small as mice, cunning as foxes, exuberant and full of mischief, the Brownies go to the zoo, toy shop, seashore, circus, etc., in 24 verse adventures and 266 illustrations. Long a favorite, since their first appearance in St. Nicholas Magazine. xi + 144pp. 6⅝ x 9¼.
21265-3 Paperbound $1.75

SONGS OF CHILDHOOD, Walter De La Mare. Published (under the pseudonym Walter Ramal) when De La Mare was only 29, this charming collection has long been a favorite children's book. A facsimile of the first edition in paper, the 47 poems capture the simplicity of the nursery rhyme and the ballad, including such lyrics as I Met Eve, Tartary, The Silver Penny. vii + 106pp. 21972-0 Paperbound $1.25

THE COMPLETE NONSENSE OF EDWARD LEAR, Edward Lear. The finest 19th-century humorist-cartoonist in full: all nonsense limericks, zany alphabets, Owl and Pussycat, songs, nonsense botany, and more than 500 illustrations by Lear himself. Edited by Holbrook Jackson. xxix + 287pp. (USO) 20167-8 Paperbound $2.00

BILLY WHISKERS: THE AUTOBIOGRAPHY OF A GOAT, Frances Trego Montgomery. A favorite of children since the early 20th century, here are the escapades of that rambunctious, irresistible and mischievous goat—Billy Whiskers. Much in the spirit of Peck's Bad Boy, this is a book that children never tire of reading or hearing. All the original familiar illustrations by W. H. Fry are included: 6 color plates, 18 black and white drawings. 159pp. 22345-0 Paperbound $2.00

MOTHER GOOSE MELODIES. Faithful republication of the fabulously rare Munroe and Francis "copyright 1833" Boston edition—the most important Mother Goose collection, usually referred to as the "original." Familiar rhymes plus many rare ones, with wonderful old woodcut illustrations. Edited by E. F. Bleiler. 128pp. 4½ x 6⅜. 22577-1 Paperbound $1.25

TWO LITTLE SAVAGES; BEING THE ADVENTURES OF TWO BOYS WHO LIVED AS INDIANS AND WHAT THEY LEARNED, Ernest Thompson Seton. Great classic of nature and boyhood provides a vast range of woodlore in most palatable form, a genuinely entertaining story. Two farm boys build a teepee in woods and live in it for a month, working out Indian solutions to living problems, star lore, birds and animals, plants, etc. 293 illustrations. vii + 286pp.

20985-7 Paperbound $2.50

PETER PIPER'S PRACTICAL PRINCIPLES OF PLAIN & PERFECT PRONUNCIATION. Alliterative jingles and tongue-twisters of surprising charm, that made their first appearance in America about 1830. Republished in full with the spirited woodcut illustrations from this earliest American edition. 32pp. $4\frac{1}{2}$ x $6\frac{3}{8}$.

22560-7 Paperbound $1.00

SCIENCE EXPERIMENTS AND AMUSEMENTS FOR CHILDREN, Charles Vivian. 73 easy experiments, requiring only materials found at home or easily available, such as candles, coins, steel wool, etc.; illustrate basic phenomena like vacuum, simple chemical reaction, etc. All safe. Modern, well-planned. Formerly *Science Games for Children.* 102 photos, numerous drawings. 96pp. $6\frac{1}{8}$ x $9\frac{1}{4}$.

21856-2 Paperbound $1.25

AN INTRODUCTION TO CHESS MOVES AND TACTICS SIMPLY EXPLAINED, Leonard Barden. Informal intermediate introduction, quite strong in explaining reasons for moves. Covers basic material, tactics, important openings, traps, positional play in middle game, end game. Attempts to isolate patterns and recurrent configurations. Formerly *Chess.* 58 figures. 102pp. (USO) 21210-6 Paperbound $1.25

LASKER'S MANUAL OF CHESS, Dr. Emanuel Lasker. Lasker was not only one of the five great World Champions, he was also one of the ablest expositors, theorists, and analysts. In many ways, his Manual, permeated with his philosophy of battle, filled with keen insights, is one of the greatest works ever written on chess. Filled with analyzed games by the great players. A single-volume library that will profit almost any chess player, beginner or master. 308 diagrams. xli x 349pp.

20640-8 Paperbound $2.75

THE MASTER BOOK OF MATHEMATICAL RECREATIONS, Fred Schuh. In opinion of many the finest work ever prepared on mathematical puzzles, stunts, recreations; exhaustively thorough explanations of mathematics involved, analysis of effects, citation of puzzles and games. Mathematics involved is elementary. Translated by F. Göbel. 194 figures. xxiv + 430pp. 22134-2 Paperbound $3.00

MATHEMATICS, MAGIC AND MYSTERY, Martin Gardner. Puzzle editor for Scientific American explains mathematics behind various mystifying tricks: card tricks, stage "mind reading," coin and match tricks, counting out games, geometric dissections, etc. Probability sets, theory of numbers clearly explained. Also provides more than 400 tricks, guaranteed to work, that you can do. 135 illustrations. xii + 176pp.

20338-2 Paperbound $1.50

MATHEMATICAL PUZZLES FOR BEGINNERS AND ENTHUSIASTS, Geoffrey Mott-Smith. 189 puzzles from easy to difficult—involving arithmetic, logic, algebra, properties of digits, probability, etc.—for enjoyment and mental stimulus. Explanation of mathematical principles behind the puzzles. 135 illustrations. viii + 248pp.

20198-8 Paperbound $1.75

PAPER FOLDING FOR BEGINNERS, William D. Murray and Francis J. Rigney. Easiest book on the market, clearest instructions on making interesting, beautiful origami. Sail boats, cups, roosters, frogs that move legs, bonbon boxes, standing birds, etc. 40 projects; more than 275 diagrams and photographs. 94pp.

20713-7 Paperbound $1.00

TRICKS AND GAMES ON THE POOL TABLE, Fred Herrmann. 79 tricks and games—some solitaires, some for two or more players, some competitive games—to entertain you between formal games. Mystifying shots and throws, unusual caroms, tricks involving such props as cork, coins, a hat, etc. Formerly *Fun on the Pool Table*. 77 figures. 95pp.

21814-7 Paperbound $1.00

HAND SHADOWS TO BE THROWN UPON THE WALL: A SERIES OF NOVEL AND AMUSING FIGURES FORMED BY THE HAND, Henry Bursill. Delightful picturebook from great-grandfather's day shows how to make 18 different hand shadows: a bird that flies, duck that quacks, dog that wags his tail, camel, goose, deer, boy, turtle, etc. Only book of its sort. vi + 33pp. 6½ x 9¼. 21779-5 Paperbound $1.00

WHITTLING AND WOODCARVING, E. J. Tangerman. 18th printing of best book on market. "If you can cut a potato you can carve" toys and puzzles, chains, chessmen, caricatures, masks, frames, woodcut blocks, surface patterns, much more. Information on tools, woods, techniques. Also goes into serious wood sculpture from Middle Ages to present, East and West. 464 photos, figures. x + 293pp.

20965-2 Paperbound $2.00

HISTORY OF PHILOSOPHY, Julián Marías. Possibly the clearest, most easily followed, best planned, most useful one-volume history of philosophy on the market; neither skimpy nor overfull. Full details on system of every major philosopher and dozens of less important thinkers from pre-Socratics up to Existentialism and later. Strong on many European figures usually omitted. Has gone through dozens of editions in Europe. 1966 edition, translated by Stanley Appelbaum and Clarence Strowbridge. xviii + 505pp. 21739-6 Paperbound $3.00

YOGA: A SCIENTIFIC EVALUATION, Kovoor T. Behanan. Scientific but non-technical study of physiological results of yoga exercises; done under auspices of Yale U. Relations to Indian thought, to psychoanalysis, etc. 16 photos. xxiii + 270pp.

20505-3 Paperbound $2.50

Prices subject to change without notice.
Available at your book dealer or write for free catalogue to Dept. GI, Dover Publications, Inc., 180 Varick St., N. Y., N. Y. 10014. Dover publishes more than 150 books each year on science, elementary and advanced mathematics, biology, music, art, literary history, social sciences and other areas.